At the approach of danger there are always two voices that speak with equal force in the heart of man: one very reasonably tells the man to consider the nature of the danger and the means of avoiding it; the other even more reasonably says that it is too painful and harassing to think of the danger, since it is not in a man's power to provide for everything and escape from the general march of events; and that it is therefore better to turn aside from the painful subject till it has come, and to think of what is pleasant. In solitude a man generally yields to the first voice; in society to the second.

— Leo Tolstoy
War and Peace

Working for Peace

A Handbook of Practical Psychology and Other Tools

Neil Wollman, Ph.D., Editor

Impact Publishers
SAN LUIS OBISPO, CALIFORNIA 93406

Library of Congress Cataloging-in-Publication Data
Working for peace.

Bibliography: p.
Includes index.
1. Peace.   I. Wollman, Neil, 1950 —
JX11963.W72   1985   327.1'72   85 — 19706
ISBN 0-915166-37-2

Publisher's Note
This publication is designed to provide accurate and authoritative
information in regard to the subject matter covered. It is sold with the
understanding that the publisher is not engaged in rendering psychological,
medical, or other professional services. If expert assistance or counseling is
needed, the services of a competent professional should be sought.

Cover by Sharon Schnare, San Luis Obispo, California, based on a design by
Sharon Davin Skinner.

Printed in the United States of America

Published by

Impact 🔊 Publishers
POST OFFICE BOX 1094
SAN LUIS OBISPO, CALIFORNIA 93406

Contents

Dedication

To George Miller, who said that we need to give psychology away; to Ken Brown, friend and mentor, who led me on the road to peace; and to my loving parents and sister, Joe, Bettye, and Kelly, who always support me.

N. W.

Acknowledgements

The only people who read acknowledgements are those whose names might appear within them. Nevertheless, for those people and for the appreciation I have for them, let me proceed.

First, let me thank colleagues Ken Brown and Gary Zimmerman, along with the Manchester College peace studies students who helped inspire me to do what I could for peace. Then there is Jerry Oster, who introduced me to the idea of applying what I learned in psychology textbooks to the "real world." I received valuable suggestions on what authors and topics to include from Jeri Seese-Green, Gary Zimmerman, and Jamie Newton. Specific information for a few of the chapters was provided by Ed Heddeman, Jim Gratz, and Dick Linbarger. A number of people assisted in editing various components of the entire project. They include Jo Keller, Paul Keller, Gary Zimmerman, Carol Stuart, and Jeri Seese-Green.

Special recognition for his editorial and production contributions goes to Jeff Hunn, the person who spent literally hundreds of hours with his computer and my perfectionistic tendencies. He added many, many valuable ideas to make the papers more clear and understandable.

There are also those who helped in typing, a skill I have not yet mastered: Karen Myers, Jack Hill, Kary McVay, Karen Lawson, and Jeff Hunn.

I thank those who have given me financial support (notably Manchester College and its psychology department) and moral support (the Wollmans, the Nelsons — including Kimberly —, Joan Gildemeister, Jeri Seese-Green, and members of Manchester's Psychology and Peace Studies Programs).

I want to formally acknowledge the authors who worked hard on their contributions and accommodated many changes by me and by the publisher. Unfortunately, there were a few papers written for the book that for one reason or another do not appear. I thank those authors for their efforts, and am sorry we could not include them.

Finally, of course, there is Impact Publishers' head, Robert Alberti, and his advisor for the project, Linden Nelson. Bob saw merit in this venture where some others did not, and he moved me along while shaping this sometimes unwieldy project of thirty-five chapters. Linden's diverse psychological knowledge pointed out material that was originally lacking. He "beefed up" and helped guide the papers so that they accomplished their intention.

So many people now thanked, yet I fear some may have been missed. I trust they know how much I appreciate their help as well. May our collective efforts bring the world just a little closer to lasting peace.

N. W.

About the Authors

CHARLES T. BROWN, Ph.D., is a long-time researcher and teacher in the field of interpersonal communication (presently Professor Emeritus, Western Michigan University). He introduced the study of conflict into the Western Michigan curriculum. (Rt. 2, Box 261, Eureka Springs, AR 72632)

CHERIE R. BROWN, M.Ed., is the director of the National Coalition Building Institute. She is a trainer and consultant in inter-group conflict resolution, coalition building, and prejudice-reduction workshops. (National Coalition Building Institute, 38 Dartmouth Street, Somerville, MA 02145)

BARRY CHILDERS, Ph.D., is a clinical psychologist by trade, and a peace activist by choice. He lives in Geneva, Switzerland, where his wife works for the World Council of Churches. His duties as househusband, with two small children, give his life added zest and his peace activities added importance. (Av. Amazones 10, 1224 Chene-Bougeries, Geneva, Switzerland).

BARBARA DATE', works as an educational consultant to organizations and individuals for learning interpersonal peacemaking and conflict resolution; she is completing her doctoral dissertation on conflict prevention and resolution at the University of Oregon. (996 Ferry Lane, Eugene, OR 97401)

WILLIAM ECKHARDT, Ph.D., psychologist, peace researcher, director of research with St. Louis Peace Research Laboratory. Staff member, Canadian Peace Research Institute, 1967-1980. Author of three books and over 100 peace-related articles, he is married (Maggie) and the father of three sons. (2000 Main Street, #211, Dunedin, FL 33528)

WENDY FORMAN, Ph.D., is a family therapist in private practice, a peace activist, and a parent to her two children. (Family and Psychological Services, 140 E. Butler Ave., Chalfont, PA 18914)

DONELSON R. FORSYTH, Ph.D., an associate professor of psychology at Virginia Commonwealth University, works with groups as both a member and consultant. (Department of Psychology, Virginia Commonwealth University, Richmond, VA 23284)

LAUREN FRIESEN, Ph.D., is Director of Theater at Goshen College, Vice-Chair for the Playwrights Program of the American College Theatre Festival, and the author of the published three-act play *King David*. (Goshen College, Goshen, IN 46526)

JAMES GANONG, a member of Computer Professionals for Social Responsibility, has helped the organization Witness for Peace with its membership list, word processing, and electronic mail. (Computer Professionals for Social Reponsibility, Box 7708, Santa Cruz, CA 95061)

JOAN GILDEMEISTER, Ph.D., is an Associate Professor of Educational Psychology. Her research interests include the memory, problem solving, and critical thinking of Black children, and the components of effective peace education. She is an active political educator on behalf of a more effective United Nations. (Department of Psychoeducational Studies, Howard University, Washington, D.C. 20059)

RONALD E. HOLTZMAN, Ph.D., is an experimental psychologist. (1700 Rockville Pike, Suite 500, Rockville, MD 20852)

JOANNA T. HOSKINS, Ph.D., stresses skill enhancement for conflict resolution in her private psychotherapy practice. She is particularly interested in applying such skill when medical illness changes family systems. (2095 Fairmount Blvd., Eugene, OR 97403)

JEFF HUNN, a peace worker and jack-of-all-trades, plans to be teaching lower elementary school children in the near future. (601 Wayne Street, North Manchester, IN 46962)

JOHN S. JAMES, a member of Computer Professionals for Social Responsibility, developed *The Conference Tree* electronic-meeting software for the CommuniTree Group in San Francisco. (Computer Professionals for Social Responsibility, Box 7708, Santa Cruz, CA 95061)

JO KELLER, Ph.D., teaches communication theory and interpersonal communications at Manchester College in Indiana, where she also enjoys her two energetic children. (Manchester College, North Manchester, IN 46962)

PAUL W. KELLER, Ph.D., is a long-time teacher of speech communication, and has offered courses in conflict resolution since 1962. He is Professor Emeritus, Manchester College. (504 N. Sycamore, North Manchester, IN 46962)

GEORGE LAKEY, M.A. (Sociology), is an organizer, writer, and teacher whose first time in jail was for a civil rights sit-in. He is presently Pennsylvania coordinator for the Jobs with Peace Campaign. (Jobs With Peace, 1425 Walnut, 3rd Floor, Philadelphia, PA 19102)

MARK LUDWICK, M.A., is a private consultant in industrial and organizational psychology, and is completing his Ph.D. in that area at Wayne State University. (Psychology Department, Wayne State University, 71 West Warren, Detroit, MI 48202)

HELEN MARGULIES MEHR, Ph.D., is a clinical psychologist in private practice who has been Chair of the Committee on Social Issues of the California State Psychological Association and serves on the National Steering Committee of Psychologists for Social Responsibility. (1240 Scott Blvd., Santa Clara, CA 95050)

VALERIE MELBURG, Ph.D., is Assistant Professor of Psychology at Westfield State College. She has carried out research on self-presentation and human aggression. (Psychology Department, Westfield State College, Westfield, MA 01085)

ED NELSON is a freelance author and political consultant. (938 N. Austin, Oak Park, IL 60302)

LINDEN NELSON, Ph.D., is a professor of psychology who is currently involved in research, writing, and curriculum development concerning the psychology of the nuclear arms race. (Department of Psychology and Human Development, California Polytechnic State University, San Luis Obispo, CA 93407)

JAMES W. NEWTON, Ph.D., is a Quaker who has been involved in peace activities since childhood, developed a program for training in nonviolent methods during the movement to end the Vietnam war, and completed his doctorate in Psychology at Stanford University in 1977. (Department of Psychology, San Francisco State University, San Francisco, CA 94132)

GERALD OSTER, Ph.D., is a licensed psychologist involved in individual and family therapy with children and adolescents and is a co-author of books on psychological testing and on using drawings in assessment and therapy. (Regional Institute for Children and Adolescents, 15000 Broschart Road, Rockville, MD 20850)

ROBERT PETTIT, Ph.D., is a sociologist with widespread interests ranging from magic and pop culture to the promotion of social justice. (Department of Sociology, Manchester College, North Manchester, IN 46962)

MARIANNE PHILBIN, Curator at The Peace Museum in Chicago, has organized a number of special events and benefits related to music and peace, including a major exhibition on the history of folk and rock music and its relation to peace efforts. (Peace Museum, 430 W. Erie Street, Chicago, IL 60610)

INGRID ROGERS, Ph.D., is a writer, peace activist, and pastor; she has authored or co-authored a collection of peace plays, a peace and justice songbook, and a book on the Salvadoran refugee situation (*In Search of Refuge*). (707 N. Sycamore, North Manchester, IN 46962)

LAURA SLAP is a graduate student in clinical psychology at Hahnemann University who has been active in working for peace and social change for the past ten years. Currently she is the treasurer of Philadelphia Psychologists for Social Responsibility. (c/o Psychology Dept., Hahnemann University, Broad and Vine Streets, Philadelphia, PA 19102)

JAMES T. TEDESCHI, Ph.D., is Professor of Psychology at State University of New York at Albany. He has written books on social power and impression management. (Department of Psychology, State University of New York - Albany, Albany, NY 12222)

LORENA JEANNE TINKER, Ph.D., Quaker, mother of 6, psychologist, peace and social justice researcher and activist. Researcher with St. Louis Peace Research Laboratory and Corpus Christi Peace Research Laboratory since 1979. She initiated peace and Central American justice groups in South Texas, and is involved in the U.S. Sanctuary Movement in 1985. (P. O. Box 703, Corpus Christi, TX 78403)

LEONARD WILLIAMS, Ph.D., is Assistant Professor of Political Science at Manchester College. He is active in local party politics, the Religious Society of Friends (Quakers), and the Fellowship of Reconciliation. (Political Science Department, Manchester College, North Manchester, IN 46962)

NEIL WOLLMAN, Ph.D., is a peace worker-psychologist at Manchester College who believes the time has come for people to pool their knowledge and resources to work for peace. (Psychology Department, Manchester College, North Manchester, IN 46962)

ELAINE YARBROUGH, Ph.D., formerly a professor in the Department of Communication at the University of Colorado, now runs a consulting business that helps individuals and organizations improve their communication and manage their conflict. (Yarbrough and Associates, 1919 14th Street, Suite 330, Boulder, CO 80302)

GARY ZIMMERMAN, Ph.D., is chair of the Psychology Department and a professor in the Peace Studies Program at Manchester College. (Psychology Department, Manchester College, North Manchester, IN 46962)

I

Introduction

Working for Peace

Neil Wollman

What This Book Is About
As you pick up this book, you may ask yourself, "Why another book about peace? Aren't there enough books about war and peace? Aren't there enough manuals about fundraising, writing letters, canvassing, and holding meetings and demonstrations?"

I agree, if you're only interested in facts and theories about war and peace, or the "nuts and bolts" of political organizing, the existing books are sufficient. But, there is far more involved in being a successful peace worker than understanding the issues and knowing how to prepare a press release, run a meeting, or set up a speaker system. This book presents *personal and interpersonal psychological principles* that will help you effectively put your knowledge and organizing skills to work.

Psychologists certainly have no corner on the market on how to make peace workers more effective. (Indeed, the last section of this book covers a number of non-psychological tools.) But psychologists do have a valuable perspective to offer — one that has worked well in other situations but which has been only minimally applied in the peace movement. Psychologists must, in my opinion, give more of the knowledge they possess. At the same time, peace workers must be more open to all of the tools that are available to them.

In general, the suggestions here will help you, as a peace worker, to improve three aspects of your peace work:
your personal skills (for example, you can use certain "time management" techniques to improve your productivity and confidence),

the internal workings of your peace group (for instance, your group decision making will be better if you take steps to avoid "groupthink" — a process resulting from group pressure for members to conform), and

your ability to communicate sensitively and persuasively to friends, government officials, or the general public (for example, you should avoid using "hidden antagonizers," those words and phrases that aren't intended to hurt or exclude others, but do).

Each chapter is written by an expert in a particular area and is intended to be practical and readable, rather than filled with theory and technical language.

Is This Book for You?

This book is intended principally for those actively working for world peace. In addition, the chapters are generally written so they can be used by those who are new to peace work or those who only occasionally talk with others about the topic.

Though the examples here are geared to peace, I believe the book also will be useful to those working for other causes. The basic principles of good organization and effective communication remain essentially the same, regardless of the issue with which you are dealing: calling an opponent of bussing a "racist" is just as likely to hinder attitude change as is calling a peace-through-strength supporter a "war-monger."

You will also find a number of chapters helpful in your own personal life. Everyone has some conflicts that need attention: marriage squabbles, problems with the boss, hassles with the garage mechanic. There are also suggestions that will improve your own psychological health and the inner workings of any group to which you belong.

Finally, the book will also find its way into the classroom, where it can be employed by instructors in psychology, sociology, political science, and communication. In addition to teaching psychological techniques, it demonstrates useful application of social science knowledge to the needs of the "real world."

How To Use This Book

This volume will serve its purpose best if used as a handbook. While each chapter has much valuable information, and a cover-to-cover reading is recommended as time allows, most peace workers will choose to refer to appropriate material as it is needed to help with different aspects of their work. When you are concerned with a particular topic, go to the relevant chapter or chapters (use the Contents, Section Introductions, and Index to help find what you need).

At times you will want to combine information from more than one paper. For instance, to help yourself or others select peace activities of interest, consult the chapters on setting life priorities and building confidence for social action. You can also use chapters for more than their original purpose. For example, chapters dealing with communicating with the public can help communication within your own group. Ideas for using the material are found in the book, but these are offered only as examples; you will have to apply the principles to your own situation. The greater your creativity and the more you work with the book, the more you will gain from it.

Creative application of these techniques will help your peace work, and can be fun as well. I would much enjoy hearing from readers who discover imaginative ways to apply this material.

Each chapter includes References and/or Suggested Readings, should you want to pursue the topic further. Or, the ideas here may lead you to consult with a peace-oriented psychologist or other professional with the expertise you need.

I'd like to close this section with a caution. Every person is unique and his/her actions cannot be influenced with perfect reliability. The techniques discussed here will generally hold, but they will not help you *every* time or in *every* situation. I am confident, however, that through experience, creativity, and the use of a full range of techniques, you will make progress toward your peace goals.

Manipulating Others in the Pursuit of Peace

At least one moral issue arose for me at times while preparing this book. A few chapters offer procedures which seem to suggest "manipulation" of others, or at least of others' attitudes about militarism. Peace is a just cause, but you will need to decide whether the techniques discussed meet your own ethical standards.

As you make these ethical decisions, keep in mind that *everyone* tries to influence others, whether the listeners or speakers are consciously aware of it. Parents raising children, advertisers selling products, teachers instructing students, politicians making speeches, charities seeking donations, friends giving advice — all are attempting to influence in some way. In this book, our intent is to help readers to *become aware* of those ways of influence which are most effective, and to *employ* those methods in the service of peace.

In Closing

You'll find that *Working for Peace* contains several different approaches to some topics. As with other complex life issues, there is usually no "one, right way" to do things. There are different approaches to making group decisions or changing attitudes about peace, just as there are different approaches to successfully raising children. You can't use all the techniques suggested here for any given topic — you don't need to in order to be successful. Choose and combine the techniques which best fit your needs, abilities, situation, group, and moral beliefs. Take from the book what best fits you and work with it.

I hope *Working for Peace* can help you, and in so doing help our country and our world turn toward peace.

I wish peace to you and all those you touch.

Creating a "Peaceful Climate" for Peace Work

Jo Keller

During speeches or sermons on peace, many of us sympathetic to the peace position find ourselves thinking, "I sure wish the president (or my conservative neighbor, Rick) could hear that!" Although we are quick to agree that communication problems are at the heart of many misunderstandings, most of us also focus on areas in which the *other* person needs to change.

Consider the persons with whom you are most likely to disagree about peace issues, and you probably come up with a variety of rich images:

-a paranoid uncle who thinks that the "commies" are out to rule the world.

-a condescending church friend who thinks peace advocates are well-meaning, but much too idealistic to be taken seriously.

-a smart, conservative Senator who contends that peace people, while they have a right to speak, do not have access to pertinent, classified information which would cause them to change their views.

-a local evangelist who preaches acceptance and even encouragement of the nuclear build-up because it is "prophesied" in the Bible.

-a neighbor who thinks that peace advocates should "stop harping about peace and get jobs!"

When you discuss peace with these people, you can easily see their communication faults. This chapter won't tell you how to change them. Instead it will discuss how you can improve yourself. You cannot directly change the behavior of others, but you can change your own.

Each of us needs to improve our own communication habits when we talk about such a controversial issue as peace. Effective communication is often defined as "shared meaning," a situation in which both parties have similar ideas of the message that has been spoken. When a State Department official clearly understands a reporter's question, then we say they have communicated effectively, because they have shared meaning. The suggestions in this chapter are based on the assumption that you genuinely want to achieve more shared meaning, more effective communication. If you adopt this "shared meaning" definition of communication, then you should ensure that the messages you send about peace issues are clear. Moreover, as a listener you should listen to messages carefully in order to share meaning with the people who are speaking to you. In other words, work to change your own communication behaviors.

First, although the general tone of all interpersonal exchanges is affected by everyone involved, just one person in the dialogue can make the communication climate more open. If a discussion about nuclear weapons has become a shouting match, the climate can improve if even one of the parties begins to listen with an open mind. A communication researcher who studied small group communication noted that most groups have primarily either "defensive" or "supportive" communication climates. [1] Defensive climates are those in which people feel threatened. As a human, you likely respond to perceived threat with self-protection; and whether the threat is real (e.g. a car pulling out in front of your own car) or imagined (e.g. the shadows in the bushes which are spookier after you've seen an Alfred Hitchcock movie), you will work to protect yourself. This self-protection is obvious when the perceived threats are physical; it is less obvious when the threats are verbal.

What happens to communication when people feel defensive? A person who perceives a threat and puts up defenses against the threat is less likely to listen well, especially on controversial topics such as peace. As is often experienced in arguments with spouses or children, one may feel so heavily attacked verbally as to develop a verbal "battle plan" even while the other is talking. At the first pause for breath, the already well-rehearsed verbal attack is launched! This practice hurts communication effectiveness because time that could be spent on listening and comprehending is instead spent mentally developing one's own arguments.

Poor listening and comprehending will not help you speak openly with others about peace. What then can be done to improve your own role in a dialogue so that the communication can be as effective as possible? What can you do to have a "supportive" climate and make shared meaning possible?

Certain behaviors lead to openness, while others lead to defensiveness. We all need to develop skills for making the climate more trusting and more supportive. The following sections will cover such behavior and skills.

Use Descriptive Words: Avoid Judging

One behavior which leads to more trust is using *descriptive* words and phrases rather than those which *evaluate* or *judge* another person. People like to hear their ideas and work responded to descriptively, and they feel threatened when people judge them.

I overheard a recent discussion about peace in which a college student said to her mother, "I know you're sincere, but you are so gullible and stupid to believe everything the President says." The mother naturally responded by becoming defensive. What could the student have said to keep communication channels open? A better statement would have been: "I've read in several places that the President just reads a one-page summary of these daily issues, rather than studying them in depth. I hope you will look at the issues more thoroughly than that and not assume that the President is always right." This statement leaves room for the mother to disagree and does not pass judgment on her for taking a "stupid" position. No one likes to be called "stupid" or "naive."

I also overheard a professor, a long-time advocate for peace, describe one government official as a "total idiot." While the professor may feel that his evaluation is accurate, the remark will make any person sympathetic toward the official feel defensive. When such judgment occurs, the communication effectiveness decreases. Although most of us do not think we are judgmental toward others, we would do well to become more aware of our own comments and those of our peace movement friends to make sure we are not making judgmental remarks that might hurt communication.

Be Open-minded: Avoid Rigidity

Communication improves when the parties are open-minded, open to each others' views. An open-minded person is not wishy-washy, but rather is willing to hear opposing arguments, even while staying strongly committed to a particular position. Being open-minded is difficult for many peace movement people, especially those who are well-read but who limit their reading to such peace position sources as *Sojourners* and *The Progressive*. Ironically, we want our opposition to read sources other than *Readers' Digest* or *U.S. News & World Report*! We will all benefit from reading a variety of sources, those with which we disagree as well as those with which we agree.

Reading only those sources with which one agrees tends to foster certainty, a rigid "I know what is right, don't confuse me with the facts," attitude. When faced with such rigidity, other people's defensiveness increases. When open-mindedness is exhibited, open discussion is likelier — in part because people sense that their ideas will be heard, even by their opponents.

In a recent class at a college with an active peace studies program, a business major presented a well-researched, well-reasoned speech on the necessity of "balance of power" for world-wide nuclear stability. He used historical analogies and supported his views with good research. Two peace studies students nearly hooted him from the room. Their criticisms of the speech were not based on what he had presented, but on a standard line about peace and the craziness of balance of power arguments. They were rigid in their own views and did not give serious consideration to his. It was apparent that the speaker, a man somewhat moderate in his political positions, was defensive — so defensive, in fact, that I suspect he moved further away from the peace position because of the closed-minded attacks from its supporters.

Persons with a strong peace commitment need to exhibit openness to opposing views. If our ideas about peace are sound, we need not see such views as serious threats to our own. Moreover, we can grow by welcoming those views. We may decide to subscribe to journals which present an alternative view; we may read columnists who consistently support military build-up; we may occasionally find ideas within these and other "enemy" sources with which we can agree! Such openness will enable those with whom we talk to speak freely, knowing that they will be heard with an open mind.

Display Equality: Avoid Appearing Arrogant

People who treat others as equals produce trust in those with whom they communicate. Perhaps because the issue of peace is so vital to us all, some (or many) of us who are long-associated with the peace movement feel morally superior to the rest of "misguided" humanity. If other people detect that superior attitude, as they usually will, they may be frightened by our arrogance. That superiority may be expressed in different ways: sometimes it is a "know-it-all" attitude in discussions about the U.S. government and its involvement around the world; sometimes it is in-group jokes which exclude the non-peace people present. The inverse of the golden rule seems good advice here: if you do not like people acting morally superior and arrogant toward you, you would do well not to act that way toward them.

Use Sensitive Language: Avoid "Hidden Antagonizers"

Language has considerable impact on communication effectiveness. All peace workers who have been called "Commie-lover" know that certain words arouse people. Often, however, words operate with more subtlety; one writer refers to these words as "hidden antagonizers." [2] These are words or phrases that are not intended to hurt or exclude anyone but which, nevertheless, have that effect. The speaker means no harm, but the listener takes offense and becomes less open to the message. For example, many peace workers find themselves labeled "idealistic." While that label is not necessarily negative, and the person using it may not intend to be critical, the phrase may still be a hidden antagonizer. Why? Because my being called "idealistic" might suggest that I am also naive or uninformed, and thus easily disregarded.

Peace workers also use words that hurt clear communication, words that function as hidden antagonizers. Abbreviations, such as O.M.B. and I.C.B.M., may make listeners feel excluded if they don't know the meaning of the initials. Emotional statements like "you wouldn't kill your own children, would you?" breed powerful defensiveness because of the implied judgment about the listener. While the speaker may intend to make a point rather than provoke anger, the overall effect still harms the quality of communication. What can you do to be more sensitive in your use of language?

-Avoid unnecessary use of abbreviations. Provide full names of agencies and weapons, assuming that not everyone is knowledgeable of the abbreviations.

-Avoid technical words; talk directly and clearly about the issues. If your aim is good communication then you should adapt to your listeners.

-If you have a choice, use short words rather than long ones.

-Do all you can as a speaker to keep the doors of communication open by careful language choice.

If your goal is to share ideas about peace with others, then you must work hard to create a communication climate which allows good discussion. To do that you need to reduce (or eliminate) judgment, rigidity, attitudes of superiority, and use of antagonizing language; and you need to increase your descriptiveness, open-mindedness, equality, and sensitive language (see the exercise below to practice this). By making these skills more a part of your daily communication, you can work toward peace in your interpersonal relations. You can then help that peacefulness move to wider circles.

The Andy Murray song which says, "What can one person do is a very good question if you don't do nothing at all," lets us know that each step toward peace, whether in Moscow or over our backyard fences, will help.

A Communication Exercise

In small groups, label the following statements as exhibiting judgement, rigidity, superiority, or hidden antagonizers. After doing that, rephrase them to be more descriptive, open-minded, equal, or sensitive in language.

(a) "The Republican plan for moving tanks through the desert will never work."

(b) "Those Civil Defense planners are absolutely crazy if they think we can evacuate New York City to Syracuse!"

(c) "Joe's reasons for joining the Army are stupid."
(d) (on the phone): "All right, Ms. Winter, I'll get the material in the mail today. Good-bye, honey."
(e) "You may think you understand the complexities of the East-West problem, but I know when something is over your head."
(f) "Oh, Susan. You're so funny for thinking you can believe what the State Department says. Well, I guess that's a woman for you."
(g) "1984 was a banner year for girls — Geraldine Ferraro was on the Democratic ticket!"

References
1. Gibb, Jack (1961). Defensive communication. *Journal of Communication*, 11, 141-148.
2. Brooks, William D., & Emmert, Phillip (1980). *Interpersonal Communication* (2nd ed). Dubuque, IA: Wm. C. Brown.

Suggested Readings
Adler, R., Rosenfeld, L.B., & Towne, N. (1980). *Interplay: The process of interpersonal communication.* New York: Holt, Rinehart, and Winston. This introductory interpersonal communication textbook devotes an entire chapter to communication climate, providing clear explanations and earthy personal examples of its application.

Stewart, J. (Ed.) (1982). *Bridges not walls* (3rd ed.). Reading, Mass.: Addison-Wesley. This collection of readings adopts a humanistic viewpoint to interpersonal communication, and includes Gibb's original article (cited in the References above) as well as related articles and exercises.

PeaceWorkers:
Getting Yourself Together

You will be more effective in your peace work if you develop personally in various ways, including making certain decisions about your life, acquiring particular knowledge and skills, and learning how to remain psychologically healthy while doing your work. This section is opened by Gildemeister, whose paper will help you sort out your personal priorities if you have decided to change your life by putting more time into peace activities. She gives suggestions for determining how much time to give, and how such a commitment will affect other life activities.

In the next chapter Childers focuses on how to decide what peace activities to pursue, and how to build confidence for doing them. Included in his chapter is a valuable list of 101 things you can do for peace. Wollman's paper on "personal appeal" assumes that your effectiveness will be determined not only by your arguments, but by how you come across personally. Included are specific suggestions on how to improve your own personal appeal as a bearer of the message of peace.

The next two papers in this section deal with the peaceworker's psychological well-being. Oster presents a few simple but powerful techniques to help you be more positive and confident as you plan and work toward achievable goals. Mehr covers a number of difficulties peace workers often face, such as dealing with anxiety, anger, and depression and helplessness in the face of current world conflict.

The chapter by Yarbrough emphasizes the need for changing yourself internally if you are to be an effective communicator and worker. She discusses several internal conflicts that peace workers must resolve. Finally, Forman and Slap concentrate on preventing "burnout." Keep their suggestions in mind as you plan your own work for peace.

Adjusting Your Priorities:
Make Room in Your Life for Peace

Joan Gildemeister

Becoming more politically active requires some life adjustment. To work effectively for peace, you will need to rearrange your time and other personal resources to meet your new commitments. If you don't, you'll probably encounter conflicts and tensions. If you do, your increased commitment to peace can improve your self-esteem and make you feel less helpless about the gloomy world situation.

This chapter offers some help for the difficult process of adjusting your priorities to "make room in your life for peace." It covers two basic formats for setting priorities: working on your own, and working with the help of a group. You'll eventually need to make your own decisions in line with the realities of your life, but both individual contemplation and group work are useful tools.

Undertaking more peace activities will require personal and financial sacrifice. There is no big paycheck waiting after a peace workshop has been arranged, a speaker obtained, or a mailing list brought up to date. Any additional action you choose for peace will compete with other activities which result in more immediate benefits, financial and other. Increasing your peace activities means that time spent in other areas, sometimes important ones, will have to be decreased.

Rearranging your priorities can take place without a major disruption of your life, however. You can allow peace work to replace some of the less rewarding areas of your current routine. The important thing is to begin to change that pattern.

Look at the way you currently use *time*. Few people ever do a systematic assessment of how they spend their time. Most of us waste a good deal of time, and some careful time management may make it possible to add peace activities to your schedule without much disruption of your current interests. Nevertheless, as you increase your involvement, you will probably find it necessary to sacrifice time spent elsewhere. Can you identify the priorities you place on your time? Time spent for sleep, food, and work is a fairly fixed requirement for most of us. But could you spend less time on hobbies? Recreation? Entertainment? Could you hire someone to do your chores for you? Could you eat less well and thereby spend less time preparing and cleaning up? The way we spend our time determines what get accomplished. Look creatively at your schedule, and make the tough choices which will allow you to allocate some of that precious resource to peace. [1]

Relationships are a second key area which will be affected by increasing your involvement in peace activities. Let's take one example of this and see how you might deal with it. Most of us are involved in at least one close personal relationship. Intimacy does not survive without time together, but you've decided to begin spending some of your time working for peace. One solution to this difficulty would be to have a frank and open discussion with your partner and explain that you plan to begin reordering your priorities. Not that you value or need closeness less, rather that for a period of time peace activities will be put on the "front burner." If your friend reacts defensively, feeling that love has been withdrawn, perhaps you can negotiate. Find a third party if necessary — a mutual friend or counselor — to hear both sides and help you reach agreement. Read about negotiation [2] so you two can come to terms. (See chapter 14.) You may need to set limits for how long these new activities will occupy a high priority place and how intense your involvement will be.

Make a list of your *activities* and group them in terms of how they meet your personal needs, such as being around others, feeling good about yourself, and gaining knowledge. It is true that putting peace actions in front of movie-going might deprive you of valued companionship. And you may not be able to bring uncompleted work home from your job if you have to attend a peace group meeting at night. But as you review your list of activities you may find that some of them just bring you momentary satisfaction. Such pursuits may be put aside on an experimental basis. You will then be free to replace them with new or extra responsibilities within peace organizations.

Have you considered how peace activities might change your *beliefs*? Your view of the world, other people, organizations to which you belong, religion, politics, ... all are likely to be affected by your resolve to work for peace. Perhaps your church refused to take a stand on the nuclear freeze. Or your favorite congressman may have voted for the MX. Or members of your service club may be so caught up in "patriotism" that they refuse to acknowledge any errors in our national foreign policy. Where are your loyalties in such circumstances? You'll need to take a hard look at your priorities to avoid much confusion and turmoil when these inevitable conflicts occur.

Does your *career* get in the way? A young stockbroker recently became so convinced of the dangers of nuclear war that he became active in a local peace group. When he came to work with the group's emblem on his lapel, his colleagues ridiculed him. It required all the courage of his convictions to stand up for his new concern in the light of this challenge to his career. Others have taken leaves of absence to work full time for peace. Do the demands of your career permit you to be an active peace advocate? If a direct conflict occurred on the job, what path would you take? Do you have a choice, or does economic survival demand that you put your job first? Or perhaps your career permits you special opportunities to work for peace; teachers, writers, clergy, and some entrepreneurs, for example, have unique roles and somewhat flexible schedules which can accommodate peace activities. One's job presents important challenges to personal priorities related to peace work.

The old expression, "Put your *money* where your mouth is!" takes on special meaning when applied to the peace movement. Certainly one way we can all work for peace is to contribute financially to the work of organizations we believe in. Yet making such contributions diverts that money from other purposes: family, home, other social causes, investments, even subsistence.

A great deal of psychological research has focussed on identifying patterns of an individual's *interests*. Studies of interests have tended to emphasize their relevance for a person's vocational choice. Indeed, peace work may be thought of as a "vocation" (for some people it is a full time occupation!), so you might use some of the vocational interest work to clarify how your interests fit with the type of peace work you do. There are many approaches to assessing vocational interests. If this idea appeals to you, look at the "References" for these resources: John Holland's *Self-Directed Search* [3]; the *Strong-Campbell Interest Inventory* [4]; and the career search work of Richard Nelson Bolles. [5]

A person's *values* are often considered to be connected with his or her religion. While religious values are certainly a powerful force in the lives of many individuals, religion is not the only source of values. Honesty, integrity, loyalty, dedication to a cause, decency, concern for the human family — all are values worth supporting, and all will affect your commitment to peace work. Psychologists have developed a number of procedures which may be helpful in clarifying your own value priorities. One method which can help in examining and sorting out those values which you hold most dear is "Values Clarification." This is an extensive complex of activities and procedures which requires you to make forced choices among alternatives in hypothetical, value-laden circumstances. If you must choose between your life and that of another, for example, your values begin to become clearer to you. Additional material on Values Clarification may be found in the "References" at the end of this chapter. [6, 7]

Group Procedures for Priority Setting

Setting priorities and making good decisions can be easier with the help of a support group, ideally composed of some who are and some who are not heavily involved in peace activities. The following suggestions are adapted from organizational psychology and the writing of Sites and Blossom. [8]

Five steps are to be taken by you and the group. A recorder and "referee" should be appointed to help with these steps.

The first step calls for you to consider with the group what goals and values are important to you regarding peacemaking. For instance, goals may involve supporting existing institutions for peace (say, the United Nations or the new U.S. Peace Institute), contributing to peace education for youth, helping others become more effective in their peace work, working for peace through the political process, or promoting cooperative activities between individuals and groups. The moral and political values you feel are important should be identified and clarified through these wide-ranging discussions.

The second step is for you to discuss what peace activity choices are actually available to you that are consistent with the goals and values you discussed in step one. Begin by brainstorming among the group, but then narrow your choices to a number of activities which appeal to you.

A further narrowing of choices will occur as you evaluate the activities in the remaining stages of this exercise.

The third step calls for the group to assist you in anticipating the present and future consequences of your choices for your life. Creativity sometimes results in improbable or ridiculous conclusions; however, the purpose of this step is to open up exploration of all possible consequences, not just the most obvious, so open discussion should be encouraged and criticism declared off limits.

The fourth step involves discovering who will be affected, and in what ways, by the particular form of peacework you choose. For example, if you choose to do promotional work, you will need exclusive use of a telephone and a place where messages may be received. How will housemates, friends, relatives, or a spouse be affected? Will they be expected to answer the telephone or take on other responsibilities? How many of those close to you will have to limit their expectations of you during that time? If an activity will bring about a major realignment of many of your support relationships, perhaps a different activity should be explored. Here you discover the repercussions of some major changes may be negative, and yet you may not see this on your own because of your preoccupation with peace-oriented goals.

After the evaluations in steps three and four, you will probably have narrowed the choices to those few which are most desireable. In the fifth and final step, you and the group should discuss how you can begin carrying out your choices. Both potential difficulties in implementation and the positive goals expressed in the choice must be considered. You need to be supported and encouraged to carry out the choices you made.

Consequences
Decision Making. Once you have set aside the time to begin peace activities (or take on more), you must decide what specific actions to engage in. Ask yourself some questions: Have I looked carefully at my goals and the values each choice implies? For example, selling tickets to a benefit will finance a newsletter and result in circulation of information within your peace network; arranging a peace-oriented discussion group among college students and professors may help change values in higher education, but this latter goal will be much harder to reach and may require skills you may not yet have.

To what extent have I weighed the known costs and benefits of an activity? For example, if I am considering civil disobedience, how likely is it that I will receive a fair decision from the court? And is that important? If I go into politics, how expensive will it be to mount a campaign for public office? If I noticeably shift energies from my regular job to peace activities, will my boss understand? If I engage in particular peace activities, what is the likelihood they will result in immediate or long-term success? Will the activity I am considering be enjoyable to me, and within my capacities and abilities to accomplish? You may need to seek advice to answer some of these questions.

Monitoring the Effects of Your New Priorities
After implementing the decisions you make, keep a record of successes (or failures) in peace projects and then revise your priorities for the future. Continue to keep in mind your specific interests, personal abilities, and other factors discussed earlier. And as you make life changes, don't forget to tell others about them; for by doing this you will gain company for the long journey of social change.

By defining the number and range of your interests and by clearing the personal front, you are free to make changes in priorities. Check on the soundness of your new priorities in light of your long-term goals and values, and review them often. Think through how resetting priorities will bring your daily activities into line with your peace interests.

Ask whether you have a realistic plan for carrying out your decision. Will the group I join hold together? Will the peace candidate in whose campaign I work vote consistently? What will I do if pressures at work cause too much stress? What will happen to this project if my romantic partner suddenly demands more time and attention? The soundness of your decision depends on how thoroughly you have asked such questions and evaluated the answers.

Reinforcement

Sources of Support for Changes. There are a number of sources of support that should be sought when making changes in your life. Keeping a journal may help in charting the path to goals. Certainly you should discuss your plans with others and gain their perceptions of your actions for peace. But your biggest source of support may well be found within yourself. Develop an inner dialogue. Be willing to learn about yourself and why you want to make intentional changes. You may wish to use some sort of meditation technique (you don't have to be an accomplished yogi!). Contemplate how goals of peace can be achieved, and how you can help achieve them.

Elise Boulding of Dartmouth College has developed an imagery technique through which individuals envision changes in the world situation which in turn lead to a nuclear-free future. (9)

Psychological resistance to change is powerful, but it can be overcome. The challenge is to find a peace-making activity that you find so inspirational you cannot leave it uncompleted.

References

1. Lakein, A. (1974) *How to get control of your time and your life.* New York: Signet/New American Library.
2. Fisher, R., and Ury, W. (1983). *Getting to yes: Negotiating agreement without giving in.* New York: Penguin Books.
3. Holland, J. L. (1985). *The Self-Directed Search.* Odessa, FL: Psychological Assessment Resources (P.O. Box 98, 33556). *Note: It may be necessary to obtain the SDS through a professional counselor or public counseling service.*
4. Strong, E. K., Campbell, D. P., and Hansen, J. C. (1984). *Strong-Campbell Interest Inventory.* Stanford, CA: Stanford University Press. *Note: The SCII is available only through a professional counselor or counseling service.*
5. Bolles, R. N. (1985/Annual) *What color is your parachute? A*

manual for job hunters and career changers. Berkeley, CA: Ten Speed Press.
6. Howe, W. L. (1977) *Taking charge of your life*. Allen, TX: Argus Communications.
7. Simon, S., Howe, L., and Kirschenbaum, H. (1978). *Values clarification*. New York: A & W Publishers.
8. Sites, W. K., and Blossom, B.C. (1972). *Ethics in perspective and practice*. Dobbs Ferry, NY: Oceana.
9. Boulding, E. (1982). Envisioning the peaceable kingdom. *Fellowship*, (April/May), pp. 3-5.

Suggested Readings
Sites, W. K., and Blossom, B. C. (1972). *Ethics in perspective and practice*. Dobbs Ferry, NY: Oceana. Three types of ethics are set out in this book: man-centered, natural law, and theistic. Of particular value is the brief presentation of John Dewey's method of ordering personal values before taking action.

Tough, A. (1982). *Intentional changes: A fresh approach to helping people change*. Chicago: Follett. This book identifies the processes by which people achieve personal growth. The reader benefits from data supplied by a survey of 150 adults from three different countries. These interviews attest to the fact that many individuals can successfully reorder priorities and undertake new and constructive activities.

Williams, R. L., and Long, J. D. (1975). *Toward a self-managed life style* (2nd ed.). Boston: Houghton-Mifflin. Williams and Long set forth in a straightforward manner the behavioristic approach to personal change. Their method in brief: record behavior, analyze it in terms of current rewards, and undertake exercises to change it through imaging positive or negative consequences.

4

Building Confidence for Social Action

Barry Childers

Like anyother kind of learning, learning to be active and effective in response to peace issues takes time. You can learn by reading and by talking with others who are more experienced, but most of all, you learn by doing. Social action at its best represents an attempt by you (alone or with others) to bring your particular interests and talents to bear on a problem of your own choosing. Generally, social action can be classified as research, education, or direct action.

Following is a list of social actions in which people engage. You will need to duplicate the list in some form. There are several purposes for the list. It is intended to help you (a) assess your unique interests and skills in relation to social action, (b) evaluate the difficulties that particular kinds of activities present, so that you can better understand them, and (c) help you choose the most appropriate tasks and build confidence in undertaking them.

The list can be used most effectively in a support group, with sharing of experiences and mutual exploration of problems and options, but it can also be used alone. In the former case, there should be no pressure to achieve or to conform. The best results will be obtained if you can make an honest assessment of what you wish to do, unpressured by others' expectations.

For each item on the list, mark down how difficult it would be for you to do that particular action (very hard—VH, moderately hard—MH, or fairly easy—FE). Why an action is difficult for you is not important at this point; just get a fairly quick, gut-level reaction about each item.

1. Join a national organization that is active on peace issues.
2. Write a letter to the editor of a local paper encouraging people to think about a peace issue.
3. Spend several hours a week doing volunteer office work for a peace organization.
4. Obtain a peace-related slide show to present to my church group.
5. Encourage my local political party to endorse peace policies.
6. Ask some friends to come to my home and discuss a peace issue.
7. Write a letter to my Congressperson urging him/her to vote a certain way on an upcoming bill.
8. Spend time learning about organizations that work on a particular issue so that I can discuss the groups with others.
9. Circulate among my friends a petition supporting action on a peace-related problem.
10. Raise funds for a cause by organizing an event (a garage sale, a bake sale, a walk or run, a book sale, a craft fair, etc.).
11. Write a letter to a government official, criticizing her/his decision on an issue.
12. Set aside 20 minutes a day to think about and study an issue, and consider what I can do about it.
13. Talk about a peace issue with someone I just met at a party.
14. Write a letter to the editor of a local paper criticizing actions of the city council or a local business firm.
15. Join a social action group that is not too popular in my community because of its outspokenness on a peace issue.
16. Make it a point to bring a peace issue into conversations whenever the opportunity presents itself.
17. Think about my own particular interests and skills, and figure out how I can contribute to solving a global conflict problem and enjoy myself at the same time.
18. Organize a speakers bureau in my community.

19. Persuade several friends to join a group to which I belong.
20. Take an unpopular position on an issue that arose during a local civic group meeting I attended.
21. Send a gift subscription of a peace-oriented magazine to a friend that might be interested.
22. Explore how people in my profession can contribute to peace.
23. Withhold a percentage of my taxes to protest government spending that contributes to a military conflict.
24. Talk with my minister about directing certain church funds toward peacemaking.
25. Write a letter to a magazine journalist criticizing her/his article.
26. Stop buying a product that I know is produced by exploiting poor people in another country.
27. Write a letter to my Congressperson criticizing militaristic statements he or she made at a news conference.
28. Join a non-violent demonstration obstructing the gates of a nearby defense plant.
29. Call in to radio talk shows to express a peace concern.
30. Set up a booth at a community or county fair to provide literature and talk with people about militarism.
31. Help a group to which I belong plan a public meeting on a peace issue.
32. Volunteer for a low-paying job with a peace group overseas.
33. Run a newspaper ad regularly about world conflict.
34. Prepare an annotated reading list on an issue to distribute among friends and groups to which I belong.
35. Join a peace demonstration marching through the middle of town, knowing the stance is not popular with local people.
36. Telephone my Congressperson to convey my peace concerns.
37. Canvass local businesses, asking permission to place a peace sign (or a sign publicizing a local group) in their window.
38. Actively help plan a demonstration at a local defense-related industry.
39. Feed and house people who come to my area to speak or do other peace work.
40. Write a letter to the president of a large corporation to complain about its ties to military defense.
41. Canvass the neighborhood door-to-door to raise funds or survey attitudes about peace.

42. Try to arrange a dialogue between opposing factions in a dispute about peace.

43. Appear on a TV talk show to discuss a peace issue.

44. Be a part of a phone tree to alert people to a peace issue needing urgent action.

45. Organize a rally in a local park to protest government action in a conflict somewhere in the world.

46. Write to national radio and TV networks urging them to carry a program on war and peace.

47. Contribute part of my monthly budget to a peace-related cause.

48. Explore ways to introduce war and peace issues into the curriculum of elementary schools.

49. Purchase and distribute materials on conflict wherever I think they might create some interest.

50. Write a grant proposal for money to develop a local peace program.

51. Take part in a march across the country to make people more aware of an issue.

52. Become known as a person willing to speak about peace.

53. Organize a benefit concert with area musicians to raise funds for a cause.

54. Volunteer my vacation time to work on a peace project.

55. Spend several months learning all I can about a peace issue.

56. Start refusing when people ask me to do things that I know contribute to world conflict.

57. Do library research on a peace issue for our local group.

58. Contact a local TV or radio station and try to persuade them to give some time to a peace issue in the public interest.

59. Chair a committee in my church to decide what my congregation should do to promote peace.

60. Help write materials for a local organization (descriptive flyers, meeting announcements, calls to action, etc.).

61. Stand on a busy street corner to distribute leaflets and talk with passers-by about militarism.

62. Bring in a speaker or show a film on peace, arranging for publicity in the local media.

63. Talk with the local high school principal to find out how peace and conflict issues are covered in the curriculum, and encourage more attention to them.

64. Start a peace-oriented newsletter among people I know.

65. Attend a conference on a peace issue held in a nearby city.

66. Do in-depth research on a peace issue and write a report for a local or national organization.

67. Speak to a junior high or high school class about a peace issue.

68. Volunteer one day a week to work with a state peace group.

69. Organize a meeting to start a local chapter of a national peace organization.

70. Help organize a guerilla theatre group to dramatize issues at public events.

71. Wear a peace symbol button or lapel pin.

72. Engage in a house-to-house petition campaign for a peace issue.

73. Simplify my lifestyle as a contribution to solving global conflict problems.

74. Write an article about a peace issue for a national magazine.

75. Create a photo-display about a peace issue and show it at a local shopping center once a week.

76. Try to persuade friends to join a social action group to which I belong.

77. Organize a letter-writing network to focus on peace action.

78. Join an organization that I know is considered radical by many community people, including my friends.

79. Write an article on peace for the local newspaper.

80. Attend a rally in the center of town protesting local government action.

81. Ask a local civic group to which I belong to have one of their meetings focus on a peace issue.

82. Talk with people at a local college or university and try to persuade them to offer a course on peace and conflict.

83. Write a will leaving some of my assets to a peace group.

84. Personally confront a board member of a corporation to explain my concern about the corporation's activities.

85. Organize a telephone lobbying network to influence my Congressperson on peace-related legislation.

86. Stand up in a question-and-answer period following a speech and express criticism of something the speaker said.

87. Give a talk promoting peace to a local civic group.

88. Organize a vigil in front of the governor's mansion to call attention to an issue.
89. Serve as a contact person in my area for a peace group.
90. Give up a large portion of my leisure time to do peace-related activities.
91. Participate in a small non-violent protest, knowing that I will probably be arrested and jailed.
92. Solicit funds from local businesses to support a peace group.
93. Boycott a company that contributes to a conflict somewhere.
94. Take a job with a social action organization, even if it would mean a drop in income.
95. Speak at a local rally that is protesting government action.
96. Attend a meeting of the city council and speak to them about declaring a day for peace.
97. Travel a long distance to attend the annual conference of a national or international peace organization.
98. Participate in a panel discussion on peace given by a local group.
99. Quit my job if it is contributing to world conflict.
100. Make a speech promoting peace to a large audience at a church conference.
101. Prepare and teach a class on peace and conflict at a community college.

Now that you have completed the list, go back and find the items you marked *very hard* (VH). Try to get a sense of what makes them difficult for you. If you're in a group, do a sharing-discussion with one or two other members of the group. Afterwards, briefly write what you think makes them difficult for you — just a few words to identify the difficulty. Examples: "I find writing very difficult — I'm more of an action-oriented person"; "I enjoy talking with individuals, but talking in front of a group really scares me"; "I tend to shy away from situations where there might be conflict"; "I prefer intellectual activities and tend to avoid action groups"; "I've never had much experience at organizing and think I'd be very poor at it"; "I'm a procrastinator"; etc.

Now that you have a better idea what things are difficult for you and why, begin to think about what you would like to do. Choose an item of moderate difficulty that appeals to you and that represents something you could, in fact, do now. Think through a plan for doing it, or discuss a plan with your small group. If it is something that cannot be done alone, include in your program a way of joining with others to do it.

After you have finished, write a brief description of your plan, including a time schedule for following through on it. If you are part of a group, you may want to get together with others after you complete your activity to share your experiences. You may want to talk about (a) how easy or difficult the activity was, and why, (b) what problems arose that you hadn't foreseen, (c) what things you might want to do differently to be more effective if you repeat the activity later, and (d) your plans for the next step you want to take.

Through this exercise you are engaging in a learning and confidence-building process that you can continue at your own pace. Choose activities that will keep you moving gradually in the direction you want to go, and stay with each level until you feel fairly satisfied with your performance. Comments from others can be helpful, but remember that you are the final and best judge of your own progress.

A Final Note: One thing that discourages many people unnecessarily is the feeling that they don't know enough to participate in social action. They feel that many of the actions require that one be an "expert." It is true, of course, that a few of the listed actions require some knowledge and experience, and the more you know about an issue, the more effective you can be. But one can learn in the process of doing, and most actions can be undertaken by anyone, at any stage of understanding.

5

Improving Your Personal Appeal

Neil Wollman

Though you might hope that others' opinions will be affected only by the strengths of your position, this will not be the case. The greater people's liking for you, whatever the reason, the more likely they will be open to your arguments. The importance of personal characteristics goes beyond just being friendly and sympathetic during conversations. Even seemingly trivial characteristics will have an effect — are you aware that every U.S. Presidential election except for one since 1900 was won by the taller of the two candidates?

Though personal traits and other nonpolitical factors will not single-handedly determine someone's views toward peace, they will have some effect on it. These secondary factors will most likely affect opinions for a short period of time, and primarily in people for whom the issue is of minor importance. [1] On the surface it may seem that if this is the case, it's not worth worrying about, but such factors are worth considering for several reasons.

First, for some of your projects, a short-term attitude change (without deep commitment) is all that may be needed; a brief change of opinion on an issue not critical to someone may be enough to get them to sign a petition, give a financial contribution, or vote favorably in an immediately upcoming election.

Secondly, it will be easier to bring about a deeper commitment once you've changed an opinion temporarily.

Finally, secondary factors can be applied along with other attitude change techniques to make a more effective overall appeal.

Even if personal characteristics have their greatest effect in only certain situations, they will likely have some effect in all circumstances. Why not use all the appeal that is available to you?

The following is a presentation of principles which are most likely to make others like you, and thus be more open to your message. These principles can be divided into four types of factors which lead to greater liking: favorable personality traits; rewards; similarities between people; and amount of contact between individuals.

Personality Traits

The most powerful traits that cause liking seem vaguely similar to the Boy Scout pledge: loyalty, honesty, sincerity, competence, and physical attractiveness. [2] The more you have (or appear to have) these qualities, the greater the chance that people will like you. Presumably, it will not be difficult to be sincere and honest when talking to others about your concern for peace. If it is, it will probably become obvious to listeners in the long run (and perhaps even in more limited interactions). Likewise, if people think you are insincere, they will have negative feelings about you and your message.

It may be more difficult to establish your competence with listeners if contacts are brief. Try to show it through the actions you take and the knowledge you express. If appropriate, mention your training, awards, work accomplished, degrees, etc.

Physical attractiveness, for better or worse, is a particularly important factor. Appearance may be improved by use of appropriate clothing and grooming. Whether you wish to be concerned with such matters is your own choice, but you should be aware that they will have an effect on others' acceptance of you and your message. One needn't necessarily be "clean-cut" to be best received; listeners are usually most receptive to those who are dressed and groomed similar to themselves. I'll go more deeply into the effects of similarity later on.

Rewards

People like others who provide them with pleasant things. [3] Rewards can take many forms. For example, you could praise listeners for their openness and their giving of time, or you could

compliment them on something not directly tied to the topic —
clothing, a personality trait, some statement made during the
course of conversation. People like to be liked, and you can certainly
find something in your listeners to like. The more your liking can be
conveyed in a genuine manner, the more your audience will like
you. Depending on the circumstances, other rewards might include:
(a) providing food or some other material goods, (b) doing or
promising a favor, or (c) relieving some sort of stress or bad feelings
that another is experiencing. Be aware of the needs of those you
contact; by helping someone out, not only will she be better off, but
you might be doing a little something indirectly for the cause of
peace.

Interestingly, research also shows that when someone is
rewarded, he will begin feeling good about other people who
happen to be around at the time, even if they had nothing to do with
the good feeling. [4] Taking this a step further, if you happen to be
around someone who is feeling good (regardless of what caused the
good feeling), that person will like you more; thus when you talk to
others about peace, try to catch them when they are feeling good.
Plan on approaching them at times and places when they are likely
to be in a good mood. It turns out that this will cause them to better
like not only you, but your ideas as well.

Another interesting finding is that we like not only those who
give us rewards, but also those to whom we give rewards. [2] If this
is the case, it seems logical that those people working together
cooperatively (and thus rewarding each other by helping) would like
each other; this turns out to be true. Working cooperatively has such
a strong effect on liking because not only are both parties giving
rewards, but they are also receiving them.

Thus, the more you can cooperate with people or groups in any
way, political or otherwise, the more they will like you. Cooperation
could involve anything from your peace group working with a local
service club to register voters or raise money for charity, to working
cooperatively with someone while fixing a car or a meal. The type of
cooperative ventures you undertake will depend upon whom you
wish to approach about peace.

Finally, be aware that through cooperation you will also like the
other person or group more, and some of their ideas may rub off on
you as well.

Similarities

There is strong evidence that we like others who have opinions similar to our own. [3] Surprisingly, the importance of the topic often does not matter. There is also a tendency for people with similar personalities to like each other; as the saying goes, "birds of a feather flock together." This is usually true unless the similar personalities tend to be conflicting; for instance, two very talkative people might not get along well if they had to compete for talking time.

Try applying these principles of similarity by having your peace message delivered by someone from your group who has similarities with the audience. Additionally, wherever possible mention any similar interests or opinions you have with your listener(s), whether politically related or not. Sometimes something as simple as wearing a t-shirt with the name of a pro sports team can make others feel some identification with you, and make you seem like a similar, average citizen. (See Chapters 10, 23, 24.)

Contact

The more time people spend together in neutral or pleasant circumstances, the more they will like each other. [5] Only under unpleasant circumstances will greater contact lead to less liking. What this means is that the more times your listeners see you, the better, be it listening to a speech or just seeing you at a restaurant. There are many ways to be seen more often; some examples: scheduling many formal or informal political contacts; becoming involved in nonpolitical events and gatherings in the community; and being pictured on television or in newspaper photographs.

One final point: though you will be liked more the more often you are seen, be aware of the importance of making a good first impression. Research shows that first impressions are sometimes hard to shake — for better or worse. [3]

Conclusion

I did not attempt here to present all the factors which increase liking, but I have described the most important ones. By applying what is known about the effects of personality traits, rewards, similarities, and frequency of personal contact in your work for peace, you and your message can have more impact.

References
1. Petty, R.E., & Cacioppo, J.T. (1981). *Attitudes and persuasion: Classic and contemporary approaches.* Dubuque, IA: Wm. C. Brown.
2. Berscheid, E., & Walster, E. (1978). *Interpersonal attraction* (2nd ed.). Reading, MA: Addison-Wesley.
3. Middlebrook, P. (1980). *Social psychology and modern life* (2nd ed.). New York: Alfred Knopf.
4. Baron, R., & Byrne, D. (1980). *Social psychology: Understanding human interaction* (3rd ed.). Newton, MA: Allyn & Bacon.
5. Zajonc, R.B. (1968). Attitudinal effects of mere exposure. *Journal of Personality and Social Psychology Monograph Supplement,* 9 (2, part 2), 2-27.

Suggested Readings
Baron, R., & Byrne, D. (1984). *Social psychology: Understanding human interaction* (4th ed.). Newton, MA: Allyn & Bacon. Baron and Byrne have a chapter which summarizes the basic literature in attraction.

Berscheid, E., & Walster, E. (1978). *Interpersonal attraction* (2nd ed.). Reading, MA: Addison-Wesley. This is a less recent, but more complete summary of research and theorizing in the area.

Hendrick, C., & Hendrick, S. (1983). *Liking, loving, and relating.* Monterey, CA: Brooks/Cole. The authors present a well-written summary of the area, which focuses on the development of relationships.

6

Peace Work and Your Mental Health

Helen Margulies Mehr

If I am not for myself, who will be for me?
But if I am for myself alone, what am I?
And if not now, when? — Hillel

When I told my husband that I had been asked to write a chapter on how to stay mentally healthy doing peace work, he said, "How is it possible for people who understand the nuclear danger to the planet and humanity to remain mentally healthy and *not* work for peace?"

There are a number of problems which are common to those working for peace, whether they are working to prevent nuclear war, end U.S. intervention in Central America, or otherwise reduce international conflict. Working for peace and justice can often be exceedingly discouraging. People feel powerless to effect change, and experience hopelessness and resulting depression in the face of horrendous world problems. It is not surprising for a person to develop a "what's-the-use" attitude and say, "What can one person accomplish?" There may also be a sense of being alone, of being unable to elicit support or give it.

In our work for peace we often experience other situations and emotions affecting our health, such as being the object of others' anger, or feeling hurt, anxious, or angry. This chapter will discuss these problems and give some basic suggestions on how to deal with them.

Overcoming Feelings of Despair
— *Acknowledge and accept* feelings of hurt, depression, or grief. Confronting a world filled with warring nations, where people are tortured, and where so much injustice prevails, naturally results in reactions of overwhelming anger and grief. Accept these feelings as natural, normal, and healthy. Set aside a little time for reflecting or writing whenever these emotions develop, even just five to ten minutes.

— *Release* these feelings. Most of us are inclined to repress unpleasant feelings. When skidding on an icy road, your first reaction may be to slam on the brakes. But the way to handle a skid is to take your foot off the brake pedal and gently steer the car. (This expresses the principle of "going along with a feeling." See [1].) In a similar vein, one can be emotionally "safer" by expressing strong emotions. Many people in our society are ashamed of crying and showing emotions, considering it weakness. Yet if we think about our violence-ridden planet, crying is an appropriate reaction. Accept these feelings as natural, normal, and healthy.

— *Express* feelings to others. If you are depressed, words of cheer from others are usually not helpful. Rather, just having others listen and acknowledge your pain can many times bring relief.

I remember seeing a woman whose daughter was murdered. It was with apprehension that I approached her, asking myself what could I do to help her. She said her friends had told her to stop crying and go on with her life. I told her to tell her friends they were wrong. We both had tears in our eyes, and putting my arms around her, I supported her deep grief and her right to express it for as long as she needed to. This affirmed her need to express the hurt within her, and her pain was relieved. To think she had not allowed herself to grieve over the death of her own daughter!

If pain and depression become severe, you may need to seek professional help and express your feelings to a therapist. Find a counselor who sees your concern for other people as appropriate, someone who feels it fitting that you experience pain for human suffering. Any therapist who sees such concern and pain merely as symptoms of personal problems will likely not be helpful to you.

— *Seek out* individuals or groups who have similar views. This will provide support and encouragement. I find comfort in knowing there are over 4500 peace groups in our country alone, and the correspondence I engage in with other activists revitalizes my energies. The American colonists set up the "Committee of Correspondence" before the Revolutionary War so they could secretly keep in touch with each other while struggling to uphold their rights. This network played a big part in drawing the colonists together for their struggle with Great Britain. By staying in contact with other individuals and groups who are working for peace, we feel an interconnectedness that builds our personal strength. [2]

— Stay physically fit. Taking care of yourself physically has a positive effect on mental health. For instance, physical activity is a good way to deal with depression, as well as other problems such as stress. Staying healthy requires effort, for it means engaging in a number of behaviors, and doing so over a period of time. It involves taking time for exercise, proper nutrition, relaxation and fun, and enough sleep; it also means avoiding or limiting smoking and alcohol. [3] These behaviors will improve your mental attitude and help give you the mental and physical energy to more effectively do your peace work.

— Develop and maintain hope. Finally, the best antidote to feelings of discouragement and pain is hope. But how can we stay hopeful? Where can we look for hope? In the story about the opening of Pandora's box and the releasing of evil, it is often forgotten that at the bottom of the box was hope. "Hoping is hard, active work. A person must use images and weave a pattern of ideas which presents the future in a potentially positive light." [4]

Each day, at a regular time, take 10 or 15 minutes (or longer) for reflection and/or prayer. [5] During this time, close your eyes and allow an image to form, actually see the way you would want people to live if the world were at peace. Visualize symbols as well, like an image of the planet earth as seen in totality by the astronauts. A colleague of mine visualizes a long rainbow of circling colored scarves; for her it represents a personal commitment to the idea we are all one. There was an organization in the early '60's in Berkeley, California, called "Acts for Peace." Their idea was to do an act for peace each day — write a letter, talk to a person, read a book — do something. I elaborate on this; loving the beach, I think each act then becomes like a grain of sand making up a beach. When I think of all the acts going on all over the world, it helps give me hope.

During times of reflection, also think of the people who inspire you: friends and colleagues, people you know personally who have shown courage in overcoming obstacles, public figures who helped advance peace and social justice through individual initiative, like Gandhi, Martin Luther King, Jr., Thomas Merton, Cesar Chavez, and Bishop Tutu.

It is also inspiring to read about the accomplishments of individual (and often unknown) citizens who have brought about changes in their communities and beyond. [6,7] Helen Caldicott, as an Australian pediatrician, became concerned about radiation levels found in milk. She persuaded a majority of Australians to boycott French products, succeeded in stopping above-ground nuclear testing in the South Pacific, and went on to influence millions as President of Physicians for Social Responsibility in the United States.

Think of important victories in the past, victories which were won through the efforts of ordinary people, and which overcame what appeared to be insurmountable obstacles: the Quakers' 100-year struggle to abolish slavery, women's achievement of the right to vote in the U.S. after 70 years of effort, the ending of monarchies as the world's dominant political force, and the gradual deterioration of imperialism through the years.

History teaches us that many things that had once been unimaginable have come to pass. Such knowledge can inspire not only yourself, but perhaps also those you meet who say they might support your cause if it were not a "hopeless dream."

Dealing With Your Anger and Hostility

Perhaps some might assume that those who work for world peace are not the kind of people who get angry. But, of course, we know that this is not the case. As with the emotions of discouragement and grief, anger should be regarded as normal and natural. There will always be times when we feel annoyed, angry, or even enraged. Disagreements and arguments among peace workers and with others are inevitable. Unfortunately, peace workers (particularly pacifists) have a particularly hard time acknowledging and accepting anger in themselves.

When you start to get angry, sometimes it's beneficial to directly communicate that anger, in which case you can start by saying, "I feel angry because..." and end up with, "...and I would like you to..." Don't blame the other person, but instead talk about *what needs to change* on the other person's part to improve the interaction. Better yet, if the circumstances allow it, say "I feel angry because..., and I would like us to ..." Talk about what needs to change on both persons' parts to improve the interaction (see Chapters 2, 15, and 16 for more on maintaining good communication).

Whenever your anger has risen such that your body is becoming tense, perhaps feeling as if it will soon "explode," or whenever you begin feeling very frustrated or out of control, say to the other person, "I'm feeling angry and I need to take a break. I'll be back soon." Leave the other person and go for a brief walk or run, or do something else physical; doing so will help discharge the tension in your body. [8] Taking a "break" is hard to do initially but it becomes easier with practice. And just acknowledging your anger to yourself, which taking a break first requires, will in fact make you feel less angry. The more you are aware of your anger and what effect it has on you, the more control you will have in dealing with it.

While alone, take a number of deep breaths and relax your muscles. Then, rather than blaming the other person (or yourself) for the conflict, accept the anger that you feel ("I'm not happy about the situation, but that's how I feel"). If you begin again to get angry about the conflict, say to yourself, "I'm beginning to feel angry again, and I need to take a break." Take a few more deep breaths. Finally, come back and ask if the person is willing to first discuss why the hostile situation developed before getting back to the original topic of discussion.

There are some people who have difficulty recognizing when they are feeling angry. One reason is that many people were taught as children that anger is a "bad" emotion. As a result, they try to ignore or suppress their anger. Anger that is not acknowledged often gets expressed in unhealthy ways, such as in violence or in trying to make other people feel inferior. You will better understand and be able to deal with your anger patterns if you look at messages you received in the past. How did your parents or siblings behave during conflicts? How did you behave when you got angry? What signals did you get from your parents or guardians regarding your expression of anger — was it O.K. or not O.K.? Many people discover that their angry behavior as adults is similar to that which they observed or were taught as children. Having insight into your anger patterns makes it easier to recognize, understand, and deal with your anger. [8, 9, 10]

Dealing With Others' Anger, Ridicule, or Abuse

It is difficult to listen to others getting angry. When people express anger toward you, you are apt to give another, and often inaccurate, meaning to what they are conveying, such as, "You're stupid." The first step in dealing with others' anger is to avoid assuming that the angered party is putting you down. If you view another's anger as a personal attack, you may become defensive and either retaliate automatically or think you have to respond in kind in order to "save face." In either case, a contest will likely develop in which you feel pressure to defeat, hurt, or prove wrong your "opponent."

Sometimes, of course, others will make personal attacks in the form of ridicule or criticism. But whether you falsely assume a personal attack or are directly ridiculed does not matter; you will likely feel defensive to some extent. The trick then is to stop the cycle, which leads from feeling defensive to becoming angry to creating or intensifying a conflict.

Develop an "emergency kit" — through practice — which you can use in the midst of a barrage of another's anger: *take a deep breath*, and another. *Count to five* to yourself while inhaling; count to five to yourself while exhaling. This helps relieve the tension inside you which normally builds during another's attack. Then, *consciously decide* not to give the other person the power to upset you. Eleanor Roosevelt once said that no one can make you feel inferior without your consent. Finally, *concentrate on your conviction* that if others are indeed attacking you personally, it is due either to their own insecurity or to the weakness of the position they are espousing. [8, 9, 10] (Also see Chapter 18 on how to stay calm during potentially violent confrontations.)

Handling Anxiety
Exercises for dealing with everyday anxieties. It is unrealistic to think you can eliminate anxiety. The types of activities that peace workers typically engage in will not allow that. For instance, you

may plan a major event involving a great deal of time and energy; as the day approaches, it is likely you will experience a great deal of anxiety about the outcome. And there are times you will be anxious about talking to certain citizens or legislators who are important to some aspect of your work, such as the passage of a Congressional bill.

— To deal with your worries, set aside a time each day for 10 or 15 minutes, or whatever time you need, to *actively worry*. Think of the worst thing that could happen for the events you'll be involved in, and what you would do about them. Then later, when you become aware of a worrisome thought, say to yourself, "I've already done my worrying." Then take several deep breaths and internally count each inhalation and each exhalation you take. Switch your thoughts to pleasant experiences in which you have felt totally relaxed — lying at the beach, in the garden, whatever. Use all your senses, and if, for example, you imagine the beach, feel the warmth of the sun, hear the waves against the shore, and see the beauty of nature. Doing so will enable you to recapture a relaxed feeling. Learning to reduce worrying requires practice, as every skill does, but I have never found anyone who could not switch their unpleasant thoughts to more positive ones.

— Practice the following relaxation technique so it will work for you when you need it — you can't just *tell* yourself to "relax" and expect it to happen. Sit in a comfortable chair or lie down, and take some deep breaths. Don't make a conscious effort to *try* to relax because that only increases the tension. Instead, just *let go*; imagine what a noodle looks like when you throw it in the water. It goes limp, and that is the message you want to give your muscles. After several deep breaths, start at the top of your head, loosening up the scalp muscles. Then proceed downward, systematically relaxing each set of muscles — face, chest, shoulders, arms, back, thighs, lower legs, and feet and toes. After this progressive relaxation you may wish to visualize a relaxing scene, as discussed in the section above.

Nuclear war anxieties and dealing with them. The specific anxiety associated with nuclear war issues is a special problem. To become awakened to the fact that our species is in great and immediate danger of extinction invokes a sense of incredible pain, despair, fear, and bitterness — all the negative emotions and feelings our minds can conjure up.

But how can we deal with such negative emotions? Many have taken the route of blocking them out and not "really" thinking about the horrors and ever-present danger of nuclear war; they have engaged in "psychic numbing" or "nuclear numbing." [11] Such a process, though perhaps beneficial to the person's mental health, may eliminate any motivation on the person's part to actively support the anti-nuclear movement. We in the peace movement can do three things to lessen nuclear numbing and then attempt to gain support from these people: continue to spread the word about the horrors of nuclear war; stress that through public support it is possible to change current nuclear policies; and present anti-nuclear proposals that seem feasible (Chapter 9 offers ideas on the latter).

There are some things we ourselves can do to better deal with our own nuclear war anxieties and despair, and to give us more hope and confidence for the future.

— Employ the previous suggestions dealing with discouragement and despair, particularly those on developing and maintaining hope. The exercises already given for reducing anxiety will help when worries surface.

— Imagine the gradual steps necessary over the next ten to fifteen years which would culminate in a nuclear-weapon-free world; what changes in U.S.-U.S.S.R. policies and relations would be necessary? Start ten or fifteen years in the future and work backwards. You'll become more confident that a nuclear-free world is possible.

— Cultivate a sense of humor (relating to nuclear issues and otherwise) to better accept nuclear anxieties (see Chapter 33).

— Acknowledge that we have at least the present moment, and we should enjoy life fully, taking encouragement in knowing we have committed the time and resources we can to help save our planet.

Conclusion

Psychologists have worked with individuals who have had the most terrible childhoods and yet have become truly remarkable people. The research about these "super children" who have survived tragic childhoods shows that in some way they made a decision not to be engulfed in their past. [12] As did these children, we can see our circumstances as a challenge; we can *decide not to be victims* — to work for peace, regardless of failures in the past and many likely ones in the future.

Thomas Merton said, "When you are doing the sort of work you have taken on... you may have to face the fact that your work will be apparently worthless and achieve no result at all, if not perhaps results opposite to what you expect. As you get used to this idea, you start more and more to concentrate not on the results but on the value, the rightness, the truth of the work itself... Insisting on evidence of success might quickly lead to despair and paralysis. The big results are not in your hands or mine, but they suddenly happen, and we can share in them." [13]

Sebastiane Olguin, a co-worker of Cesar Chavez, said at a conference on non-violence that he didn't know whether the farm workers would ever get what they needed, but the process was in itself rewarding for him.

We can find rewards in the friendships we make with caring, fun, and interesting people who open up new vistas for us by telling about their lives.

Finally, Dr. Alan Nelson, a psychologist who closed his clinical practice in order to work full time for peace, told me after five years of full time peace work: "I feel much greater hope, and my mental health and joy and peace of mind increase the more I do work on peace issues." Thus, although peace work has its times of despair, anger, and anxiety, it can also be filled with much joy and hope.

References

1. Fisch, R., Watzlawick, J ., & Weakland, J. (1974). *Change: Principles of problem formation and problem resolution*. New York: W.W. Norton.

2. Mehr, H.M., & Webster, M. (1984, December). Peacemaking works. Association of Humanistic Psychology *Perspective*, p. 21.

3. Shealy, N. (1977). *90 days to self-health*. New York: Dial Press.

4. Breznitz, N. cited in Carol Turkington (1984), Israeli researcher finds hope eases stress, affects outcome. *APA Monitor* p. 18.

5. Nelson, A. (1984). Prayer for peace: Meditation, contemplation and nonviolence in our nuclear age. *Journal of Humanistic Psychology*, vol. 24, No. 3, p. 93.

6. Kresh, P. (1969). *The power of the unknown citizen*. New York: J.B. Lippincott.

7. Boulding, E. (1969). *The underside of history: A view of women through time*. Boulder, CO: Westview Press.

8. Sonkin, D.J., & Durphy, M. (1982). *Learning to live without violence*. San Francisco: Volcano Press.
9. Bower, S.A. and Bower, G.H. (1976). *Asserting yourself: A practical guide for positive change*. Reading, MA: Addison-Wesley.
10. Tavris, C. (1982). Anger defused. *Psychology Today* Nov., pp.25-35.
11. Lifton, R.J., & Falk, R. (1982). *Indefensible weapons: The political and psychological case against nuclearism*. New York: Basic Books.
12. Pines, M. (1979, January). Superkids. *Psychology Today*, p. 53-63.
13. Faust, J. (1980). *Thomas Merton: A pictorial biography*. New York: Paulist Press. p. 79.

Suggested Readings
Ferguson, Marilyn, (1980). *The aquarian conspiracy*. Los Angeles: J. P. Tarcher. Personal and social transformation in the 1980s. The author speaks to those who are experiencing a growing capacity for change in themselves and know that it is possible for others. There is evidence for hope that our society can be changed.

Hunter, Allan A. (1962) *Courage in both hands*. New York: Ballantine Books. This book has examples of people who used daring and creative actions in crisis situations and illustrates the fact that each person can accomplish more than he or she believed possible, turning from violence.

Macy, Joanna R. (1983). *Despair and personal power in the nuclear age*. Philadelphia: New Society Publishers. Macy presents a clear and perceptive analysis of the psychological problems that peace workers must face, and provides good methods for coping with these problems.

Rass, Dam, and Gorman, Paul (1985). *How can I help? Stories and reflections on service*. New York: Alfred A. Knopf. Chapter six expresses the importance of understanding that we need a strong sense of who we are. The authors stress that we need to be free of self-righteousness and grounded in a kind of inner clarity and quiet self-assurance. There is also a good chapter on burnout.

Acknowledgements

I wish to express my appreciation for their suggestions to Dr. Amal Barkouki, Dr. Virginia Dupraw, Dr. Wendy Martyna, Ms. Annie Head, Dr. Joanna Macy, the Board of Northern California Psychologists for Social Responsibility, and members of the San Jose Chapter of the Fellowship of Reconciliation.

For specific ideas in the section on *anger*, I wish to acknowledge my indebtedness to D.J. Sonkin and M. Durphy [8], Sharon and Dr. Gordon Bower [9], and Dr. Carol Tavris [10].

7

Overcoming Feelings of Helplessness and Depression

Gerald D. Oster

Mary worked actively for peace-related causes. She had been involved in peace organizations since her high school days, doing everything from writing articles and soliciting petition signatures to marching in demonstrations and speaking at rallies. Now, at 23, Mary found herself taking on so many reponsibilities that she could no longer meet all her commitments. Rather than realizing that she was just taking on too big a load, she began criticizing herself for not being able to accomplish all she could. A pattern of self-criticism followed over the next several months.

Before a demonstration which was projected to be exceedingly large, Mary suddenly became anxious for no apparent reason and expressed many feelings of sadness and an uncharacteristic pessimism regarding the movement's success. Her once-hectic life came to a standstill, and despite the support of her friends, Mary became increasingly depressed and inactive.

John yearned to be more of an activist but stayed in the background, yielding to his lack of confidence and shyness. He agreed with many of the peace-related issues but felt ineffective, helpless, and overwhelmed by the extent of the problems. After joining an organization which was attempting to stop the

Editor's Note: *The focus of this chapter is on the kind of helplessness and depression that can result from frustration in one's day-to-day peacework. See Chapter 6 for suggestions dealing with the possibility of despair and hopelessness in the face of world problems.*

construction of a weapons-related facility, his feelings of self-worth dropped even further due to an unfortunate incident. Before the first major rally, a legal injunction against the event was enacted, which had the effect of halting any demonstration. John took this defeat very personally, thinking that if he could have worked harder or had known someone in the legislature, the rally would have taken place as planned. After this perceived failure, John felt that he was powerless to change the issues and he avoided all further involvement.

Learned Helplessness

Although the two fictitious individuals described in the above situations are of very different temperaments, both experienced similar feelings of helplessness and depression. Both felt that they had lost control of the outcomes in their lives, and this feeling began a cycle of self-degrading thoughts in each of them (e.g., "I am powerless to control any situation"). This culminated in a belief system consisting of negative feelings about themselves and about the world in which they live. They became less active as they began to view themselves as powerless people who were unable to help themselves, let alone help change problems in society.

This perceived loss of control sometimes leads to a form of clinical depression called "learned helplessness." [1] Even though the above examples might be considered extreme, it is likely that everyone has at one time or another experienced a similar situation and has felt this negative thought process begin.

The Thought-Feeling Connection

Many theorists of modern psychology believe that how individuals view the world and themselves will ultimately determine how they will feel and act, and that thoughts and disturbed feelings are interrelated. Rarely, they suggest, can one feel upset without also having associated disturbance-creating thoughts. [2, 3, 4] For instance, such unrealistic views as "I must be a success in everything I do," will ultimately stir up feelings of anxiety or sadness when faced with any failure. Conversely, sad feelings may produce irrational beliefs, e.g., "I'll never experience success from now on." This type of thought-feeling connection can happen fairly regularly to peace workers, who often run into "brick walls" in their efforts for peace. Fortunately, much psychological research has shown that when people are able to alter their flow of disturbing thoughts, their feelings and subsequent behaviors become much more positive. [5]

Monitoring Your Activities and Associated Feelings and Thoughts

If you happen to find yourself in the early stages of this cycle, what can you do to avert these negative thoughts and resulting feelings? You might first attempt to create what is termed an "activity schedule." [6] This technique calls for you first to make an hour-by-hour list of your daily schedule, peace-related or otherwise, keeping record of those activities which you find enjoyable and rating (on a scale of 1 to 5) how much pleasure you get from them. From this information you should soon realize that you are deriving more satisfaction from your daily activities than you had previously thought; this will disprove any notion you might have had that your situation was hopeless. Next, you should rate the negative moods you experience during your day's activities, e.g., how much anxiety you felt during your telephone conversation with your boss. From these various ratings you will discover that positive and negative feelings tend to be limited in time and are associated with specific activities. [6] You will also discover that your mood improves when you have completed assignments or have engaged in particular activities. You can then begin to do more of those pleasureable activities and schedule more accomplishable tasks. Doing so will improve your mood and productive energy. (Hints for engaging in accomplishable tasks are covered later in the chapter.)

You can take these suggestions a step further by becoming more aware of those negative thoughts which lead to bad feelings. To begin, pay attention to your negative moods and replay in your mind exactly what went on before the bad mood began. Try to recall the thoughts that led to those feelings. For example, when you find yourself becoming nervous when planning a peace activity for your organization, examine the thoughts which preceded the anxiety. You might have been thinking about how you were criticized the last time you did planning, and perhaps you had attributed that criticism to a lack of ability on your part. Ask yourself whether the criticism was valid, i.e., whether the peace activity really turned out to be that bad. A past criticism can infringe on your present efficiency;

you need to realize that things probably have changed since the original criticism.

Questioning Your Assumptions About Yourself

It is most important at this point to also begin questioning your assumptions. Are you: (1) falsely assuming that your negative thoughts or self-criticisms are valid (i.e., confusing thoughts with facts)?; (2) holding beliefs without checking out your ideas with others?; (3) overgeneralizing failures (i.e., thinking that you will fail at everything)?; (4) not becoming aware of factors beyond your control which may have caused a failed project?; (5) overlooking your obvious strengths or underestimating the impact you might have on others?; or (6) thinking that the present negative situation will never change?

A case illustration might emphasize the above points and also provide another means to overcome destructive thoughts:

Sue was beginning to believe that she had nothing valuable to contribute in group meetings as she always listened to someone else's view rather than expressing her own. Although she privately differed on many of the ideas being expressed, she had always taken criticisms of her opinion very personally, which led to increasing feelings of anxiety. When she attempted to understand why she always felt so nervous when wanting to say something, she discovered that she would say to herself statements like, "What would the other group members think of my ideas?" "Will I be able to influence anyone with my ideas?" "Will the others just think I am jealous of the person I oppose?" "Does what I have to say really have any relevance?" "Wouldn't it be awful if I made a mistake in public?" (It is these self-imposed statements which many psychologists hypothesize cause feelings of anxiety. They believe that emotions nearly always are created by personal thoughts and beliefs.) [7]

Fortunately, after receiving advice from a friend, Sue began questioning the assumptions she was making and thoughts she was having about her problem with public speaking. This led her to make an agreement with herself to increase the proportion of time spent expressing personal views in meetings. It was only after she tried this and discovered that nothing terrible happened when she made a mistake (and that she was not a terrible communicator even if she failed to influence anybody), that she overcame her fear of public speaking and participated actively in group meetings.

Although this is an isolated example, you can use the same basic technique in other situations to monitor and question the thoughts which lead to negative moods. Try to think of some examples in your daily life where different moods may have been precipitated by your thoughts or beliefs.

Plan Accomplishable Activities

Another practical strategy you can use to improve your mood and increase your energy is to plan more accomplishable activities, and then reward yourself for even minor successes.

Say, for instance, that you have been wanting to write a pamphlet concerning the atrocities of war, but have never found the time to do it or do not know where to begin. If you don't break the task down into small steps, you may feel overwhelmed and give up before trying. By breaking the activity down into smaller parts, you are more likely to accomplish it. In writing the pamphlet, you could begin by going to the library and using the card catalog for 15 minutes to discover what books are available on the topic. Then on the next visit, go inside and skim several relevant books and articles for 30 minutes, taking notes on which sources deserve further use. Return to the library for an hour to study and outline, and so on.

As you progress through the project, you should reward yourself for each success, perhaps stopping for ice cream or a beer after visiting the library, or going someplace special at the end of a productive week. The actual writing of the pamphlet may also be a stumbling block; again, break it down into small accomplishable steps — write for ten minutes and not more on the first night, fifteen minutes on the second, twenty on the third, etc. This time-management technique of breaking activities down into easily accomplished subgoals can be applied to almost any task you might want to attempt.

The following scenario demonstrates another method of establishing goals and subgoals, and how they can enhance feelings of success:

Tom was in charge of a large political organization which seemed to be getting bogged down by its own weight. Because of constant phone calls, distractions from visitors, and meetings which seemed unfocused, very little work was getting done, and Tom began blaming himself for the group's inefficiency. In order to accomplish more objectives and thus feel better about the job he was supposed to be doing, he rearranged the group's structure in the following manner:

1. He identified as many goals as possible for the organization;
2. He listed the goals in order, from the most important to the least, and put his energy into them accordingly;
3. He broke down all complex tasks into simple steps (e.g., to prepare a report he went to the library for background information, then checked previous reports, next used someone as a "sounding board," and finally set a deadline and began writing);
4. He assigned as much work as possible to others;
5. He established a quiet time for two hours of the day when he would not be interrupted by phone calls or visitors. [8]

With the introduction of this program, the organization became much more effective and Tom overcame his disturbing thoughts which were beginning to be self-defeating.

Conclusion

This chapter began with examples of two persons who became disappointed and discouraged at their performance during peace-related activities, resulting in self-defeating thoughts and behaviors.

Psychologists have learned that it is a person's distortion of actual facts that begins a vicious cycle of thoughts and moods which lead to the expectation that nothing can change the situation and any attempts to change will always fail. The result usually produces less motivation and possible feelings of helplessness.

Techniques reviewed here encourage positive beliefs and expectations by incorporating pleasureable activities and accomplishable tasks into the peaceworker's life. Small task successes increase feelings of mastery and control and, in turn, the chances for further success. It is also necessary to question negative faulty beliefs and assumptions about onesself which lead to anxious and sad feelings.

Appropriate use of techniques such as those described can help peace activists keep positive attitudes about themselves and their work.

References
1. Seligman, M.E. (1975). *Helplessness*. San Francisco: W.H. Freeman.
2. Ellis, A. (1985). Cognition and affect in emotional disturbance. *American Psychologist*, 40, 471.
3. Beck, A.T. (1976). *Cognitive therapy and the emotional disorders*. New York: International Universities Press.
4. Burns, D. (1980). *Feeling good: The new mood therapy*. New York: Morrow.
5. Meichenbaum, D., & Jaremko, M.E. (Eds.) (1983). *Stress reduction and prevention*. New York: Plenum
6. Emery, G. (1981). *A new beginning: How to change your life through cognitive therapy*. New York: Simon & Schuster.
7. Ellis, A., & Harper, R.A. (1975). *A new guide to rational living*. Englewood Cliffs, NJ: Prentice-Hall.
8. Davidson, J. (1978). *Effective time management: A practical handbook*. New York: Human Sciences Press.

Suggested Readings
Ellis, A., & Harper, R.A. (1975). *A new guide to rational living*. Englewood Cliffs, NJ: Prentice-Hall. This is a revised edition of a pioneering self-help book which demonstrates that people have many more solutions to their problems than they actually realize. The authors offer a wide range of educational techniques to show how people can change from their style of self-defeating behaviors.

Davidson, J. (1978). *Effective time management: A practical handbook*. New York: Human Sciences Press. This is an easily consumable guide for persons with managerial responsibilities who need hints for bringing to their workers better methods of managing their time. It provides a basis for changing structure and its effect on subsequent behaviors.

Emery, G. (1981). *A new beginning: How to change your life through cognitive therapy*. New York: Simon & Schuster. This is a practical and easy-to-use self-help book that emphasizes the use of cognitive techniques for aiding in problems of weight control, drug abuse, suicidal thoughts, and feelings of depression.

8

Making Peace with Yourself

Elaine Yarbrough

We often search for interpersonal and international solutions in our work for peace. However, no amount or type of interaction with others is likely to bring world peace unless we first find peace within ourselves. This chapter is about promoting internal peacemaking in order to improve our work and communication with others; it describes internal conflicts which peace workers often experience, the consequences of ignoring such conflicts, and the steps to take to promote internal peace.

Conflict Within Yourself

Internal conflict may be described as a clash between different aspects of ourselves. [1,2] For instance, one part of you may think you should spend every waking moment working for peace, while another part wants some relaxation. If such a conflict develops, each part will negatively affect your life or work. The desire to relax will slow down your work to some extent and you will not feel as productive as you could be when you are working, while the urge to work will make you feel guilty when you are relaxing. Further, if you see others relaxing, you may judge them as being uncommitted, just as you do to yourself. The result is that you become dissatisfied with your co-workers, feel frustrated about work in general, and hurt your group's productivity by causing interpersonal conflict. And all of these external events are but a mirror of your own internal conflict.

Internal conflict often comes from seeing the world in

incompatible opposites. You may, for example, believe that conflict and peace are opposites. If you see yourself as peaceful, you don't feel you can be in conflict with others. When conflict does emerge, then, you have to psychologically deny or distort it in some way, but this denial will eventually erupt in unproductive ways, like time-consuming debates with co-workers over trivial matters within your peace group.

There are four types of internal conflict that often affect peace workers, the most central of which is between *power* and *love*. For many of us power is negative, and in opposition to equality, democracy, peace, love, and all the other values we hold dear. The irony is that when the need for power (control over one's environment) is not satisfied, it goes underground and increases, making it difficult to deal with issues and persons in a peaceful and just way. [3] In practice, that may mean being nice on the surface but gossiping to others about co-workers after a meeting, holding up decisions during group discussions, or being upset when another group member has influence.

A second internal conflict is between *inclusion* and *exclusion*. As a peace worker, you probably believe that "the system" excludes certain citizens from resources or influence in society. To counter that exclusion, you may include people in some tasks better left to others. For instance, a person in your group may want to speak to public audiences about peace issues, but you know that she does so in judgmental ways that inevitably turn audiences off. As a result of not coming to terms internally with how to properly balance inclusion and exclusion, you do the movement more harm than good by allowing that person to speak on behalf of your group.

A third battle is between *strategy* and *honesty*. Feeling you must be absolutely honest and aboveboard in all interactions can lead to inflexibility in employing social change strategies. For example, it is sometimes appropriate to be tough privately, like demanding that a weapons facility manager respect your right to protest at the facility, while publicly being polite and accommodating with plant officials during the protest itself. Or you might have to use a different communication style when you talk to a conservative group than that you would use with a liberal group. In both cases, you may balk at changing your manner because it seems dishonest; consequently you always communicate in your one preferred style, appealing to those who already share your values and making no headway with others.

A fourth internal conflict typical to peace workers is between *selfishness* and *altruism*. Your altruistic side thinks, "So many millions are suffering out there, I can't take any time for myself to relax; I can't look at the suffering in my own family because there are others worse off." Then what happens? You burn out, and your family wishes peace could begin at home.

When we deny certain parts of ourselves (power, exclusion, strategizing, and selfishness), they often gain influence rather than disappear. They "leak" into our communication, and our words and nonverbal behaviors don't match. You may be saying, for instance, "I respect your opinion," while clenching your fists and interrupting the other. Such inconsistencies in communication lead to confusion and mistrust.

If instead of denying them, we were to embrace the so-called "negative" aspects of ourselves (power, selfishness, etc.), we could defuse the detrimental influence they have over us, [1] and could instead use them in positive ways. We could use power in situations where it was needed, we could make difficult decisions that might hurt people's feelings in the short run but are necessary in the long run. We could vary our communication styles to influence the many kinds of groups that could be supportive of peace, and we could take care of ourselves. By reducing conflict within ourselves, we will be better able to reduce conflict in the world.

Five Steps to Internal Harmony

What, then, can you do to create internal harmony and thus use all your strengths? Here is a five-step plan that can help you deal not only with the four major conflicts thus far discussed, but also with other aspects of yourself which you may be denying and which may be hindering your peace making:

-AWARENESS — identifying the parts of you in conflict.

-ACCEPTANCE — believing all parts of you can be used for good.

-EMPOWERMENT — developing the parts of yourself that have been under-used.

-INTEGRATION — making peace between the conflicting parts so that they can help each other.

-SYNTHESIS — communicating with others with empathy, responsibility, and flexibility.

These steps of internal peacemaking are meant to help you recognize, understand, legitimize, and use parts of yourself that you do not now accept. As with interpersonal conflict, all parties must feel accepted and understood if the conflict is to be constructive.

Awareness. How do you gain awareness? First, notice the kinds of people you consider extremely objectionable. I am not speaking just about those who are irritating, but those to whom you instantly respond in a very negative way, those you want to set straight and reform. This strong response often means they embody traits you are denying in yourself. When you say, "I can't stand that arrogant weapons facility official — he won't listen to any idea other than his own," it may be that you are also arrogant and stubborn. You may be clashing so dramatically with him precisely because both of you are so dogmatic. Though you are aware of the flexible, open-minded side of yourself, you cannot use it well because you are blind to the effects of your dogmatic side.

Once you recognize your own obstinance, you may still be in conflict with the official, but at least you realize that other arguments besides your own could have merit. You might now understand the official's feeling that the facility should be kept open to save jobs, and that you will need to take this into consideration as you formulate a plan for relocation of workers. You will be more effective as a peace worker (and will be more likely to reach agreements) because you are now more able to listen to others.

You can also increase your awareness of internal conflict by noticing emotions within yourself you find unacceptable. Can you accept anger within yourself? How about hate, sadness, joy, or humor? If you find an emotion unacceptable in yourself, you will usually find it unacceptable in others. The result is that when others express your unacceptable emotion, you may try to talk them out of it ("You aren't really angry,"), penalize them for it ("You can't participate in this group"), or indicate that their emotion is inappropriate to the situation ("You shouldn't be laughing about such a serious political issue"). You end up both failing to deal with your own feelings about an issue and preventing others from expressing theirs.

Third, notice the kinds of individuals who surround you.

Oftentimes the people you choose as friends, co-workers, or mates may reflect what you have not dealt with inside yourself. For example, if you have not dealt with or accepted anger within yourself, you may keep selecting friends and co-workers who are consistently angry.

Finally, to increase your awareness, pay attention to feedback from others about your behavior. You may think you are always gentle with people, but others may tell you they feel threatened by you. By acknowledging your use of power you can begin to use it more responsibly, rather than spending your energy denying it.

Acceptance. The second step of internal peacemaking goes beyond acknowledging a certain part of you to welcoming it, understanding its potentially positive side. For example, selfishness, once accepted, becomes the need and right to take care of yourself. With this acceptance, you likely will be less over-extended and more effective in your work. Also, dominance, once accepted, becomes the direct and legitimate use of power. You realize that you needn't run everything in your peace group in order to satisfy the power aspect of yourself; you can gain satisfaction by gently guiding others on tasks which you have delegated to them.

To gain acceptance, imagine the disliked part of you as a small child that may have misbehaved. Treat that part of yourself firmly but with love, coaching it to use more positive means to meet its needs. Also hang around others who can accept those parts of yourself that you see as negative and perhaps overwhelming — their acceptance may help you begin to accept yourself.

Empowerment. The third step involves developing under-used parts of yourself. After identifying the positive quality behind a negative aspect of yourself, you are ready to develop its use. Do so by finding role models who demonstrate responsible use of power, for example. They can be colleagues, friends, public figures, or even media or historic personalities. Notice how they act, what choices they make, how they affect people over time. Doing this will diminish your fears about using certain aspects of yourself.

Try new behaviors in low-risk situations to test their effectiveness. Get direct coaching from respected others on being powerful, yet not overpowering. Set a time-share plan for different aspects of yourself. For example, determine that you are free to relax at certain times if you can work without interruption at other times. As more aspects of yourself are empowered, it feels natural to use the different parts, and to do so more responsibly.

Integration. The fourth step deals with actual conflict between parts of yourself. Since power is a central issue for most of us, the conflict between power and love is used as an example. As you manage your internal conflict, ask the two parts of yourself some questions:

Q1: *What does each part want and need?*

The love side may need to be connected in cooperative ways with others, may want to care for others. The power side may need to have influence — it understands that there are some hard-ball players out there who can't be soft-soaped by love. It may recognize the need to push to solve certain problems.

Q2: *What does each side have in common?*

Both want to see a more peaceful world. They may also share the desire to be connected to other people, though they have different ways of reaching out to people.

Q3: *What is in conflict? Where do the sides differ?*

The love side believes anything can be accomplished with gentleness and enough nurturing. The power side believes it's a dog-eat-dog world where you'd better watch out or people will take advantage.

Q4: *What would each side be without the other, and what can each contribute to the other?*

Love without power would be naive and sentimental, like the well-meaning but sometimes ineffective flower children of the sixties who tried to achieve peace by putting flowers into the barrels of guns raised against them. The power side without love would become manipulative and lacking in regard for others. When both sides are recognized and allowed to have their say, each contributes to the other, and becomes modified in the process.

The power side can become more flexible — knowing some people can and some can't be trusted, knowing "easy-going" as well as "tough" strategies work, knowing when to push and when to be silent. The result is that power becomes more compassionate. For instance, instead of trying to influence weapons facility workers by calling them "murderers," you might strive to find them alternative employment, or you might get them to examine their involvement in militarism by demonstrating how such involvement affects people they love, e.g., money going to weapons manufacturing is redirected from the Social Security system, which provides for the workers' parents.

Likewise, the love side becomes wiser, learning that love is not the only human motivation, and understanding that love is sometimes best communicated by setting firm guidelines.

When you can truly integrate power and love, you will reach a wholeness that will allow you to deal effectively with your world. Gandhi was a good example, for he was willing to push the system when it was necessary, yet was sensitive enough to realize when certain protest actions were best stopped because they were having negative effects on the opposing side. For instance, he halted the civil disobedience in Bardoli when 22 British police were killed by Indians.

Q5: *What will each side threaten to do if not given a voice?*

It is often frightening to recognize internal conflict, especially when one part of you dominates at the expense of the other. It helps to introduce internal dialogue, which includes asking each side, "What will you do to prevent the other side from reaching its goal if you are not able to reach yours?" In response, the power side may threaten to be unnecessarily harsh on co-workers who don't complete their tasks for your group. The love side may threaten to be confused and inarticulate when the power side is trying to persuade an unsympathetic community audience. These threats are beneficial, because they ensure that each part has its say.

Synthesis. When the first four steps of internal peacemaking are achieved, synthesis, the final phase, is automatic. Internal decision-making and interpersonal communication are changed; they become flexible and responsible. You are not unintentionally "leaking" hidden messages, and you are not fighting with others who represent unacknowledged parts of yourself. The result is that you are a better peace worker.

Conclusion

We don't usually view our internal processes like a community, where every part must be recognized, utilized, and kept in dialogue with each other. However, interpersonal and international peace will come only through people who have a different vision of how things should and can be. That vision must encompass what you have allowed yourself to become internally. When you are whole and understand how to recognize, appreciate, and integrate your internal differences, you will have a special understanding of how to integrate differences among people in the world.

References
1. Delazlo, V.S. (Ed.) (1959). *Basic writings of C.G. Jung.* New York: Random House.
2. Yarbrough, E. (1985). Intrapersonal conflict: A neglected and necessary level of intepersonal conflict analysis. In A. Goldman (Ed.), *Public communication* (pp. 361-375). Malabar, FL: Robert E. Kreiger Publishers.
3. May, R. (1967). *Power and innocence.* New York: W.W. Norton.

Suggested Readings
Bandler, R., & Grinder, J. (1982). *Re-framing: Neuro-linguistic programming and the transformation of meaning.* Moab, UT: Real People Press. This is a detailed and practical overview of how internal parts of the self can be re-defined so that peoples' communication is more effective. It would help to read *Frogs Into Princes* by the same authors for a fuller understanding of Neuro-Linguistic Programming, upon which reframing is based.

Jampolsky, G. G. (1979). *Love is letting go of fear.* Millbrae, CA: Celestial Arts. A simple and practical guide to experiencing peace in our lives; it combines personal examples with daily lessons.

Polster, E., & Polster, M. (1973). *Gestalt therapy integrated.* New York: Random House. This book provides a psychological basis for viewing the personality as multiple parts that must develop effective communication for mental health and good interpersonal relationships.

Yarbrough, E. (1985). Intrapersonal conflict: A neglected and necessary level of interpersonal conflict analysis. In A. Goldman (Ed.), *Public communication* (pp. 361-375). Malabar, FL: Robert E. Kreiger Publishers. This article includes theoretical background, a model, and examples of internal conflict management; it should be read for more understanding of the processes discussed here.

9

Preventing Burnout

Wendy Forman and Laura Slap

Many who devote a significant portion of their time to peace work find themselves occasionally feeling they just do not have any more energy to devote to the cause. They are suffering from burnout. For some it is an occasional experience that requires a nonpolitical recovery period; for others, it may even signal the end of their active involvement in peace work. In this chapter we'll explore the nature of burnout, what causes it, and some suggestions for making it less likely to occur.

Understanding Burnout

Burnout can best be understood as a reaction to stress, [1] and as the end product of unsuccessful coping strategies. Stress can be defined as a "nonspecific response of the body to any demands" (p. 369) [2], and can result merely from the wear and tear of daily living. Peace workers, however, are even more likely to suffer burnout because our work requires the maintenance of idealistic values [1] in the face of constant awareness of the dangerous world situation; being aware of such danger naturally causes stress. Becoming politically active has the potential to reduce this stress, because activism helps us feel we are doing something to make the world more peaceful. The way we go about our activism, however, will determine whether it helps us successfully cope with the stress. We actually increase our stress when we add too many commitments and activities to our schedules, when we expect to immediately change all unjust laws and policies, and when we ignore our own mental and physical needs for rest and enjoyment.

Stress progresses in three stages: an initial alarm reaction of anxiety, an attempted coping ("resistance"), and a stage of exhaustion in which the depletion of energy leads to fatigue. [3] These three stages repeat themselves throughout our life's activities and it is important to recognize when we are approaching the final stage (burnout) and to replenish our energies.

Unfortunately, the body itself complicates matters; during the initial stage, tension and excitement lead to an increase in the production of adrenalin, which may lead to a kind of euphoria or intoxication. This intoxication can be addicting and can lead to an attempt to be constantly active without allowing time for relaxation. The euphoria is sometimes followed by depression, because the body stops producing adrenalin at some point after the stressful feelings end.

One strategy to avoid these consequences is to become more aware of our progress through these stages, to regulate our stress levels by monitoring what activities produce stress, and to limit stressful activities. [1,4] Also, try to see stressful situations as challenges to be overcome; such an attitude will help you maintain a sense of control and thus better cope with the situation. [5]

In your peacework you will often be trying to change things in your environment (changing others' attitudes about peace, passing government bills, trying to bring coalitions of people together); these activities can all cause stress, but they can also be seen as challenges and thus help you cope with them. Accept, however, that you cannot control everything in your environment, and the world will not dramatically change in the near future. Thus you will need to deal with your frustrations and stress with specific sorts of activities so that burnout can be prevented. Below are some group and individual coping techniques which may be helpful. Chapter 6 gives suggestions for maintaining good mental health in doing peace work; some of those suggestions will help in preventing burnout as well.

More Suggestions for Preventing Burnout

Support Groups. [1,6] Form your own personal support group — not an official organization, but friends and colleagues you can call on at any time to share frustrations, fears, depressions, and even hopes and fantasies. It should be a group that celebrates and reinforces your successes and gives you encouragement for the future. The people in this informal small network do not necessarily need to be working for peace themselves. In fact, some non-activist friends who are basically sympathetic to the cause can often be exceptionally helpful precisely because they are not going through the same thing.

One Day at a Time. Most people, when they first become active, go through a hectic period of frenzied, constant motion. Though it is hard to say no to any request or project at this time, you need to turn *some* down; if you are not able to stop your frantic pace, instant burnout will inevitably result. Try not to apologize for what you have not done or cannot do. It will help to get some hints from "veterans" who have already been through this stage and survived. Also, begin considering the quest for peace as a lifetime project; this will help you realize the need to conserve your resources and choose priorities more carefully. Each day schedule only what you can reasonably accomplish, and where possible, start with tasks you have already prioritized as most important.

After the initial period of frenzy, consider the possibility of becoming more of a "specialist." [4] If you are a good and persuasive speaker, think about taking on more speaking engagements and fewer commitments to stuffing envelopes. There are some people who would be petrified to speak in public but actually do not mind stuffing envelopes. Chapters 3 and 4 can help you in deciding on which peace activities to pursue.

It is also helpful to keep a Peace Journal, even one with only brief entries; it can be a real boost to return to it occasionally and realize just how much you've already done for peace. And if you have done that much, be gentle with yourself and don't feel guilty about not doing more; avoid the "I must save the world" complex. Give yourself permission to nourish your personal relationships and personal life. There is an old Hebrew saying that in the World Beyond, we will be punished for every innocent little pleasure we denied ourselves. Hillel, one hundred years B.C., said, "If I am not for myself, who will be for me? But if I am for myself alone, what am I? And if not now, when?"

Attendance at Fewer Meetings. [1] Because of the abundance of excellent peace organizations, you will soon realize that you could easily be attending one or more meetings daily if you desired. But it is important to keep in mind that it is not necessary to attend every meeting to which you are invited. You can sometimes contribute input by way of letters or phone calls.

Many of us go through a period in which we say to ourselves something like, "If I don't go to the planning committee meeting tonight, then surely our group will never reach its goals." It is good to realize that the world, and meetings, can go on without your physical presence. While it may be hard to give up this kind of control, you stand to gain a lot by keeping a lean schedule of meetings.

Natural Ebbs and Flows in Work Loads. [1] Although peace work is not exactly seasonal, there are periods of greater and lesser activity on the local level. After putting a lot of time into a specific project, make sure to take a mini-vacation afterwards. During this break, you will become rejuvenated and be ready for the next planning session, demonstration, or campaign. Recognize that depression can sometimes accompany these quieter periods. Depression can come from many things: exhaustion, anger that others aren't doing more and then denial of that anger as unacceptable, or the realization that despite your round-the-clock efforts, there is not yet peace in the land. (See Chapters 6 and 7 for further discussion of depression and anger.)

Burnout Workshop. It might be helpful to hold an activist burnout workshop. [4] Our local group sponsored one and included a picnic lunch and swim to stress the point that working for peace should not just be drudgery. Both peace workers and those who are in personal relationships with them can benefit from attending such a workshop.

Here is the format for a workshop designed to promote a better understanding of and a release of feelings stemming from burnout:

Participants should be seated in a circle, and each one should tell his/her name and reason for coming. Next do an exercise called "Telling your activist story," which is an adaptation of Joanna Rogers Macy's "Telling your nuclear story" (p. 98). [7] Put the following questions on a blackboard or flip chart:

1. When did I first become aware that warring among peoples was an accepted fact of life for most individuals? What did I do with this awareness?

2. What is the history of my activism or my relationship with an activist? How have I already experienced "burnout?"

3. How have my relationships with others been strengthened and/or weakened through my activism or my relationship with an activist?

Have group members divide into smaller groups of four or five people who are not well acquainted. Have each participant spend about five minutes telling his/her "story" to the others in the small groups. Then bring everyone together again in the circle and have a few participants share what they got from the activity.

For the next exercise, go around the circle again and have everyone complete this sentence: "I feel most burned out when........" Follow this with a role-playing procedure, also borrowed in part from Macy (p. 108). [7] It is called "I Am a Rock." First, write on the flip chart:

I don't care. I am a rock.
I don't give a damn. Leave me alone.

Then encourage everyone to tune in to that part of themselves which wants to say "No," or "I don't care," when they are confronted with something else they could do for peace. Going around the circle, have each person say aloud the written statement or a similar one of their own invention. End the exercise by having everyone yell "No!" simultaneously.

Complete the workshop with a brainstorming session [7], after first putting the following rules on the flip chart:

1. Say whatever occurs to you that is relevant to preventing or curing burnout.

2. Do not explain or defend your ideas.

3. Do not judge or discuss the ideas of others.

Open the floor for ideas and write them down on the chart. Give participants time to jot down those ideas from the chart which appeal to them, then the meeting should be adjourned.

Fun As a Healing Agent [1,2]

One of us (Wendy Forman) and three other family therapists are involved in research projects and workshops on the psychological aspects of living in a nuclear age. We really enjoy each other's company, both professionally and personally, and our work together has blossomed into much more than we had originally expected.

The major factor which has prevented our burning out is the invention and existence of Hedonists for Social Responsibility (HSR). While our professional group (Peace Research Associates) is a tightly-knit group, HSR is open to anyone who wishes to participate. Unlike other peace groups, there are no meetings, no dues, no newsletters, and no fund-raisers. Most HSR events are fairly spontaneous and tend to resemble parties or vacations. Dancing and music, while not part of the original group charter, are strongly encouraged. It is useful (for summer meetings) to find someone who has a swimming pool or access to a beach or lake; a sprinkler on a lawn will do in a pinch. We are hoping that other people will follow our lead and start their own chapters of HSR. If your focus is not on nuclear issues, why not start a new organization to serve the same purpose?

Though you'll certainly burn out if you spend all your waking hours doing peace work, if you make good choices with your time and use certain strategies, you can still do much for peace and yet eliminate or at least limit burnout. The suggestions provided here should help.

References
1. Doohan, H. (1982). Burnout: A critical issue for the 1980's. *Journal of Religion and Health*, 21, 352-358.
2. Selye, H. (1978). *The stress of life.* New York: McGraw-Hill.
3. Selye, H. (1974). *Stress without distress.* Philadelphia: J.B. Lippincott.
4. Pines, A., & Maslack, C. (1984). Characteristics of staff burnout in mental health settings. *Hospital and Community Psychiatry*, 29, 233-237.
5. Lazarus, R. (1966). *Psychological stress and the coping process.* New York: McGraw-Hill.
6. Thacker, J. (1984). Using psychodrama to reduce "burnout" or role fatigue in the helping professions. *Journal of Group Psychotherapy, Psychodrama, and Sociometry*, 37, 14-26.
7. Macy, J.R. (1983). *Despair and personal power in the nuclear age.* Philadelphia: New Society Publishers.

Suggested Reading
Selye, H. (1978). *The stress of life.* New York: McGraw-Hill. This book presents an excellent and highly readable analysis of stress at both the physiological and behavioral level, and contains valuable suggestions for regulating stress.

PeaceGroups:
Getting Organized

A great deal of significant research has been conducted on groups and how they function. Your peace group can turn to this information for help in getting volunteers, organizing itself, determining what it wants to do, and working smoothly together and with other groups.

Wollman begins this section with ideas on how to get donations, volunteers, or other help for your cause (some suggestions might even help in motivating your own group members).

Ludwick covers basic organizing processes: setting goals and specific activities, determining group structure, satisfying and motivating group members, and dealing with group decline. The Forsyth chapter focuses on such aspects of group meetings as conflict, communication, and leadership. He also presents and evaluates various techniques for making decisions.

The final paper in this section, written by Brown, examines facets of building coalitions with other peace or justice groups. Suggestions such as those on decision-making can be of help with the internal operations of your group as well as in cooperation with other groups.

(Don't forget that any chapters relevant to dealing with the *public* are potentially applicable to processes *within* your group as well — for example, discussion of conflict reduction in Section IV.)

10

Motivating Others to Work With You

Neil Wollman

People become active in working for peace for many reasons. A series of interviews with peace workers revealed five principal factors: *modeling* (repeating the actions of others), *being affected by the media* (e.g., small group film showings, books, commercial movies), *belonging to a group in which activism is encouraged*, *being motivated by an historical event* (napalming in Vietnam, the bombing in Hiroshima), or *responding to an important personal event* (identifying with a victim of war, travelling overseas, experiencing childbirth). [1] Though the latter two factors occur spontaneously, you can encourage political activity by using the other three factors in this list, and some additional ones presented in this chapter.

The purpose of this chapter is to help you bring new people into the peace movement. The ideas presented here should assist you in such activities as recruiting new people to join your group, getting volunteers for specific needs, obtaining donations, convincing people to write their representatives, encouraging the public to come to demonstrations, and getting support for your cause from those in government. A number of the ideas can also be used to motivate regular group members, but they will not be directly applied that way here.

Factors Relating to the Volunteer
Moods and feelings. Research has found that people will be more likely to help if they are experiencing certain moods or feelings,

such as feeling guilty or being in a good mood. [2] Even if you do not feel comfortable in purposely making others experience these things, at least be aware that the chances for receiving help are greater if you make your request when they are already feeling good or guilty.

Moral obligations. People are also more helpful when they experience certain moral obligations. [3] For instance, most of us feel that we should be socially responsible — that we should help those in need. Use this principle by expressing the needs you are experiencing, the justness of your position, and the good deed your listener(s) would do by contributing in some way to your need. When you do this, keep in mind that people tend to help more when they are alone than when they are in a group. People in groups frequently experience what has been called "diffusion of responsibility." This results in a tendency for individuals to rely on others in the group to fulfill the need. Thus when you appeal to a group, it is important to state that *each person's* contribution is necessary. Saying this to an individual listener is also desirable, for whenever you can emphasize individual responsibility, your chances of succeeding increase.

Another moral obligation is termed *reciprocity*; it is the belief that we should help those who have helped us. This effect is less likely to hold if someone feels you did him a favor only to pressure him into returning one, but even then it might hold. When you employ reciprocity to get some help on a peace project, be aware that the help you gave previously to the person needn't relate to the kind of help you are requesting now — though chances are even better if they *are* related. However, the amount of help you request should approximate the amount you gave before.

Besides those moral obligations that hold for society as a whole, others may hold only for a specific person. [3] Concerning nuclear war, for example, one person may feel strongly about the need to protect future generations, while another may feel an obligation to protect the environment from destruction. If these types of specific interests are known, mention them in your request.

When you address a special interest group (or an individual member of a group) try to find that particular moral appeal to which most members will likely respond. For instance, when you talk with any "child-related" groups (PTA, Boy Scouts and Girl Scouts, youth athletic clubs, etc.), stress the need to protect future generations. Stress the terrible nature of permanent war injuries with handicapped-related groups (military veterans' organizations, or any group tied to a crippling disease). Do research beforehand to find out a group's basic moral beliefs — whether it is a political group or a service club. Then tie your appeal for money, signatures, volunteers, or whatever, to some aspect of peacework that relates to those moral beliefs.

Attributions. In whatever way possible, suggest to potential volunteers that they are the type of individuals who give assistance to others in need. This suggestion could result in their "attributing" that characteristic to themselves. If this happens, they will likely *become* so in reality. This type of attribution effect has been shown in several studies. One experiment found that telling children that they were tidy individuals was an effective way to improve their neatness — in fact, it even worked better than trying to convince them that they *should* be neat. [4] In applying this method, perhaps you could briefly state that your audience is of "the helping type" whenever you communicate with them in presentations, printed materials, and conversations.

The attribution effect will be enhanced if you can get the person to do even one small action for peace. Perhaps the volunteer can write one postcard to the President, or talk to one neighbor about peace, or work for half an hour in a peace group's office. By doing so, the volunteer will further take on the self-image of a helper, and will be more likely to do such things in the future.

One further attribution-related effect: a volunteer whom you can convince to urge *other* people to work for peace will become an even more dedicated worker. Research shows that publicly endorsing a particular action makes the endorser more likely to take that action herself.

Factors Relating to You and Your Peace Group

Research has shown that we aid those who are truly needy, who are similar to ourselves, and whom we like (psychology often seems to verify the obvious!). [2] Because people lead busy lives, they will not give assistance unless you can establish a genuine need. Appeals should point out the needs of your group (financial, volunteer work, etc.) and the important human needs your group is attempting to fulfill (saving innocent citizens from the war in Central America, or ending the dangerous arms race, for instance).

There are many ways that the principle of similarity can be employed. When your group is asked to talk with particular professional, religious, racial, or special interest group members, you could send someone from your organization who is similar to them in one or more of these dimensions. Show by word and deed the resemblances between yourself and your listeners. When you address certain women's groups, for example, point out that you and many others in your peace group are concerned mothers, or make a few comments about sports when talking to groups that are likely to have many sports fans (this procedure can be used in one-to-one conversations as well). Another tactic is to dress and otherwise appear similar to those you contact.

That we help those we like is not an astounding fact, but you should keep it in mind. No matter how good your cause or specific message, a disagreeable personal style will be detrimental (Chapter 5 gives hints on increasing your likeability).

Factors Which Increase the Desire to Help
Rewards. A well-researched theory states that we will give assistance only when the benefits expected to be gained from helping outweigh the expected costs. [4] Such potential benefits can take many forms: hoping to feel good about oneself, wanting to help with something one believes in, expecting to receive praise or finances. Costs might include the possibility that the help would do no good, and that time and resources would be lost. It is also true that if someone gets something beneficial after helping, he is more likely to help in the future — even for totally new kinds of requests.

How might you employ these ideas? First, try to make your appeal so that those you approach will expect psychological or material benefits from their helping. Then do whatever possible to deliver those benefits in return for the help given. What you tell a potential volunteer depends on what you have to offer and what sorts of things are appealing to that person. Some volunteers may find it rewarding to work behind the scenes for praise or inner satisfaction; others may want to deal directly with the public and receive a minimal salary. Some may want to be assured that they will feel good by helping out, or that their costs in time and effort will not be great. If you know what someone will find appealing, offer it (if you can); otherwise, give some options regarding what contributions are needed and what sorts of compensation are available.

One of the best compensations for peace work is knowing that one's actions will have an effect, so if at all possible make known the success of specific peace campaigns, and/or how a volunteer's assistance has helped and will help in future activities.

One psychologist recommends a way that volunteers can begin to get involved and feel they can have some effect: start small. He suggests that volunteers concerned about peace first take on small assignments with a high probability of success, such as collecting signatures for a nuclear freeze. Because the anti-nuclear movement is building, the person will likely get some signatures, feel successful, and accept additional assignments. The volunteer may be encouraged to work on projects of gradually increasing difficulty if she continues to receive self-satisfaction, praise from others, and perhaps even media coverage. [6]

If you have volunteers working on a long-term basis, there is one more thing to keep in mind. What is rewarding at one point may not be so in the future. [7] The long-term peace worker should be offered a variety of challenging tasks with opportunities for varied rewards. The suggestions in Chapter 9 may also be helpful for avoiding the possibility of burnout.

Modeling. There is a psychological principle which states that we learn new behavior by watching others (models) take particular actions. [2] We can also learn simply by hearing about others' actions. If models are rewarded for their actions, we are even more likely to perform them. These findings can be applied specifically to peace work in a number of ways. First, you can talk to potential volunteers about others who have previously donated time or resources. The modeling effect can be enhanced by mentioning models whom the listeners identify with or respect, such as friends, governmental leaders, or celebrities. Though it works best if those models aided your specific peace group, it can still work if they didn't. The important thing is that they have been involved in the same basic kinds of activities you want volunteers to do.

There is also another approach to modeling: First, schedule activities in which regular group members and others engage in demonstrations, fund raisers, leafletting, letter writing, etc. Then, to utilize the modeling effect, publicize the event afterward so that the helping actions are emphasized. You can do this through stories and pictures in newsletters, leaflets, posters, advertisements, and, if you plan it right, in news coverage. If the contribution of non-group members can be pointed out, so much the better.

Finally, have potential volunteers actually witness acts of working for peace: schedule activities in places visible to the public, invite friends and acquaintances of group members to your activities, and publicize your political events to draw an audience.

A "Foot in the Door"

Two more principles will be briefly noted. The "foot in the door" effect states that if you need to ask someone for a lot of help on something, first make a small request that will be granted. [8] The volunteer will then be more likely to continue helping with the bigger project. On the other hand, other research has indicated that the "door in the face" technique may be even more effective. [8] This involves first making an unreasonably large request that will likely be rejected; then when it is rejected, ask for a smaller favor — the one you really wanted in the first place. You may find these tactics too manipulative to use, but that is your choice. It should be obvious that any means you use which potential volunteers see as purposely manipulative may not work.

A Few Concluding Hints on Getting Help

Causes for noninvolvement. One study identified seven basic beliefs or experiences of many citizens which seemed to block their involvement in peace concerns: the "irrelevance" of peace to more pressing personal concerns; the repression and denial of the horror of war; not wishing America to be so heavily involved in foreign affairs; the feeling of powerlessness given the world situation; the inevitability of war given human competitiveness; fear of the Soviet Union; and not being aware of organizations existing specifically to advance the cause of peace. [9,10]

Obviously anything you can do to counter these can help. The study gave three basic recommendations on what peace workers should try to communicate: war is a personal threat both in the long and short term; there are efforts already underway attempting to reduce the likelihood of war; and the organizations that are making these efforts have achievable goals.

Options and plans for helping. In as many ways as possible, let the general public know that there are plenty of opportunities for them to get involved with your group and with the peace movement in general. Mention projects that can be worked on and exactly what people should do to get involved. Many people want to do *something* for peace, but they don't know whether their participation is needed, how they can get involved, or what they can do to help. (See Chapter 4 for an extensive listing of peace activities.)

Two hints for applying principles. There are two other things to remember when you apply the ideas presented here. First, take a little time to determine which principles are the best to apply to the given situation and potential volunteers involved. For example, if your group members are only vaguely similar to a potential helper, do not expect an appeal based on similarities to work. Secondly, your best bet in most situations is to combine different principles; you might assure your audience that your peace group is in need (moral obligation), and that they as individuals will get specific benefits (rewards) from their participation.

Recruiting group members. If someone joins your peace group, do not expect him to necessarily become heavily involved. People join groups for many other reasons than just furthering the group's goals; for example: to increase personal interactions, meet psychological needs, and gain status. [2] Expect different types and levels of involvement depending on the reason(s) for joining, although involvement may well change as membership continues and circumstances change.

If you want to increase your group's membership, you can probably do so by adding dimensions that are not directly tied to promoting peace, such as incorporating extra social activities, adding group goals besides peace, increasing group status by recruiting prominent community citizens who may be minimally interested in peace, etc. However, first consider how the new membership and activities will affect your peace work.

One creative way of reaching new people combines and modifies the "house meeting" concept taught by organizer Fred Ross and the "peacemeals" strategy of Wendy Forman. Have each group member choose five or ten friends and invite them over for a meal (each meal would have five or ten guests, and would be hosted by a separate group member). During the meal the host/hostess presents the peace concerns of the moment, and encourages each guest to become active to some degree. The guests could even write letters to Congress or donate money that very evening. Each guest should then be encouraged to invite her own friends to similar meals. It doesn't take much mathematical figuring to realize that if you successfully follow this procedure through a few cycles of meals, you've gotten quite a few people involved!

On that optimistic note, I will conclude and wish you good luck in recruiting.

References
1. Mehr, H.M., & Webster, M. (1984, December). Peacemaking works. Association of Humanistic Psychology *Perspective*, p. 21.
2. Middlebrook, P. (1980). *Social psychology and modern life* (2nd ed.). New York: Alfred Knopf.
3. Schwartz, S. (1977). Normative influence on altruism. In L. Berkowitz (Ed.), *Advances in experimental social psychology* (Vol. 10) (pp. 221-279). New York: Academic Press.
4. Miller, R., Brickman, P., & Bolen, D. (1975). Attribution versus persuasion as a means for modifying behavior. *Journal of Personality and Social Psychology*, 31, 430-441.
5. Piliavin, I., Piliavin, J., & Rodin, J. (1975). Cost, diffusion, and the stigmatized victim. *Journal of Personality and Social Psychology*, 32, 429-438..
6. Nevin, J.A. (1984, August). Behavior analysis and the nuclear arms race. Paper presented at the meeting of the American Psychological Association, Toronto, Canada.
7. Mehrabian, A. (1970). *Tactics of social influence*. Englewood Cliffs, NJ: Prentice-Hall.
8. Harari, C., & Kaplan, R. (1982). *Social psychology: Basic and applied*. Monterey, CA: Brooks/Cole.
9. Yankelovich, Skelly, & White, Inc. (1978). *A qualitative study of attitudes toward peace and peace organizations*. New York: Institute for World Order.
10. Leake, P. (1979). *Attitudes toward peace and peace organizations* (Report from the New Manhattan Project). New York:

American Friends Service Committee. Permission for quotation from this article was granted by the New Manhattan Project of the American Friends Service Committee.

Suggested Readings

Middlebrook, P. (1980). *Social psychology and modern life* (2nd ed.). New York: Alfred Knopf. See the chapter on helping and altruism for a good brief overview of important factors in the helping process. Her two chapters on groups will also be helpful.

Fisher, J.D., Nadler, A., & De Paulo, B.M. (Eds.). (1983) *New directions in helping:* (Vol. 2, Help seeking). New York: Academic Press. This book describes research on helping that has been conducted out in the "real world," not in the laboratory.

Schwartz, S. (1977). Normative influences on altruism. In L. Berkowitz (Ed.), *Advances in experimental social psychology* (Vol. 10) (pp. 221-279). New York: Academic Press. This chapter gives an excellent perspective on the three major theoretical explanations of helping behavior: arousal, social norms (moral obligations), and personal moral codes. The chapter nicely fits various views on helping into these three categories.

11

Organizing Your Group and Setting Goals

Mark Ludwick

*(I would like to thank Donelson Forsyth
for his substantial contribution to this chapter.)*

Many peace groups seem chaotic when forming or restructuring. Although members agree that the group should promote world peace, they may not agree about how best to organize the group to achieve this. Your group will eventually pass through this stage of uncertainty, but the process will be easier if you can deal effectively with certain basic organizational needs. This chapter focuses on principles and methods that will help you do this. Although the beginning of this chapter and other specific parts are geared to the newly-forming or restructuring group, most of the material will be relevant to you no matter what your group's stage of development.

Defining Your Mission
     The value of goals. The first task of any newly forming or restructuring group is to determine the nature of the group's mission. While some members may feel most comfortable if the goals and objectives of the group are left vague, research indicates that most people prefer to specify their goals. [1] Without specific objectives to work toward, members have little way of structuring their activities, and have difficulty determining their progress. While your fundamental mission may be clear — promoting world peace — it offers little guidance for the week-to-week operations of your peace group; more specific goals must be developed. Even if

your members had specific ideas and intentions when they joined, it will be necessary to formalize those intentions.

Goals are expectations of what a group desires to achieve. They may be as broad as trying to educate the general public about the dangers of world militarism, or as specific as trying to stop production of a specific missile. Some goals should also relate to the internal processes of the group, such as maintaining morale and good relationships among members, in order to help the group function better. If your group falls apart, it will no longer be able to work for its fundamental mission.

Setting goals. You may have difficulty setting goals because members bring many diverse, and sometimes incompatible, suggestions for "what to do next." A possible solution is to hold a goal-setting session, in which members examine alternative suggestions and make a decision about the best path to take. Furthermore, if your group is large, you may want to use a special decision-making method, such as the nominal group technique (NGT), to save time and wasteful arguing. Here is how I might use NGT if I were to lead a session on defining the group's goals.

I would first introduce the problem by writing a short question on a chart which all members could see. The question might be stated as, "What goals should our group seek to best promote peace?" (If your group already has some basic focus, you would, of course, use a more specific question.) Next the members, working individually, would write down those goals that they think are the most important. After this, as each member reads one goal from his/her list, I would write them on the chart. If the group is small (seven or fewer), I would go around the participants a second time. Next, the whole group discusses these goals, eliminating overlapping ideas, and clarifying those that seem unclear. After the discussion, each member privately picks those five goals from the list that s/he thinks are best, and ranks them in priority from one to five. After the ranks are added, several goals will probably stand out; if not, the group needs to decide on a numerical cut-off point for goals to be adopted. Although the NGT limits member interaction, evidence indicates that it effectively reduces conflict, increases satisfaction, and generates more suggestions than simple "brainstorming." [2]

Translating Your Mission Into Action

Action steps. Close examination of your selected goals will reveal that they are too general to work with week-to-week. There is a way, however, to use these "general goals" to develop more specific plans: use the NGT or another decision-making method (see Chapter 12 for a discussion of other methods) to generate a number of possible "action steps" that will help achieve each general goal. Then decide which two or three are the best — those that are closely linked to the general goals, are specific in the types of activities involved, are timely, are cost-effective in terms of time and materials, and can be effectively substituted if they do not work. [3] For example, the general goal "inform the community of peace events" may have action steps like "create and circulate newsletters to interested groups," "post notices of peace events," and "schedule and plan informational events."

Working goals. Before finally getting down to the nitty-gritty of planning and doing, you should set "working goals" for each action step. For instance, the action step "create and circulate newsletters to interested groups" may have as a working goal "to create a one-page typed newsletter covering peace issues and local events and circulate it to 100 local community residents by the end of next month." Begin with easy working goals — start small to build confidence. After the break-in period, set new working goals which are more difficult, but still realistic; the challenge will benefit your group. Clearly defined, specific, and challenging working goals have been shown to bring out the best in people. [4] Be sure to choose working goals over which your group has considerable control and which allow progress toward the goal to be measured. For instance, you can control and measure the number of letters sent, phone calls made, events held, donations requested, and conferences and demonstrations attended. Keeping track of these types of actions and events will provide valuable feedback to group members regarding the progress of their efforts. [5]

Setting general goals, action steps, and working goals takes time, energy, and possibly some hair-pulling. However, it is necessary if you are to build a solid and true foundation on which to grow.

Keep Your Feet On the Ground

General goals which are idealistic can breathe spirit into a group, but you should take a realistic look at them periodically. Being honest is a key; acknowledge shortages of funds, people, time, and other resources which are not allowing you to accomplish all that you set out to do. If you do not acknowledge these problems and some goals remain unaccomplished, organizational and interpersonal conflicts will arise that will have a negative effect on your group.

If you come to realize that your goals and action steps are no longer adequate, whether due to lack of resources or because they now seem too easy or too difficult, change them. Goals should not be sacred; set new ones when necessary.

Group Structure

Informal and formal structure. Besides the need for goals, another area of concern is group structure, how to organize your group. Although newly formed groups usually lack both formal and informal structure, given time informal structure will develop regarding such things as status differences between members, general customs about appropriate behaviors, and roles for members as they interact with each other. These things will influence the political workings and effectiveness of the group. Keep the informal structure in mind as you plan who will do which assignments, which members will work together, and in what ways. Some aspects of informal structure will develop on their own, but some will follow from the formal structure (leadership, hierarchies, committees) which you directly control as you organize the group. If your group is trying to reorganize, you can certainly do formal restructuring, but be aware that you may need to deal with interpersonal conflicts resulting from informal structures of the past (such as differences in members' status).

In some ways the size of a group will dictate formal structure, for the larger an organization, the greater the need for a centralized leadership structure. Although this centralization means that only certain members will direct the carrying out of working goals and group activities, such structure may be essential because of the need for coordination of various subgroup activities. Furthermore, while some members may argue that a formally appointed leader is not needed, research suggests that satisfaction will be higher when a leader is available to coordinate activities and route communications. [6]

Goals and structure. A group's general goals will also help dictate structure. For example, let's say your group outlines five goals: maintaining group morale, keeping the community informed about peace-related issues and events, encouraging informal discussions of peace issues among members, lobbying state legislative representatives, and working to support local conscientious objectors and war tax resisters. First, look at these goals to see if there are any themes or needs which underlie some or many of the goals. In this case, communication with outsiders seems to underlie several of the goals. Also, several of the goals will require financing. Finally, a couple of the goals seem tied to the internal workings of the group. Perhaps, then, committees related to outreach, fundraising, and intragroup work would be appropriate. Your leader(s) can coordinate the efforts of different committees (and fill in missing gaps) to assure that the intended goals are being met. As you determine committee structure, look also at such things as how many members you have, how much time and energy members can devote to committees, and which goals are best achieved by the group working as a unit, rather than by a smaller portion of the members.

Another way of setting formal structure is to merely have a different committee for each general goal; however, this is usually more inefficient because similar tasks are duplicated by different committees. Chapter 19 presents a specific method for setting up group goals and structure to effect social change.

Selecting people for committees should be based upon two factors: competence/experience in the area covered by the committee, and willingness to train and work in that area. Basing committee membership on friendship ties is not advisable. It would probably lead to each committee becoming a clique because the members within it would be set apart, both as a group of friends and as a committee.

Finally, don't necessarily assume that increasing the size of a committee will increase the amount of work that gets done. As "social loafing theory" tells us, the more people working on a project, the less any one person will work. [7] When a large committee is required or when the group as a whole is working on a project, stress the responsibility of each person to do his/her part and give specific assignments to individuals.

Interaction among members. A final aspect of group structure concerns patterns of attraction and liking among members. Although establishing goals, selecting leaders, and creating committees are important steps in forming or restructuring, if your members do not like one another, the group may not even survive. Part of the pleasure of working with others comes from the friendly relations between members, and this human side of group efficiency is as important as the more task-oriented side.

Among other things (such as reaching group goals, having a warm and accepting atmosphere, and having all members share in leadership [8], positive relations among members also promotes a feeling of group identification and cohesiveness, and these help both to retain group members and to improve group performance. One reason for retained membership and better performance is that members of cohesive groups tend to participate more fully and communicate more frequently. [9] Sometimes too much cohesiveness can cause problems (see the discussion of "groupthink" in Chapter 12), but in most cases it is very beneficial; a number of chapters in this book can help you reduce conflict and promote good communication and relationships among your members.

Maintaining Your Group: Satisfying and Motivating Members
Whether or not any of your members get paid, "job" satisfaction is another prominent organizational concern. It plays an important role in keeping members in the group and ensuring their participation in activities. [10] There is no one solution to keeping members satisfied; there may be a different specific route for each person. Generally, members will be satisfied if the group and its activities are meeting those needs and values they think are important. [11] People who join your group to fulfill the need to work for peace (rather than to make friends, gain status, etc.), will want to see how their efforts and ideas help the cause of peace.

Follow five steps in trying to satisfy and motivate group members. First, discover their unique values and needs. These will likely be revealed in their comments, behaviors, and participation in particular activities. If necessary, purposely and openly discuss values and needs, perhaps in a special session. Second, help members meet these values and needs through activities that are important to them and that are likely to be successful. The discussion on rewards in Chapter 10 offers some suggestions about how this can be done. Third, promote a sense of shared responsibility; be sure each member has opportunities to play important roles in planning and performing activities. Fourth, provide assignments which are stimulating and allow for variety and autonomy. Finally, see that the results of group actions are brought to the attention of all members. Let each member know how her or his contribution helped the group reach its goals. Every member can take an active part in each of these steps; it is not just the leader's responsibility.

Group spirit. Many groups have a sense of group spirit and morale which makes members more energetic and more likely to attend meetings and participate in activities. In order to build group spirit, you could:

-frequently emphasize the importance of the fundamental mission of the group;

-share individual convictions about peace work and how important it is to be a member of the group;

-emphasize group efforts and group successes, and thus build confidence for achieving future goals;

-discuss the forces that are working against you (such as government policy) and the forces that are working with you (such as other peace groups around the world);

-share in activities that are not related specifically to promoting peace, such as parties or celebrations of group successes; and

-use music as an inspiration for your group (see Chapters 29 and 30).

Growing Up

Adding members. By adding new members, the group has the option to take on new functions, do more of what it is presently doing, or relieve members' workloads. This presents new possibilities and problems; proper planning and decision-making can reduce many of the latter.

When you consider group expansion, be sure you have enough

work, space, and other resources to support more members. If not, then wait until the situation changes before receiving new members. Assuming that new people want to join, whether initiated by you or by them, you should examine what the potential members will do and how the addition may affect the group and its activities. Talk with them to see if their values and goals and the kinds of activities they want to pursue match the needs and interests of your group. Incompatibilities can cause conflict, and unless your group members are willing to take time from the outset to work them out, some selectivity in adding members is advisable.

It is vital for new members to become well-acquainted with other members, as well as with group goals, activities, procedures, rules, and jobs. Provide adequate time and effort to work out the assignments they will have and to develop satisfactory relationships with other members.

Effects of adding members. Growth will change your group, especially when the group is in its early stages. It will tend to make the group more formal in such areas as scheduling assignments, using specific methods to complete work, and handling of leadership. Regarding the latter, as the group grows in size there becomes a greater likelihood that a leader may be somewhat separated from the rest of the group, and as a result, fail to discuss problems with other members. Also, as a group gets larger, a pattern of having small groups of intimate friends may give way to larger and less intimate groups. There are other positive and negative consequences of growth [12], and in general, you will benefit by adding members slowly so that you can adjust to changes without losing your original spirit and mission.

Recognizing Decline

Many groups go through periods in which they lose members and do not move toward their goals as well as they did in the past. Being sensitive to the reasons for decline is as important as working on solutions. Achieving all of your action steps and working goals will usher in decline if you don't choose new ones. More common reasons for decline include losing touch with community needs and interests regarding peace, using old procedures to meet new and different problems, denying that problems exist, and handling problems in an inexperienced manner. [13] Additionally, interpersonal problems between members can cause, and will often contribute to, a decline.

There are symptoms of decline that will warn you of deeper problems with the group. They include a fear of failure that prevents your group from taking risks, reduced participation by members, formation of cliques concerned with their own goals rather than the group's, boredom with tasks, and an increase in defensive and argumentative behavior. [14] These symptoms reveal a deeper problem in the group's basic mission and goals, formal or informal structure, and/or patterns of attraction and liking among members.

Patching Things Up

You can reverse decline, but it will take determination and flexibility. A typical method of handling the situation is to hold a special group meeting, scheduled apart from your usual meeting or working location if possible. Invite members personally, emphasizing that it is a "special" meeting, not for regular business, and that it is very important for members to attend. If the regular leader is seen by some members as the cause of the decline, or as partial to certain segments in the group, the meeting should be led by another person who is trusted and respected by the membership.

Holding the meeting. With all members contributing, draw up a list of problems that need to be resolved. During this discussion, the leader needs to set an atmosphere of openness toward giving and accepting constructive criticism. [15] The leader should focus discussion on problems dealing with goal accomplishment. If interpersonal problems are a key factor in your decline, they should be discussed only in relation to how they are affecting progress toward group goals. Working out personality clashes between individuals should be handled in private, in one-to-one sessions or with a trusted mediator.

The next step, and often the most difficult, is to locate the "causes" behind the problems you have defined. For instance, low morale in working toward group goals may be a symptom that members' assignments for the group lack meaningfulness. Locating the causes for a problem may require a great deal of discussion and sifting through facts and opinions. As causes for problems are generated, they should be written down alongside the problems and explained thoroughly, so that all members can see and understand them. Finally, members should vote on which two or three problems (and associated causes) are most important to deal with at the present time.

Using a brainstorming technique, generate possible solutions to these areas of concern. If at all possible, use consensus to decide which solutions to focus on, so that all members are satisfied with the new policies of the group. End the meeting on a positive note — perhaps reaffirming the group's mission. It is important not to stall, but to take significant steps to put those solutions into effect. [13] Facing decline is a frustrating experience, but if you can discover and implement constructive solutions, your work for the cause of peace will be furthered.

References

1. Zander, A. (1971). *Motives and goals in groups*. New York: Academic Press.

2. Delbecq, A.L., & Van de Ven, A.H. (1971). A group process model for program identification and program planning. *Journal of Applied Behavioral Science*, 7, 466-492.

3. Beckhard, R., & Harris, R.T. (1977). *Organizational transitions: Managing complex change*. Reading, MA: Addison Wesley.

4. Locke, E.A., Cartledge, N., & Knerr, C.S. (1970). Studies of the relationship between satisfaction, goal setting, and performance. *Organizational Behavior and Human Performance*, 5, 474-485.

5. Annett, J. (1969). *Feedback and human behavior: The effects of knowledge of results, incentives, and reinforcement on learning and performance*. Baltimore: Penguin Books.

6. Berkowitz, L. (1953). Sharing leadership in small, decision-making groups. *Journal of Abnormal and Social Psychology*, 48, 231-238.

7. Baron, R., & Byrne, D. (1981). *Social psychology: Understanding human interaction* (3rd ed.). Boston: Allyn and Bacon.

8. Middlebrook, P.N. (1980). *Social psychology and modern life* (2nd ed.). New York: Alfred Knopf.

9. Cartwright, D. (1968). The nature of group cohesiveness. In D. Cartwright & A. Zander (Eds.), *Group dynamics: Research and theory* (pp. 91-109). New York: Harper and Row.

10. Mobley, W.H., Horner, S.O., & Hollingworth, A.T. (1978). An

evaluation of precursors of hospital employee turnover. *Journal of Applied Psychology*, 63, 408-414.

11. Locke, E.A. (1976). The nature and causes of job satisfaction. In M.D. Dunnette (Ed.), *Handbook of industrial and organizational psychology* (pp. 1297-1349). Chicago: Rand McNally.

12. Starbuck, W.H. (1965). Organizational growth and development. In J.G. March (Ed.), *Handbook of organizations* (pp. 451-533). Chicago: Rand McNally.

13. Whetton, D.A. (1980). Sources, responses, and effects of organizational decline. In Kimberly, Miles, & Associates (Eds.), *The organizational life cycle* (pp. 342-374). San Francisco: Jossey-Bass.

14. Sarason, S.B. (1978). *The creation of settings and the future societies*. San Francisco: Jossey-Bass.

15. Schien, E.H. (1984). *Process consultation: Its role in organizational development*. Reading, MA: Addison Wesley.

Suggested Readings

Lawson, L.G., Donant, F.D., & Lawson, J.D. (1982). *Lead on! The Complete Handbook for Group Leaders*. San Luis Obispo, CA: Impact Publishers. This is a brief and very practical book which covers 24 topics relevant to leadership, such as "motivating members," "presiding at business meetings," and "understanding your own leadership style."

Sarason, S.B. (1978). *The creation of settings and the future societies*. San Francisco: Jossey-Bass. Sarason presents information regarding the creation and pitfalls of groups.

Schien, E.H. (1984). *Process consultation: Its role in organizational development*. Reading, MA: Addison Wesley. The first half of this book is a brief and practical guide to organizational processes and principles. It is easily adapted to a peace group setting.

12

Effective Group Meetings and Decision Making

Donelson R. Forsyth

An extraordinary amount of work and many types of decisions are handled by groups of people, for in group meetings we can pool our knowledge and abilities, give each other feedback about our ideas, and tackle problems that would overcome us if we faced them alone. Group members not only give us emotional and social support when meeting together, but they can stimulate us to become more creative, more insightful, and more committed to our goals.

Not every group, however, realizes all these positive consequences. Often we dread going to "committee meetings," "council sessions," and "discussion groups" because they take up too much valuable time as discussions get bogged down in side issues. Jokes about the drawbacks of group meetings abound; meetings are characterized as "cul-de-sacs to which ideas are lured and then strangled," or sessions where "men and women keep minutes and waste hours." Certainly there can be negative as well as positive aspects to group meetings; my hope is that this chapter can help you draw on the advantages and avoid as many of the disadvantages as possible.

During the course of any group meeting a whole host of fascinating processes unfolds. I want to focus here on four of the most critical: *leadership*, *communication*, *conflict*, and *problem solving*.

Leadership

Research indicates that leaders have two basic responsibilities:

helping the group accomplish the purpose of the meeting, and satisfying the social and emotional needs of those participating. [1] Unfortunately, evidence also indicates that these two duties are sometimes incompatible. For example, if you must constantly remind participants about their tasks during the meeting, then they may stop looking to you for support. The best leaders, therefore, try to maintain a healthy balance between "getting the job done" and helping members "enjoy themselves." Your leader will have to decide what is most appropriate for your group, but there is one rule of thumb to follow: provide a good deal of task supervision and less emotional support for recently formed groups, and more emotional support for older groups (eventually a well-established group will need little if any task structuring).

Obviously leaders can become overburdened if they have to deal with both task supervision and interpersonal needs, especially since they may be incompatible. One solution to this problem is distributive leadership. For instance, if several members are arguing, others may mediate rather than wait for the regular leader to step in. Similarly, the person who recognizes a communication problem, or a point that needs summarizing, may temporarily take a leadership role and perform the task. By distributing leadership, everyone can participate more, and the leader's responsibilities are reduced.

All group members, then, but particularly the leader, should take steps to prepare for and facilitate meetings:

-Establish a timetable for moving through the phases of group projects, while also determining how often the group needs to hold meetings (the group should meet only when necessary).

-Structure group meetings by developing an agenda and assembling necessary materials (such as handouts and charts); contacting those group members who are supposed to attend; and selecting a decision-making strategy (discussed later in this chapter). Although most meetings are structured so they start with a statement of the meeting's purpose, followed by discussion and decision-making, you may decide to modify these procedures.

-Monitor group discussions, noting both content (points raised, ideas offered, questions resolved) and process (who is talking most, what conflicts are developing, and who is not participating).

-Improve group communication by summarizing and pulling

together information, paraphrasing or restating decisions or action plans upon which you have agreed, and making certain that no one person dominates the discussion. Also, keep track of time spent on topics, and encourage resolution when necessary (it takes practice to learn what is the appropriate time for resolution).

In some circumstances, leadership can be distributed in an additional way. When your group accomplishes certain tasks and moves onto other ones, the new focus may lend itself to a change in leadership. If you don't feel the need for a permanent leader for your meetings, a useful attitude toward the role of leadership might be, "Who do we need in this situation to get this particular task done?" [2] Keeping one permanent leader lends stability to the group process and develops at least one experienced leader; sharing leadership encourages new ideas and allows many members to reveal talents otherwise hidden. This sharing approach also assumes that different circumstances create different leadership needs.

Communication

Good communication lies at the heart of effective group performance. While active, frequent participation by members, in and of itself, improves performance, members should also strive to maintain clarity in their communications. If discussion shoots off on tangents, if members ignore one another's comments, and if ideas are only sketchily presented, then your members will go home feeling very little was achieved. Effective communication requires constant attention, but it will become easier if you follow certain guidelines. [3]

-Make your statements brief and clear.

-Try to add your own suggestions, statements, and questions at the "right" point in the discussion; timing can be critical.

-Make long and more formal presentations interesting by using imaginative phrasings, colorful analogies, and eye-catching visual aids.

-Actively listen to what others are saying. Too often people seem to consider meetings a chance to talk endlessly about their pet ideas. Listening is at least as important as talking for a group to work efficiently and effectively.

-Ask for clarification of statements that you do not understand.

-Draw silent participants into the discussion through questioning; be alert to nonverbal signals that someone wants to speak but is holding back or can't seem to get into the conversation.

-Sensitively explore sources of disagreement and tension, rather than avoiding them.

-Acknowledge positive, constructive statements or suggestions which are helping the group accomplish the goal of the discussion.

-Follow the discussion carefully, remembering points that have been made while anticipating profitable directions to follow.

Conflict

Even though your group is working for peace, small "wars" may occasionally break out within the group. Conflicts arise from many sources; disagreements over basic goals, minor arguments over a particular issue, personality conflicts, and power struggles between leaders seem to be inevitable for groups.

However, for most groups conflict becomes a major problem only if you try to ignore it. As researchers have found, conflict tends to "clear the air" and leaves members more united once its source is dealt with. If, however, your members try to gloss over the problem, then it merely escalates and may surface later in a stronger and group-damaging form. [4] Indeed, evidence indicates that most groups need some conflict to maintain members' interest; if your group has no conflict, it signals that members are apathetic, and that you are examining unintriguing issues. Overall, conflict is a healthy group process that enlivens group interactions. The chapters in Section IV of this book will be particularly useful to you if conflict is becoming more destructive than constructive.

Problem-solving

When you need to plan a course of action — organizing a demonstration, correcting a financial difficulty, increasing your membership — there are some basic steps you can take to plan what to do. [5] (1) Define the problem: what is the situation now and what do you want to happen? (2) Take an inventory of talents and resources already available to your group. (3) Search for relevant facts and/or possible external resources: if you're planning a demonstration, it may be that certain days are bad for members, or that the town won't give permits for certain kinds of demonstrations, or that one member's brother has some loudspeakers that the group can borrow, or that there is a celebrity in town who might help out. (4) Generate possible alternatives for action. (5) Discuss and debate the advantages and disadvantages of each alternative. (6) Decide on the best alternative. (7) Develop a concrete form of action. (8) Determine who in the group is interested and able to do further planning, implementing and evaluating of the action (depending on the nature of the action, you may wish to form such a temporary "committee" after step 3 and have it do the remaining steps on its own). A more detailed outline of a strategy for planning direct political action is described in Chapter 19.

Making Decisions: Some Techniques

Some of the most important products your group creates will be decisions: judgments about what goals to most actively pursue, choices about group leadership, and the plans that are determined by the problem-solving method just discussed. Here are several different decision-making methods, along with a discussion of some of their advantages and disadvantages.

Delegating decisions. Your entire group doesn't have to decide simple routine matters, like where to hold meetings, what kind of stationery to order, or when to mail out a newsletter. Although delegation takes some responsibility away from members, it leaves them more time to spend discussing larger issues. Use delegation when it isn't important for all members to accept a decision, when the issue(s) involved is (are) clear-cut, and when an individual member (or a committee) is competent to make the decision. [6] Delegation is also appropriate when members know little about the issue involved; for example, if you decide to invest in a word processing computer, first seek an expert's advice. Though you might feel you can solve any question through group discussion, your group members may be merely pooling their ignorance on a subject and could make a poor decision.

Averaging individual inputs. For some decisions you might have members individually rank a number of available alternatives, and the leader would then determine the group decision by tallying the rankings for each alternative. If, for example, the group wants to award a community resident for peace efforts, members can individually rank the nominees, and the leader can then total the rankings for each nominee to determine the winner. Chapter 11 describes one particular averaging method, the Nominal Group Technique, and how it can be applied to deciding on a group's basic goals. An averaging approach minimizes interaction, so it should generally be combined with group discussion both before and after the averaging.

Voting. Many groups follow parliamentary procedure (such as *Robert's Rules of Order*) for voting. Although voting can be an appropriate method, when a vote is close some members may feel "defeated" and alienated, and consequently be less likely to follow through on the decision. Furthermore, voting can lead to internal politicking as members get together before meetings to apply pressures, form coalitions, and trade favors to ensure passage of proposals they favor. Be sensitive to these possibilities, and realize that the voting technique could be the cause.

Brainstorming. You might try brainstorming to come up with creative solutions to a problem. Brainstorming can generate a wide range of solutions by encouraging unrestricted expression of ideas, while discouraging criticism and evaluation. Brainstorming is better used to generate several possible solutions to a problem than to make a final decision. Also, unless your members are really motivated to come up with good ideas and are practiced in creative decision-making, brainstorming may be no more effective in producing good solutions than "averaging inputs" or than the combined output of individuals working alone. [7]

Discussion to consensus. Discussion to consensus — the unanimous agreement of all members — is in some respects an ideal procedure: everyone has a chance to participate and be heard, and no one feels like a loser after the vote is taken. However, discussion to consensus does have its drawbacks. Getting all members to agree on a solution is generally time-consuming, and if the leader feels a need to rush the discussion, uncertain members may feel their concerns were ignored.

Furthermore, unless you stay attuned to the group's processes, decisions can be railroaded through the group by manipulative maneuverings, leader domination, and pressures for individual members to conform to the general group opinion. For instance, there is a tendency for consensus decisions to become more "polarized" after a discussion: if individual members are already leaning a little bit for (or against) a possible solution before a discussion, the group as a whole will move more in that direction during discussion. [3] If at the beginning of a discussion many individual members have lukewarm support for some measure, the arguments presented will generally be in favor of the measure; further positive discussion ensues, and members become more favorable toward the issue. Sometimes this stronger support will reflect members' true beliefs (if the arguments really convinced them) but sometimes it will not (if members felt pressured to conform more in the direction the group seemed to be heading). The latter possibility is best minimized by the group regularly encouraging open expression of ideas and independence in voting.

Finally, with a consensus technique, each individual member wields much power and can radically affect the progress of discussion. Although this can be positive, it can also work against the group. Each member has potential veto power over the group's decision and can require the group to listen to uninformed suggestions, irrelevant remarks, and stubbornly held, but rejected viewpoints. Decision-making by consensus is most appropriate for matters that require acceptance and support by all (or most all) group members in order to properly implement resultant policy. A voting or "averaged inputs" technique becomes more appropriate when the time to decide is limited, when the need for unanimous group acceptance decreases, and when the likelihood for conflict in making the decision increases. [6]

Avoid Groupthink in Decision-Making

No matter what method of decision-making you choose, stay attuned to the phenomenon known as groupthink — a deterioration of decision-making quality that results from strong ingroup pressures to conform. [8] Groupthink is most prevalent in highly cohesive groups working under time pressures to make important decisions. It involves self-censorship of dissenting ideas, refusal to tolerate disagreement among members, mistaken beliefs that the group cannot fail, derogation of those outside the group, and a tendency to rationalize away problems and shortcomings. To avoid groupthink, a leader should: encourage independent thinking and full discussion of all sides of an issue; appoint "devil's advocates"; stress that the group is capable of making an unsound decision; and consider breaking the full group into smaller discussion groups (or have independent groups work on the same problem and report back at another meeting).

Conclusion

Group meetings can potentially bring out the best in individuals by helping them work together to produce outputs they never could on their own. Meetings can also stifle the creativity and drive that would otherwise emerge if individuals worked alone. The ideas presented in this chapter can, in part, help you take advantage of a group's strengths, while averting its weaknesses.

References
1. Bales, R.F. (1970). *Personality and interpersonal behavior.* New York: Holt, Rinehart, and Winston.
2. Fiedler, F.E. (1981). Leadership effectiveness, *American Behavioral Science* 24, 619-632.
3. Forsyth, D.R. (1983). *An introduction to group dynamics.* Monterey, CA: Brooks/Cole.
4. Bormann, E.G. (1975). *Discussion and group methods: Theory and practice.* New York: Harper & Row.
5. Lawson, L.G., Donant, F.D., & Lawson, J.D. (1982). *Lead on! The Complete Handbook for Group Leaders.* San Luis Obispo, CA: Impact Publishers, Inc.
6. Vroom, V.H. (1973). A new look at managerial decision making. *Organizational Dynamics,* 1, 66-80.
7. Bouchard, Jr., T.J. (1972). Training, motivation, and personality as determinants of the effectiveness of brainstorming groups and individuals. *Journal of Applied Psychology,* 56, 324-331.
8. Janis, I.L. (1982). *Groupthink.* Boston: Houghton-Mifflin.

Suggested Readings

Zander, A. (1982). *Making groups effective.* San Francisco: Jossey-Bass. Written by one of the leading researchers and theorists in group dynamics, this book offers a series of useful suggestions for improving groups.

Forsyth, D.R. (1983). *An introduction to group dynamics.* Monterey, CA: Brooks/Cole. This book reviews theory and research relevant to group processes. Although empirically focused, it includes chapters dealing with applications to group performance, leadership, and decision-making.

Luft, J. (1984). *Group process.* Palo Alto, CA: Mayfield. This is an examination of the interpersonal side of groups, with chapters dealing with group development, experiential learning, increasing awareness, and leadership.

13

Building Coalitions With Other Groups

Cherie Brown

There are many different peace organizations today which struggle bravely yet independently to build individual membership, raise funds, and pursue their goals of a peaceful world. What is missing is a unified strategy and coordinated effort. This can only be achieved by building coalitions, both among peace groups and with other organizations (for example, labor, feminist, cultural, and religious groups).

The benefits of forming coalitions include pooling and exchanging resources, broader participation in planning and conducting activities, sharing outside speakers and films, and psychological support. A major obstacle to building coalitions is a history of isolation, mistrust, powerlessness, and intergroup competition; this history prevents us from working together to promote peace. This chapter examines some principles of coalition building that can guide peace groups through this difficult yet essential task.

Picking the Right Groups to Form a Coalition
First Do Your Homework. Do enough research so you can draw a chart, listing prospective groups and your perception of each group's primary objectives, its current relationships with other groups, and its policies and positions that are organizational musts (those they will not negotiate on) and those that are desirable (these will be negotiable). This chart will tell you ahead of time which groups will be in conflict with others in the coalition. When you decide which of those conflicts are acceptable, you will have a better idea about which groups to join together.

Be Selective. Many coalition builders assume that in order to be democratic they must invite every group that is willing to join. Because you are trying to form a more powerful entity — rather than a strict democracy — select those groups that will work best together in meeting the expected goals of the coalition.

Be politically and psychologically sensitive. Find long-standing members within each group who will help encourage the group to join the coalition. Also, show each group how its goals and purposes can be met by joining the coalition. To do this, you will need to be informed not only about the concerns and activities of each group, but how each group expects the coalition to accomodate those concerns and activities. Minority groups, in particular, need a clear analysis of how their daily survival issues relate to various peace issues. Extra-weighted votes, veto power, or co-chairmanship of the coalition could be offered to an important group that would help the coalition. After the coalition has begun to work successfully, the different groups can work toward a more equally-shared power structure.

Single- vs. Multi-Issue Peace Coalitions

A choice facing all peace groups is whether to form a coalition committed to one specific issue, such as the nuclear freeze campaign, or a coalition devoted to many issues. Advocates of single-issue coalitions argue that they are more effective in attracting broad-based support because they usually include only those principles where there is broad agreement. Those pushing for multi-issue coalitions think they are more able to raise people's consciousness about the interconnectedness of many issues, like poverty and military spending, even if they do not attract large numbers of supporters at first.

Both kinds of coalitions are needed to effect change: single issue coalitions educating masses of people, and multi-issue coalitions analyzing in-depth the various and related factors preventing peace. There is no simple formula for deciding which kind of coalition to form, although if a coalition has formed on the basis of a single issue, it is probably best to stay that way; the various coalition members should not be forced to add new issues or concerns to previously agreed-upon policies. If certain groups threaten to withdraw unless new concerns are adopted, they should be given a means to express their views. Perhaps they could be given an evening to present their concerns and try to build a separate coalition to meet those concerns.

Who Does the Work?

Someone will need to coordinate the efforts of the coalition. In consultation with the leaders of member groups, the coordinator can determine for each group both time commitments and responsibilities which will best meet the coalition's needs. Often a staff person (either paid or volunteer) from a member organization is the natural choice to handle these tasks and then to coordinate the actual operation of the coalition. Unfortunately, many coalitions place staff in an impossible position — expecting them to make sure the coalition runs smoothly, but not allowing them to make key decisions. Staff must be given enough authority to carry out their basic assignments.

Choosing Realistic Positions

Adopt a policy on making decisions. Some peace coalitions make their decisions by consensus — only after all member organizations agree. This may work for small single-issue coalitions; larger multi-issue coalitions find attempts to reach consensus on every issue can be burdensome, and even paralyzing. Yet, a system of simple majority rule may suppress important dissent and minority opinion, especially in multi-cultural coalitions.

A good middle ground is a "working consensus." The coalition tries first to arrive at a consensus on what should be the coalition's major issues of concern. During this time there is opportunity for extensive presentation of information and a discussion on a variety of viewpoints. If it turns out that consensus cannot be reached within a specified time, the coalition then seeks a two-thirds majority approval for decisions. This procedure combines some advantages of both consensus and voting decision-making.

Don't force change. Encourage coalition members to consider new or controversial policies, but do not insist that they adopt them. It is more effective to introduce new policies informally, in a climate of cooperation and good will, than to make them immediately binding on all members. For example, one coalition lost several member groups when the leaders insisted on a vote for or against participation in a Martin Luther King march.

Later, when the coalition was struggling over whether to endorse non-violent direct action, the leaders acted less abruptly, and brought in speakers to discuss the issue. By discussing rather than insisting on a vote, the coalition kept its remaining members, and found that even more members were now supportive of a nonviolent direct action policy.

Keep member groups informed. Present early drafts of the policy statements of each group in a bulletin, so that each may be aware of the programs and concerns of the others.

Allow time for deliberation. Hold discussion sessions before coming out with formal policy statements. Forcing groups to commit themselves to positions before they are ready only lengthens the process of reaching agreement. In a coalition formed to elect a joint ticket for the state Democratic convention, neither the freeze supporters nor those seeking unionizing of public employees were required to vote for each other's platform. However, after working in the coalition together, the two groups became sympathetic to each other's issues and programs.

Use non-binding statements. When there is controversy over particular issues, add non-binding statements to the coalition policy platform. This exposes groups to new ideas without forcing them to either accept the ideas or withdraw from the coalition. The coalition's basic position paper may contain statements on which there is broad agreement, and also non-binding statements on more controversial matters.

Allow for diversity. Set up guidelines whereby groups agree to support certain positions within the coalition but are then free to have some degree of independence outside the coalition. For example, one coalition that was seeking labor support agreed that the unions would support pro-choice political candidates as part of the coalition, but that individual union members were still free outside the coalition to campaign for anti-abortion candidates.

Reduce fundraising competition. If some individuals participate in the coalition but are not members of any of the coalition's separate groups, they may be charged more for coalition dues than individuals who also belong (and pay dues) to one of the separate groups.

Seek funding for the coalition from non-local sources (such as grants) and leave local grass-roots fundraising to the member organizations. One state-wide coalition had two non-competition agreements. The coalition raised all its money from national sources, and member groups could not submit funding proposals to a source to which another member group had already applied.

On a related note, coalitions can use their influence to challenge funding sources when member organizations are victims of unfair funding distribution.

Handling Conflict

Deal sensitively with criticism and personal attacks. During coalition meetings, criticism will at times be trivial and argumentative, and it may come in the confusing disguise of "helpful suggestions" or "constructive proposals." Such criticism, at times in the form of personal attacks, is inevitable, and it must be dealt with. It often indicates that member groups feel powerless within the coalition, and you need to deal with such situations in a manner that reduces the underlying feeling of powerlessness. Provide responsible roles to the groups that are being critical so as to increase their voice in the coalition; have them chair a meeting, head up a committee, etc.

Understand inter-group conflict. Activists who are accustomed to dealing with an "opposition" often seek out areas of disagreement, even with those in the coalition who share most of their views. Asking such persons to consider the areas of agreement can be helpful in reducing tensions.

Responding to Ethnic, Cultural, and Religious Differences

Respect groups' heritages. Ethnic, cultural, and religious groups provide their members with a common background and a sense of historical continuity, a means to remain hopeful, and a feeling that they will be supported and can support others. Peace coalitions should not compete with these group commitments or belittle their beliefs. Indeed, such groups can bring unique wisdom to a coalition. For example, Native Americans, who are extremely sensitive to issues of the environment and the elderly, can help other members appreciate these concerns. In one case, a coalition of Central American peace groups had been trying unsuccessfully to attract support from mainstream churches. They finally realized that they had been unintentionally belittling certain religious values in their discussions with church members.

Challenge group isolation. For some groups, being isolated is the normal state of affairs, and it therefore seems "safe" to them because it is familiar. Thus even though they join the coalition to end their isolation, they may find the smallest point of disagreement to justify forming their own subgroup or to withdraw from the coalition. Help those groups to focus on the many areas of agreement and to understand that they are unnecessarily repeating their old patterns of isolation.

Reject excuses for inefficiency. Do not let groups defend their right to use ineffective techniques by claiming "that's our culture." Groups bring enormous resources to a coalition from their traditional heritages, but they also bring excess cultural baggage that needs to be challenged. Because of a history of oppressive male leadership, for example, some women's coalitions are rigidly anti-leadership, which only ends up paralyzing the coalition and preventing strong women from being trained to be leaders.

Be understanding of group attacks. Groups from oppressed backgrounds sometimes unnecessarily criticize their best potential partners. After trying very hard to solicit the participation of a particular minority group, a predominantly white peace group became the target of the other group's anger. The peace group did not understand that it was being given such a hard time precisely because it had begun to be an ally, and by so doing had created enough safety for the minority group to release frustrations from years of past mistreatment by other white groups. Try to be understanding of such attacks, knowing that groups working together do not often attack each other unless there is enough safety to do so. Hopefully the criticism will lessen once you have fully listened to the group.

Plan cultural evenings. Cultural evenings are an important coalition-building tool. Present special programs with songs, group skits, etc. that draw on each group's unique history of struggling for peace and justice. To bring together groups with differing interests, you must integrate at least some of their important, life-sustaining customs into the coalition.

Plan events sensitively. Schedule programs and meetings to avoid religious holidays or any group's day of Sabbath.

Utilize symbols. Seek symbols for the coalition that reflect themes of unity and cooperation; Jewish groups, for example, have used the rainbow symbol to speak about peace and God's covenant to never again destroy the earth.

Encourage separate group sessions at coalition meetings. Coalitions trying to deal with difficult issues often spend too much time in whole-group meetings; this can be counterproductive when there is a history of intergroup competition. Let member groups meet individually (at coalition meetings) to reach separate agreement on their positions. Then let each group report its position to the rest of the coalition without interruption or discussion. After each group is finished, list both the areas of agreement and the potential areas of disagreement. Then send one representative from each group off together with the task of brainstorming a number of solutions that take into account the major concerns of every group (people are often able to change their rigid positions if invited to participate in a problem solving exercise — See Chapter 14 for discussion of a problem solving method). Finally, present the list of possible solutions for the entire group to decide on the best course of action.

Get to know each other's personal concerns. Plan time for "speak-outs," where individual coalition members share personal life stories and experiences that have shaped their attitudes. During these speak-outs, other individuals should be encouraged to listen respectfully and not comment or disagree. By getting to know each other's personal concerns, individuals begin to see the real human needs, feelings, and interests from another perspective. This can also help in understanding why certain conflicts may have developed. Some leaders believe this "personal sharing" will dull the political edge of the coalition, but bringing together diverse groups requires intergroup understanding, and understanding requires time.

When Skill Training is Not Enough

A set of guidelines such as these is helpful, but not sufficient to prevent many of the intergroup conflicts that surface in coalitions. If there are deeply ingrained patterns of isolation, mistrust, competition, and powerlessness in the groups belonging to a coalition, conflicts will not simply disappear with new information and skills. The coalition will need some sort of counseling session (see the references below).

Increasingly, peace groups will be called upon to form coalitions with other organizations. The art of coalition building will need to become a significant part of any organizer's training program.

Workshop Opportunities

National Coalition Building Institute, 38 Dartmouth St., Somerville, MA 02145. This group offers training workshops for coalition leaders, and also works with organizations on reducing intergroup conflict.

Re-Evaluation Counseling, 2nd Ave. North, Seattle, WA 98109. This group offers classes and workshops in most cities on how to help each other get free of the effects of past stressful experiences. RC has a particular organizational commitment to preventing nuclear war.

Suggested Readings

Brown, C.R. (1984). *The art of coalition building: A guide for community leaders.* New York: The American Jewish Committee. (165 E. 56th St., New York, NY 10022; $3.50.) This is a training manual that takes you through all necessary steps to build effective multi-cultural coalitions.

Messinger, R. (1981, October-November). Building coalitions for change. *Center for Law and Education Newsletter.* (6 Appian Way, Cambridge, MA 02138.) Messinger describes the kinds of coalitions that activists can build to bring about effective social change.

Tydeman, A. (1979). *A guide to coalition building.* Washington: The National Citizen's Coalition for Nursing Home Reform. (1424 16th St. N.W., Washington, DC 20036.) Written for health care workers but applicable to all coalition work, this is a guide to the networking skills involved in coalition work.

IV

PeaceMaking:
Reducing Conflict

The five chapters in this section cover understanding and managing conflict. Most of the material deals with conflict between you and your listeners; however many of the techniques may be applied to conflict among your group members. Pettit, Holtzman, and Wollman contend that peaceworkers should be more willing to engage in conflict with opposing parties, and they offer suggestions on negotiating and working out conflicts.

Keller and Brown present four keys toward keeping conflict (or any communication) constructive: the self-talk monitor, the empathy monitor, the nonverbal monitor, and the punctuation monitor. Date' and Hoskins present two techniques — paraphrasing and purpose clarification/stating — which can help make communication more clear and caring.

Childers outlines a "Disagreement Dialogue" workshop for bringing opposing groups together into meaningful discussion in an intensive half-day or full-day session. Lakey's concluding paper discusses the use of nonviolence for social change, focussing on the personal dimension: how you can remain calm and unprovoking in the midst of potentially violent confrontations.

14

Using Conflict Constructively

Robert Pettit, Ronald E. Holtzman, and Neil Wollman

As a peace worker, you may feel uncomfortable when conflict arises in the course of a conversation, demonstration, or other encounter you have with those of opposing viewpoints. You may feel guilty for having been a party to conflict. You may feel you are betraying your commitment to peace if all is not forever harmonious between you and those who disagree with you. You may hesitate to speak or act boldly for fear of confrontation.

Misgivings about conflict may handicap your effectiveness as a peace worker. Nevertheless, in a world in which inequality, injustice, racism, sexism, violence, and militarism are so ingrained in our social orders, we who actively work for peace and justice are bound to encounter resistance: the pursuit of peace paradoxically entails confrontation and conflict.

As a peace worker, you need to master your misgivings about conflict; learn how to civilize it, to make it creative and constructive, to keep it humane. Quite simply, conflict can be a tool, a technique which can work to your advantage. It is a powerful tool for social change. Not only should you not fear it, sometimes you should welcome it — even foment or escalate it.

If you can overcome your fears and misgivings about conflict, you can learn to utilize it for the benefit of your peace work. You can be insistent without being abusive. You can stand toe to toe with your adversaries and press your case in the face of intimidation or coercion. You can meet the challenges of confrontation rather than shrink from them. You can grow into a more forceful and effective advocate for your ideals.

Myths about Conflict

If you want to master the use of conflict in your pursuit of peace and justice, first dispel some common myths and misconceptions about conflict [1: pp. 6-8].

MYTH: Harmony is the normal state of affairs, and conflict is abnormal. A brief survey of American history — from Revolutionary colonists and abolitionists to labor organizers, civil rights demonstrators, and Vietnam protesters — shows that conflict has been necessary time and time again to redress grievances. Conflict is just as "natural" to any social system as stability.

MYTH: Conflict is pathological, simply a result of misdirected anger. This misconception reduces real grievances to personality problems or emotional disorders. However, when you're confronted with real unfairness, injustice, or oppression, anger and frustration are not inappropriate responses.

MYTH: Conflicts are just disagreements, simply "failures to communicate." Certainly, clear communication helps dispel misinterpretations in a conflict. But if goals are significantly incompatible, no amount of "better understanding through communication" will resolve the conflict. In conflicts between participants of unequal power, it is no surprise that the more powerful party wants only to talk . . . and talk.

MYTH: Conflicts are harmful and should always be reduced, resolved, or eliminated. Our culture views conflict as primarily negative — we are told, "don't argue," "be nice," "stop fighting." But this is often a "pro-establishment" bias of whoever holds the power. It is why every corporate president stresses teamwork and morale, while minimizing or ignoring disagreement and discontent; why the political party in power always discourages dissent and encourages "patriotic" support for our President. Those in power want to keep things the way they are.

The Nature of Conflict

Freeing yourself from misconceptions about social conflict is only the first step toward using it effectively. Here are some suggestions that may help you further toward that end:

-*Realize that a free society cannot exist without an element of conflict.* If a conflict-free society could be achieved, the result would likely be a totalitarian society. The very meaning of "free" is the liberty to press conflicting views and rights.

   -*Realize that conflict can be constructive and creative as well as destructive and degrading.* If handled with skill and mutual respect, conflict can produce better alternatives than could either conflicting party alone. Since none of us has a monopoly on truth or virtue, it is only through serious exchange — even conflict — that we learn and grow.

   -*Realize that conflict can be beneficial for your group.* Conflict between your group and outside forces can intensify your members' convictions and commitment, help group members to come to a common understanding of your group's identity and purpose, and rally members to comfort and support one another. Conflict with a common foe on a particular issue may offer the opportunity for alliance with groups not otherwise committed to your cause. Conflict between your group and those who oppose you may be helpful for both groups: it may establish a relationship where none existed before, and it may help establish rules and norms to govern further relations. It may only be through conflict, furthermore, that your adversary can gauge the strength of your resolve and finally come to deal with you seriously.

   -*Be able to distinguish realistic and nonrealistic conflict.* Realistic conflicts occur when there are real differences over goals sought; nonrealistic conflicts merely vent frustration or aggressive impulses. [2] Realistic conflicts — like strikes and protests — can be productive, inasmuch as they seek to realize identifiable goals. Nonrealistic conflicts — like senseless riots or emotional shouting matches — tend to be destructive and meaningless, mere tension-relievers. Since most conflicts probably contain elements of both, concentrate your efforts on the realistic conflicts over goals, while trying to defuse the nonrealistic emotional elements.

Managing Conflict
   Though conflict is inevitable and even desirable in your work for peace, it is possible to reduce tensions and hostility without abandoning the political goals you seek. Through the negotiation and problem solving techniques described below, you can work toward goals such as getting a company to divest its military interests, encouraging a college or university to allow both military

recruiters and draft counselors on campus, and working out disagreements with a city council on the logistics of a protest demonstration.

Though these negotiating and problem solving strategies are geared mainly to intergroup conflict, they will at times be useful among peace group members or in one-to-one discussions with others concerning opinions on peace issues. Chapter 16, along with additional chapters in this section, gives specific suggestions for improving communication and understanding.

Negotiating. [3,4,5] Conflict situations involve not only opponent positions, but also persons holding those positions. Because strongly held positions become part of our identity, an attack on our positions becomes an attack on us and our self-esteem. But there's more. Because of this link between our attitude and our identity, if we have high self-esteem, we will think highly of our position on an issue. Conversely, we may think less of others who hold a different view, and we may attribute other undesirable traits to them. For example, we in the peace movement may view a person arguing for increased nuclear armament as a "warmonger," whereas the pro-armament individual may perceive us as "naive" or "cowardly." (See Chapter 23 for further discussion on attributions about peace workers.) When we attribute such characteristics to our opponents we are more likely to make personal attacks against them. The net effect will be to make both sides defensive, further entrench our positions, and increase the conflict.

The key to avoiding this crisis is to invite a mutual attack on the *problem*, and not the persons holding various positions. Concentrate on the issues and avoid a test of personal will; avoid forcing your opponent to try to save face. Attempt to create a cooperative posture in yourself, and in your opponent. This can be accomplished by refraining from threats, stressing points of agreement, and avoiding winner-take-all bargaining. Incorporate some goals which each party alone desires, and establish new mutual goals both you and your opponent value — goals which will require future mutual cooperation for their attainment. This will promote better relations in future interactions. You are more likely to elicit cooperation and trustworthiness in your opponent when you exhibit those traits yourself.

Mutual success depends on your ability to understand and

appreciate the opposing view. Avoid attacking your opponent's stated position or defending your own; concentrate discussion on the real interests and concerns that underlie those bargaining positions. Ask an opponent *why* she is taking her position. Listen carefully and let the other party know that you are trying to understand, perhaps by asking for clarification or repeating what has been said. Try putting yourself in your opponent's shoes to fully capture her perspective and feel the impact of your proposed remedies.

If both parties can talk about their own interests, fears, and frustrations, and actively listen to the self-disclosures of the other, some shared interests and an appreciation for the opposing point of view may surface. Thus, for example, a city council and those planning a demonstration may find that they both fear nuclear war, value free speech, and wish for citizens and property at the demonstration site to remain safe. After such acknowledgments, compromises can be discussed to determine how the interests of each side can best be satisfied.

Compromise solutions should be based on merit — that is, their ability to satisfy the interests of both sides. Merit is based on objective criteria, much as the merit of a selling price for a used car is based on a *Blue Book* quotation. Thus, both sides of a defense expenditure issue or military intervention issue must evaluate options based on a fair standard. A good one in this case might involve determining in what ways the options jeopardize national security or whether they escalate tensions.

Holding meetings in private is also helpful since the presence of a bargainer's constituents will tend to invite a hardline approach. A bargainer may be less likely to grant concessions in public because a concession involves a ''come-down'' from an original position and may not be reciprocated. He risks being perceived as weak. Along these lines, be aware that you can more easily sidestep the perception of being weak by granting a concession if your new proposal seems just for the situation (e.g., based on a legal or fair standard) rather than just appeasing the other side. Your side is always helped by appearing reasonable.

Negotiation can be particularly difficult if either side questions the motives of the other. If you wish to establish trust, you might first make some small, unilateral concessions which don't make you vulnerable. Do so without saying that you expect reciprocations. Such concessions are often reciprocated as trust replaces suspicion, and then future concessions are given in turn until a final settlement is reached.

Negotiation of this nature is the backbone of the GRIT (Graduated and Reciprocated Initiative in Tension reduction) strategy [6], and works best with adversaries of equal strength. A classic case of using GRIT occurred in 1963 on the international scene. The United States unilaterally halted nuclear testing in the atmosphere. This was followed by the Soviets allowing U.N. observers into war-torn Yemen and several other reciprocated actions between the nations. Unfortunately, other incidents halted further progress. The GRIT strategy is just as applicable to the bargaining table as it is to international foreign policies. Of course, if either party is bent on self-promotion at the other's expense, such a strategy will not work. You should note, too, that if you have doubts about the motives of your opponent, then all promises and concessions should be monitored and safeguarded for compliance.

If both parties are willing, a third party can often be helpful in settling a dispute. Third parties can analyze the conflict, stimulate self-diagnosis, control disrupting behavior, encourage openness and accuracy of information, support participants, and encourage the parties to cooperate to solve their problem. The third party should be expert at focusing both sides on interests, inventing intermediate options, and establishing fair standards for evaluating options.

There will be times when those with whom you are negotiating will not respond to your attempts to solve the conflict cooperatively. They may adamantly stand behind a position or employ manipulative bargaining strategies. There are some things you can try once you recognize the uncooperative stance of your opponent. Explicitly assert to your opponent what she is doing, and question the validity and desirability of her behavior if the conflict is to be resolved. Ask why she is taking such an extreme position or why she is using certain tactics; it is more productive to ask why than to merely reject the proposals and tactics. Find the true interests behind the position and behavior.

There will be occasions on which your opponent simply will not negotiate in good faith no matter what you try. For that reason it is always good to have or develop as good an alternative as possible to negotiation with the other party. Such an alternative, if you see it as a reasonable option, will lessen the likelihood you will give in to undue pressure rather than end the negotiations if your opponent remains uncooperative.

If you must end negotiations, don't end all contact with the other side. You may be able to bargain later if the relationship improves. Establish constructive channels of communication and patterns of trust. Keeping channels of communication open is beneficial in any conflict situation, whether or not any formal negotiations are ever a part of the interaction. One of the greatest temptations in dealing with adversaries is to restrict and/or filter communication so that it confirms our cherished negative impressions of them. Contact and openness with those we dislike and distrust is difficult, but it is essential if we are to avoid the tendency to read only treachery into all our adversary's actions, and only virtue into our own.

Problem Solving. [5,7,8] The chances for successful negotiation will increase if you and your opponents can adopt a "problem solving" mentality. This involves both parties trying to reach a mutually satisfying solution rather than trying to "defeat" each other, or get the best results only for themselves. Researchers have identified a number of stages in the problem solving process. The negotiating suggestions above may also be incorporated into a number of the steps in this process.

1) Gain a commitment from all negotiators to take responsibility for helping to reach a solution. This involves an agreement to fully participate in all steps of the problem solving.

2) Accurately identify and understand the problem. Divide the conflict into more manageable parts to be worked on one at a time, explore reasons for the problem, recognize the needs and constraints of both sides, and reach consensus on behaviors or policies that must be changed.

3) Generate a number of alternative solutions for each part of the conflict. You might try a brainstorming approach which encourages free expression of ideas without evaluation or discussion (see Chapter 19 for more on brainstorming).

4) Reach consensus on a solution for each part of the conflict. This involves evaluating solutions to see whether they are feasible and

whether they meet the needs and constraints of both parties. Negotiating, modifying, and combining solutions will likely be necessary.

5) Engage in action planning. Set specific steps, commitments, and responsibilities for all individuals concerned.

6) Do evaluation planning. Develop objective measures to evaluate the success of the solution; set the timing for when to evaluate and decide who will collect what information and do what particular tasks. If you can't determine an objective measure of success, or can't work out the logistics for doing evaluations, it probably signals that the planned solution is inappropriate.

7) Share perceptions and feelings about resolving the conflict. This builds further trust and openness which helps in carrying out the solution.

8) Implement, evaluate, and modify the solution. Institute the solution; evaluate progress (Step 6); monitor both side effects and social processes such as the level of involvement and satisfaction of participants; make adjustments in commitments and responsibilities if necessary.

Conclusion

In the Chinese language the written character for the word "crisis" is made up of two symbols: one stands for "danger," the other for "opportunity." So it is with conflict: its potential for both danger and opportunity is great. It is what we make of it.

C. Wright Mills' challenge still stands as a call to arms: "If you do not specify and confront real issues, what you do will surely obscure them. If you do not alarm anyone morally, you will yourself remain morally asleep. If you do not embody controversy, what you say will be an acceptance of the drift to the coming human hell" [9: p.7].

References

1. Wilmot, J.H.F., & Wilmot, W.W. (1978). *Interpersonal conflict.* Dubuque, IA: William C. Brown.

2. Coser, L. (1964). *The functions of social conflict.* New York: Free Press.

3. Fisher, R., & Ury, W. (1983). *Getting to yes: Negotiating agreement without giving in.* New York: Penguin Books.

4. Rubin, J.Z., & Brown, B. (1975). *The social psychology of bargaining and negotiation*. New York: Academic Press.
5. Fisher, R.J. (1982). *Social psychology: An applied approach*. New York: St. Martin's Press.
6. Osgood, C.E. (1962). *An alternative to war or surrender*. Urbana, IL: University of Illinois Press.
7. Morris, W.C., & Sashkin, M. (1976). *Organization behavior in action: Skill building experiences*. St. Paul, MN: West.
8. Miller, G.D., & Zoradi, S.D. (1977). Roommate conflict resolution. *Journal of College Student Personnel*, 3, 228-230.
9. Lee, R., & Marty, M.E. (Eds.) (1964). *Religion and social conflict*. New York: Oxford University Press.

Suggested Readings

Coser, L. (1964). *The functions of social conflict*. New York: Free Press. This is the classic work on how conflict can serve useful functions for social groups.

Fisher, R., & Ury, W. (1983). *Getting to yes: Negotiating agreement without giving in*. New York: Penguin Books. This is a brief, and very practical and readable guide for making negotiating successful for both sides of disputes.

Kriesberg, L. (1982). *Social conflicts*. Englewood Cliffs, NJ: Prentice-Hall. Kriesberg presents one of the most comprehensive analyses of group conflicts, incorporating theory and research from sociology, psychology, anthropology, economics, history, and political science. For illustrative purposes, he focuses on women's liberation, student protests, collective bargaining, the fight for racial equality, the Cold War, and the Arab-Israeli conflict.

15

Promoting Peaceful Interaction

Paul W. Keller and Charles T. Brown

During his stay in South Africa, Mahatma Gandhi did battle over racial injustice for years with General Jan Smuts, that country's Minister of Finance & Defense. Yet Gandhi fought in a way that kept the two talking to each other while fundamental changes took shape in that society, and the two men came to understand and respect each other. [1]

It seems strange, but peace workers often have difficulty getting along with people. They can be so determined to make everybody non-violent that they will knock their opponents' heads together to do it. Sometimes they even struggle among themselves so intensely that their peace groups are destroyed. In short, instead of creating peace and uniting people, they often create conflict and alienate people by their actions.

Why? How do people inspired by such high ideals so often turn off the very persons they would like to persuade? What is it that builds barriers between peace workers and the rest of the world? What are the characteristics of those human contacts — such as Gandhi's — which *nourish* both parties in the face of conflict?

The search for answers could focus on the philosophies or ethical standards that separate people, but we have chosen instead to examine in this chapter the dynamics of interpersonal conflict and the possibilities for improving communication in conflict situations.

The most important step in improving how we deal with each other is to become aware that conflict is not a static thing — it is dynamic. It is a flow of events between two people, a dance that may be relatively harmonious one moment and suddenly turn into sharp disagreement or dissent the next.

Consider an example: You begin talking with someone you have heard disagrees with your point of view. He seems quite open and agreeable, and you are surprised at how easy and nondefensive the conversation seems. You think to yourself that there may have been a mistake here; perhaps the disagreement was only imagined. But then the other person becomes noticeably cooler, and you begin feeling negative about what he is saying. As the negative feelings increase, you find a growing mistrust of the other, and a need to "wheel out the big guns" and arm yourself. You stand on the edge of an all-out battle.

What happened? Was it inevitable that it happen that way? Perhaps not, for it is quite possible that better communication would have prevented this exchange from turning in such a negative direction.

Four Keys to Better Dialogue

Peaceful interaction becomes possible if you become more aware of the things you are thinking, doing, and saying during the course of a conversation. To do this, turn on four powerful monitors: (1) the *self-talk* monitor, (2) the *empathy* monitor, (3) the *non-verbal* monitor, and (4) the *punctuation* monitor. They can help you gain increasing control over your behavior in conflict situations.

The self-talk monitor. Behind every emotion there is a previous assumption, said the late Irving J. Lee of Northwestern University. This is another way of saying that how you feel toward someone is not directly caused by that person; it springs, instead, from what you are thinking about that person.

One peace worker, after exploding during a phone conversation with a government official and abruptly hanging up, exclaimed, "I can't stand that man! He drives me up the wall." In conflict situations like this which lead you to negative feelings, the normal reaction is to assume that your emotion is caused by the other person and that you are powerless to change it.

Such a view has problems. Two people — as we easily observe — can react quite differently to the same stimulus. A word, a tone of voice, or a particular look can drive one person "up the wall," but affect another person positively. This difference in response is, clearly, not caused by the stimulus, but by the silent statements these persons make to themselves about the stimulus. [2]

In the situation cited above, the peace worker may be thinking ideas like these about the official: "Officials should be rational and fair at all times," "If I don't convince him, I'm a failure," "He doesn't like me, and unless everybody likes me, I am not worthy." This kind of self-talk is not very rational, and once you recognize that, you can modify your emotional reactions by developing more reasonable expectations and by thinking more rationally. You cannot control the other person, but you can begin to control what you think and do in response.

If you are saying to yourself, "They are exploiting me," and if events show they really are, then your anger is justified. But even in this situation your self-talk can reflect a problem-solving rather than aggressive motivation — ("I feel exploited. I wonder how I can best help you to understand that," rather than, "You are exploiting me. You should be punished."). Chapter 14 discusses the problem-solving approach as applied to intergroup conflict.

By refraining from blaming the other in your self-talk, you can better maintain a sense of calm and control that will help keep the conflict constructive.

The problem is that the self-talk monitor is seldom turned on. You may listen to the words you say out loud but ignore the words you say to yourself. That is the bad news; the good news is that you can change if you want to. You can change by examining your self-talk until such review becomes habit. For some people, it helps to write down what they said silently, and to do this soon after a conflict situation. For others, talking with someone about the self-talk works well. In any case, by recognizing your self-talk after an exchange, you soon become more conscious of the silent assumptions and thoughts which precede your emotional reactions and spoken words. With the self-talk monitor on, you will gain a new kind of understanding, as well as control of your thinking patterns and their effects on communication.

The empathy monitor. The cliche says, "Put yourself in the other person's shoes." Left at that, it rarely gets the desired results. But once the empathy monitor is understood and used, it makes a fundamental difference in how conflict is handled.

Empathy requires two things: *Imagination* — the ability to

imagine what the other person feels, to call on one's own experience, asking, ''What do I know that is anything like what this person is experiencing?''; and *Flexibility* — a willingness to focus on the other person, to feel good enough about yourself to step out of the focus of attention long enough to ''live'' with the other.

To become more empathic, first be aware that empathy for the other has been lost (or never existed in the first place). Train yourself — with reminders again and again — to ask yourself, ''How is the other person interpreting my words?'' and ''What does she mean by the words she is speaking?'' Or more concisely, ''What does this message mean to her?''

Isn't that what we naturally ask ourselves when we are involved in an exchange? No, it isn't. Instead — and especially in the heat of conflict — we tend to ask, ''What does this message mean to me?'' Because we feel threatened, conflict tends to promote ego-centered thinking. Therefore, injecting the question, ''What does this message mean to him?'' can have a radical effect on the way you respond; it can, in fact, produce an atmosphere much more open to constructive handling of conflict.

''But,'' said one peace activist who had been applying this approach, ''when I do that I begin to see the problem from that person's point of view, and it makes some sense, and that makes it harder for me to totally support my own position.'' That possibility is real. It seems easier to act on an absolute position — one that does not take into account anyone else's perception; but that is only the case if outright victory is the goal. If ''truth'' is the goal (as it was for Gandhi), and if ''opponents'' are instead viewed as partners in the search for truth, then conflict can be both exciting and rewarding. You can promote that search by employing an empathy that can reduce defensiveness and surprise your combatants with unsuspected openness.

The non-verbals monitor. Some psychologists estimate that non-verbals — voice, gesture, facial expression, body posture, and the like — make up more than 65% of the social meaning of any conversation; less than 35% of the meaning is actually carried by words. [3] The reason is that non-verbals are often involuntary. While words can hide feelings, non-verbals are more likely to reveal them. Words are strong, but feelings revealed through non-verbals are stronger. If words say one thing and non-verbals say another, the non-verbals, in many situations, will be believed. [3] Sometimes the face gives away one's true feelings, sometimes the hands, sometimes the voice; any part of the non-verbal channel can do it. When the verbal and non-verbal signals go in different directions, the result is increased distance and distrust between the participants. It is not as important to know which part of the non-verbal channel is "tattling," as it is to know that when either you or the other party is incongruent (that is, sending mixed messages), it can be noticed. Train your non-verbal monitor to recognize such mixed messages.

This is especially important for peace workers. If your struggle is really for world peace rather than for ways to control or defeat others, it is important that both your verbal and non-verbal messages confirm that.

Witness an actual happening: A peace worker presented herself as open, flexible, and empathic in a meeting with a college administrator. She smiled, "listened," and nodded appropriately. However, the administrator could not escape a growing feeling of mistrust in spite of the cooperative words she spoke. Something in the visual signals she was giving him made him wary (Was it the shifting of the eyes? The tension of the body? The forced laughter?). In the car going home from that meeting she said to a colleague, "We really backed him into a corner, didn't we? I think we've got him now." In subsequent meetings the administrator grew increasingly alienated and his position hardened as he realized that her non-verbal signals indicated her determination to defeat him.

It happens that many peace workers are quiet verbally even though they are committed to strong action. They see silence as a consistent feature of their "peaceful" intent. But they overlook one of the basic rules of communication: "You cannot *not* communicate." [4] Silence is a non-verbal expression, and our silence may be interpreted by others as saying we are afraid, or feel superior, or are angry — or any number of unknown possibilities. Silence has its virtues, but it does little to build trust or encourage understanding. To be authentic, that is, to have your outward appearance to others match your feelings, is to lay the foundation for trust and to make possible constructive handling of conflict.

Much more can be said about non-verbal communication. But boiled down, here are some hints for peaceful interaction:

-Make eye contact frequently, but keep from letting your eyes "go hard."

-Be aware that touching sends a powerful non-verbal signal. The context in which it is done determines how it will be interpreted. A hand placed on someone's shoulder can be seen as an assertion of status or as a sign of affection. Do not automatically assume that it will be taken as a sign of affection.

-Try to make the non-verbal signals you send — appearance, interaction distance, posture, gestures, tone of voice, touch — as non-threatening as you can.

-Remember that although non-verbal messages are more trusted than conflicting verbal ones, if you want to be precise and unambiguous, your words are more helpful than non-verbals.

The punctuation monitor. In the early part of this chapter we described conflict as a flow of events between two people. How that flow gets organized is important in determining how people deal with conflict. In every conflict, there is punctuation — a way of organizing the events that make up the exchange [4]. And people are led, by their different histories, to provide different punctuation.

In a marriage, for example, a conflict may be punctuated as follows [4]:

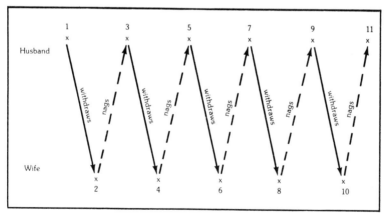

The husband sees their argument as stemming from the wife's nagging (as though to say, "Who wouldn't withdraw in the face of such nagging?"); the wife, however, sees the root problem in the husband's withdrawing (as though to say, "Who wouldn't nag a husband who doesn't say a word?''). Thus the husband punctuates the flow in clusters 2-3-4, 4-5-6, 6-7-8, etc, while the wife punctuates it in clusters 1-2-3, 3-4-5, 5-6-7, etc. This pattern can be applied to virtually any conflict. There seems to be a universal tendency to want to point a finger and say, "You started it."

In the Middle East, the Israelis say they must attack because they are being harrassed by the Arabs. The Arabs say they wouldn't be harrassing the Israelis if the Israelis hadn't pushed them out of their land. The Israelis say they wouldn't have pushed the Arabs out if the Arabs hadn't pushed them out first. The Arabs say. . . and so on.

Two things become clear: (1) When you try to punctuate a conflict you discover it is impossible to find an agreed-upon beginning; and (2)How each party punctuates the conflict makes a tremendous difference in their attitude toward the solution. If you feel the other party started it, then you probably think they are the ones who should have to back down. Turning on the punctuation monitor, then, helps us recognize that neither side is absolutely blameless, or absolutely right, or absolutely justified. It is a reminder that each side operates with a set of blinders that shuts out important understandings.

To be able to say to the other party, "I know this looks different to you. . ." is to create a different kind of atmosphere; it is the beginning of an effort to understand the other's perceptions. Such an action by one party may lead the other party to do the same.

Peace workers, who usually act out of a strong idealism, tend to blame leaders and institutions for the problems that exist: "The Pentagon is determined to plunge us into nuclear war." The Establishment, under attack, punctuates it differently: "If we didn't have to fear the Soviet Union, we wouldn't need nuclear weapons." The parties cannot seem to agree on how to punctuate the conflict, and there probably never will be agreement on that punctuation. Even so, it is good to recognize the particular punctuation occurring on both sides; being conscious of one's own biases can help develop empathy for the biases of the other person ("I can imagine how you feel; that is the way I would feel if I were in your shoes."). The punctuation monitor provides another way to build awareness.

Conclusion

Conflict is, by its nature, hard to deal with. Skills for handling it constructively are available, but they will fail unless they are based on self-awareness. To work toward awareness, follow four paths:

(1) Start listening to and examining your thoughts more deeply (a self-talk monitor).

(2) Ask yourself, "What do these messages mean to him?" (an empathy monitor).

(3) Open your eyes and ears to pick up signals you have been missing in yourself or others (a non-verbals monitor).

(4) Recognize the game of assigning blame (a punctuation monitor).

Turning such monitors on, and keeping them on, takes discipline, of course. It involves forming a set of habits that, with practice, become easier to use. Such discipline requires a strong motivation, but that motivation can be found in the very purpose of communication — to establish community. Conflict threatens community. Divorces, wars, civil hostilities are all around us. If we would have community we must know the price — there is a price for anything worth having; that price is dedication to promoting constructive conflict. Such dedication offers opportunities to establish a community enriched by the very differences from which it is made.

References

1. Fischer, L. (1951). *Life of Gandhi*. London: Jonathan Cape.
2. Ellis, A. (1962). *Reason & emotion in psychotherapy*. New York: Lyle Stuart.
3. Knapp, M.L. (1972). *Non-verbal communication in human interaction*. New York: Holt, Rinehart, & Winston.
4. Watzlawick P., Beavin, J., & Jackson, D. (1967). *Pragmatics of human communication*. Palo Alto, CA: W.W. Norton.

Suggested Reading

LaFrance, M. & Mayo, C. (1978). *Moving bodies: Nonverbal communication in social relationships*. Monterey, CA: Brooks/Cole. Rather than attempting a theoretical analysis of non-verbal messages, LaFrance and Mayo examine the ways in which non-verbals grow out of, and help shape, human relationships. This book is richly researched and is filled with useful examples.

16

Communicating Peacefully with Others: The "Foreign Language" of Caring

Barbara Date' and Joanna T. Hoskins

We are all familiar with conflict in our daily lives: we know what it sounds like, we know what it feels like. We have all said or thought words like, "You just don't understand my feelings about this! You're not listening to me!" Conflict and frustration also occur in our work for world peace as we talk with fellow peace workers and with those of differing viewpoints. Certainly people involved in dysfunctional conflict don't wish for it to happen; we would like to benefit from creative tension that challenges us to have healthy dialogue and relationships. How, then, can we explain why persons wishing for constructive interaction often end up in destructive conflict — in daily life and on a larger global scale as well?

To understand this mystery, it is helpful to examine the assumptions that many people hold about what components are necessary for relationships to be constructive and reasonably conflict-free. People tend to say, "If only others cared enough and really made an effort, we wouldn't have these conflicts!" Thus two components that are assumed necessary for positive interaction are *caring* and *effort*. However, these components, though important, are only part of the picture. They are like two legs of a three-legged stool. The indispensible element so often overlooked is *skill*. [1] In order to relate harmoniously to others while working for world peace, those in the movement need to know the skills of peacemaking and how to use them. They need to be *competent*.

Acting in peaceful ways is not so much a matter of *will* but of *skill*. We have developed a very precise educational curriculum which includes what we call the "foreign language of caring and cooperation." [2] Our program assumes that people want to be more helpful and caring, but they lack the specific know-how to put their intentions into action.

In this chapter we will focus on two of these peacemaking skills. The first, *purpose clarification/purpose stating* [3], prepares a person for skillful peacemaking interventions. The second, paraphrasing, preserves and promotes relationships. [4] Used together, these two skills minimize and manage conflict.

Purpose Clarification/Purpose Stating

By using this skill, you will be able to clarify, to yourself and then to another, what you are trying to accomplish in any given situation or over time. Skillful purpose stating is crucial to interpersonal peacemaking. Most thoughtless and hurtful behavior does not occur because people want it or plan it; rather, negative behavior occurs because people rarely think through in advance what they are trying to achieve and the probable impact of their actions. They are *reacting* rather than purposefully acting. An example is appropriate here to illustrate this problem. It will show how purpose clarification will enable you to plan actions and evaluate their likely impact on others, while purpose stating enables others to cooperate with you because they will see your goals clearly defined:

John has been dissatisfied with the way that Michael has been coordinating their neighborhood dispute mediation staff. Michael is a quiet person who withdraws during conflict. He is careful, systematic, and — in John's view — slow in the way he approaches each mediation case. John wants to move quickly and decisively in scheduling, hearing, and settling each case. As John approaches Michael, he states his displeasure in a fast and forthright manner. "We're never going to get these cases heard!!! You're creating more conflicts than helping to solve these problems!!!" Michael becomes anxious, quiet, and "shuts down." John is left feeling frustrated — the same way he felt before the conversation.

After the fact, John might justify his actions by thinking, "I wanted him to see how strongly I feel about how things are going." However, if John had clarified all his purposes before approaching Michael, he would have discovered that he had more than one purpose: "I also want Michael to keep talking with me so we can work on solving my concerns; I don't want to make him withdraw because I come on too strong. Additionally, my intention is to propose a few ideas about how things could go better."

Let's give John a chance to be more competent. First, he thinks about the situation with Michael and clarifies his purposes: "I'm upset by this situation and want to get my concerns and desires across to Michael, while still preserving our relationship. What, then, are my specific purposes? I want him to see how strongly I feel about how things are going. I also want Michael to keep talking... Additionally, I want to propose a few ideas... How can I best accomplish these? I realize Michael usually gets upset when others raise their voices around him, so it would help if I could speak calmly. If I explain to him my three purposes, he probably can understand since he is a reasonable person and also cares about me. I could ask him to *paraphrase* me so I'll know he really does understand what I'm all upset about. OK, I'm now ready to approach Michael."

At this point John can clearly state his purposes to Michael. He might say something like this:

"My purpose is to share some concerns I'm having and try to work out some problems I see. I value our work relationship and want for it to go well. I want to let you know that I'm feeling upset that we're not handling as many mediation cases as we could. I have a few ideas on how we might speed things up a bit, and still meet some of your desires about being careful. My hope is that we can work together on this to meet both our concerns."

By doing purpose clarification in advance, John was able to determine his specific purposes, to evaluate the likely impact on Michael of his actions and plan accordingly, and to then prepare and deliver purpose statements that allowed him best to accomplish his intentions.

With this illustration now complete, let's return to the nature of purpose clarification and purpose stating.

The Point (or Purpose) of Purpose Clarification

-to ensure that you know exactly what you intend to happen and what you intend not to happen (usually meaning that you intend to accomplish particular outcomes, enhancing relationships rather than damaging relationships);

-to ensure that you are not working at cross-purposes (such as intending to express strong feelings on a subject, but using words or tone that virtually guarantee others will not really listen);

-to help you assertively stick to your purpose(s) by clarifying it (them) in your mind.

The Point of Purpose Stating

-to encourage others' cooperation by clearly stating your intentions;

-to differentiate *purpose* from *method*: purpose refers to the goal or outcome, method refers to the steps for getting there (people are more willing to discuss methods when they see that they share common purposes);

-to limit conflict by limiting the conversation to the stated purposes and issues of the discussion.

The Structure of Purpose Clarification and Purpose Statements

Purpose clarification and purpose statements start with phrases like these:

"My purpose is . . ."
"What I'm trying to accomplish is . . ."
"My intention is . . ."
"I'm hoping to . . ."

Two More Examples Using Purpose Clarification and Stating

Here are two situations in which purpose clarification and purpose stating would be helpful.

1. You have just finished leading a meeting of your peace group in which several projects were discussed. The discussion became heated and some members drowned out others. Now, as you leave, a person approaches you and tells you that she is angry that her ideas weren't accepted. You wish to be helpful to her.

What are some purposes that you can clarify internally to yourself?

-You want this person to know that you are listening to and understanding her concerns.

-You want to monitor your own behavior since you are tired and a little annoyed though you still wish to be supportive.

-You want to minimize giving advice unless it is asked for; instead you want to focus on skillful listening.

Let's say you have another appointment waiting, and the person continues to speak. What might be a purpose statement you could make that would cover the intentions listed above? One might be, "My purpose is to hear about your concerns. Your ideas and your feelings are important. I have another appointment I need to go to now, but what I want to accomplish is to hear your concerns at a time when I'm not rushing off. I would like to call you."

2. You get a call from a member who recently joined your peace group. He wants some personal counseling regarding conscientious objection, and he begins to tell you his problem in great detail, evidently thinking you can solve it right then. Unfortunately, you don't know much about the topic, and there are specific people working in conjuction with your peace group who are trained to counsel on such matters. You need to inform the person about the procedure for obtaining future counseling.

What are some purposes you can clarify to yourself?

-You want your fellow member to know that his calling you is appropriate and that his concern is important—that he is not being cut short or dismissed.

-You want him to know that there is a whole procedure regarding seeking counseling which he needs to know about.

-You want him to know that you won't be counseling him on the phone — that will be accomplished by the trained counselors.

-You need to clarify to yourself whether you want to hear him describe his concerns in detail. Though you don't have particular expertise, it may help him emotionally to talk about his concerns and feelings. You, instead, may determine that you need to express — in a supportive manner — that you are not trained on the topic and that you need to refer him on.

By now you may be thinking that purpose clarification and purpose stating take considerable time. This is true only when you first try to do it; the key to lessening the time is practice. Practiced persons can clarify their purposes to themselves in seconds: "Have I accounted for all the things I want to accomplish? Have I accounted for feelings and relationships? Am I aware of all the likely effects of my actions?" A skillful purpose clarification and purpose statement saves all the time usually taken up thinking back on "how things should have been"!

Paraphrasing
　　Purpose clarification prepares a person to interact skillfully and

constructively with others. Paraphrasing builds relationships by gathering information, conveying understanding of another's statements, and showing concern and support. Since we can never really know what it is like to have another person's perceptions and experiences, the best we can do is let the person know we *wish* to understand both the content and the feelings of what s/he is expressing, and let the person know *what* we have understood her/him to have said. Some call this "empathy;" others call it "active listening" or "perception checking." We use the term "paraphrasing" and define it as "stating in your own words what you understood the other person to have said." Skillful paraphrasing requires you to do three things:

-*Focus on the speaker*: Listen carefully so that you can summarize briefly the content and feelings expressed in the speaker's message. Focusing on the speaker means beginning the paraphrase with the word "You...": "You were really angry;" "You felt overwhelmed;" "You felt the day would never end." Paraphrasing does not involve "mind-reading" or trying to figure out what the speaker "really" meant. Paraphrasing does not involve asking questions; questions imply that you want more information than the speaker gave — it shifts the topic to your particular interest and away from the speaker.

As a listener, you may occasionally experience great difficulty in understanding the speaker. Continue to paraphrase, stating what you do comprehend so far; the speaker will eagerly give you far more accurate information than you could get by asking a series of questions that could divert the speaker's "story" or even worse, could contribute to his or her feeling defensive or overwhelmed. Even when you feel lost, you can nearly always find some part of what the person said to paraphrase (for instance, one specific idea, the main feeling, or at least the "big picture"). Even if you miss the content of the speaker's statement totally, the speaker will realize you are seriously listening and trying to understand, and that s/he has not yet communicated clearly to you. You will discover that the speaker will probably assume s/he spoke in a confusing way and will then elaborate.

-*Paraphrase the content* of the speaker's statement and the feelings the person expressed in the statement if they were revealed. This will show that you have a picture of what s/he is talking about. It's also important to stick only to the content and feelings actually divulged.

-Finally, *make your statement briefer* than the speaker's original statement.

Paraphrasing is very effective, both for gaining information and for reflecting your understanding of another's ideas and feelings. However, most persons are not used to being paraphrased because few people employ the technique. You may need to prepare the person to be paraphrased. You can say, "I want to be sure I understood you, so let me tell you what I heard, using my own words." Then paraphrase the person, beginning with the word "you."

Being paraphrased. There are also skills involved in being the recipient of paraphrasing. If you are paraphrased, pause and slow your communication to acknowledge the other person's effort. If the paraphrase is incorrect or incomplete, you can say, "That's close. What I meant was . . ." or "Yes, and in addition I meant . . ." This reduces misunderstanding and promotes cooperation because the speaker corrects the listener in a constructive manner.

Conflict reduction. Paraphrasing lessens conflict because it slows the increasing rate of exchange between speakers which typifies conflict. It also diffuses hard feelings because it shows the speaker that the other person is attempting to understand what s/he said. Finally, paraphrasing lessens conflict because if each person is concentrating on understanding the other, s/he cannot at the same time be planning his/her next reply.

Some examples. Here are some statements you can try paraphrasing. Assume that these statements are directed at you, the listener. They are listed in order of increasing conflict and difficulty to paraphrase:

1. "There's already so much firepower stockpiled, it feels hopeless! It feels like the earth is a lighted firecracker ready to blow up. There's nothing I can do, except to wait. I feel paralyzed."
Your paraphrase:

2. "If we provide sanctuary for a Salvadoran family, we could get into trouble. We might get fined or arrested! People will call us lawbreakers!"
Your paraphrase:

3. "Your idea is totally unrealistic! We could never do that! It

would be impossible. We can't even consider it!''
Your paraphrase:

4. "Why in the world were you asked to help solve this problem? You don't know anything about what's going on! Just your being here is creating more conflict!''
Your paraphrase:

Now go back and review the paraphrases you have written. Check to see if you have included the three important elements mentioned earlier. Examples of effective paraphrases for each of the above statements are given at the end of the chapter.

Conclusion

These skills of purpose clarification/purpose stating and paraphrasing constitute a way of thinking and speaking that may initially seem strange, cumbersome, and time-consuming. Just as with any new skill — riding a bicycle, playing the piano, learning German — they take practice, and the first attempts feel awkward and difficult. New skills take time, patience and self- (and mutual!) encouragement. But we know from experience that both children and adults can learn and effectively use these skills. They are certainly well worth the effort.

If these techniques seem like a foreign language, it is because our society teaches both adults and children the language of competition, violence, and aggression. Purpose clarification/purpose stating and paraphrasing are part of the language of caring. When used skillfully, they can increase understanding and empathy and can reduce or prevent interpersonal conflict. They are effective in helping people be better peacemakers on a daily basis, both in peace work and in everyday interactions. They can be building blocks to peaceful problem solving between groups and nations.

Some examples of effective paraphrases for the four situations presented earlier:

1. "You feel powerless to do anything," or "You feel immobilized."

2. "You're anxious about being a law-abiding citizen," or "You're worried."

3. "You think it's out of the question," or "You believe it's not

within the realm of possibility.''
   4. "You think I'm making things worse," or "You are baffled as to why I was invited to help work out this problem."

References
1. Heider, F. (1958). *The Psychology of Interpersonal Relations.* New York: Wiley.

2. Date', B. (1984). Exploring a role clarification intervention in a health care setting: A conflict prevention and resolution procedure to increase team cooperation and reduce interpersonal conflict (Doctoral dissertation proposal, University of Oregon, Eugene, OR)

3. Hoskins, J. (1985, January). Interpersonal skill-building strategies: The executive as leader and consultant. Paper presented at the Northwest Medical Executives Conference, Sunriver, OR.

4. Gilmore, S.K., & Fraleigh, P.W. (1980). *Communication At Work.* Eugene, OR: Friendly Press.

Suggested Readings
Date', B. (1984). Exploring a role clarification intervention in a health care setting: A conflict prevention and resolution procedure to increase team cooperation and reduce interpersonal conflict (Doctoral dissertation proposal, University of Oregon, Eugene, OR) A theoretical description and practical application of a training package for conflict reduction and prevention.

Date', B., Lien, B. & Parsons, G.D. (1982). *A Vision of the Caring Community.* Eugene, OR: Author. (1475 Ferry Street, Eugene, OR 97401) This is a peacemaking curriculum for vacation church school for students grades 1-6. It teaches "how to notice opportunities to be helpful, caring, and cooperative."

Gilmore, S.K., & Fraleigh, P.W. (1980). *Communication At Work.* Eugene, OR: Friendly Press. (2744 Friendly Street, 97405) A practical guide for improving relationships in a work environment. The authors discuss assumptions, style differences, self-management, and interpersonal impact strategies.

17

"Disagreement Dialogue" — a Workshop

Barry Childers

Nowhere is the gulf between opposing views greater than on the topic of peace. Much of what passes for dialogue between those seeking less militarism and those favoring "peace through strength" is nothing more than throwing words at one another: seeing who can reason the most cleverly, produce the best "evidence," and shout the loudest. For genuine dialogue to take place, the emphasis must be on three things: listening, acquiring a genuine empathy for the other's views, and, above all, getting beyond surface positions and rhetoric to deeper levels of experience.

The opportunities to do this are rare, and it is for this reason that I developed the Disagreement Dialogue Workshop. It is intended for those individuals and groups who have clearly different basic philosophies on the topic of peace, and only a limited amount of time to dialogue. In the workshop itself, participants discuss a particular peace issue, and can come to a better understanding of each other's positions and perhaps begin to reconcile their differences. The workshop can be done in an evening, and is structured so that the usual barriers to constructive dialogue are minimized.

The workshop is typically done in a group setting, though most of the procedures involve pairs of individuals exploring a particular issue of their own choosing on which they disagree. The value of having a group is that the group as a whole can add valuable comments to the initial discussion done in pairs, and the opportunities for later cooperative action are greater. (With some minor modifications, the techniques here can also be employed by two people on their own.)

In order for your peace group (or individuals) to put the workshop into practice, you will need to find other people to join with you to discuss differing viewpoints. This may not be easy to do given that some organizations, perhaps including your own, are more interested in "converting" others than in working through differences. Other chapters in this book (such as those relating to communication, conflict reduction, and attitude change) may help in getting other groups to join you. You might arrange to dialogue with local service clubs, school organizations, political associations, veterans' and military groups, policy-making bodies (community councils, state legislatures), labor or management groups, or anyone else in your area where a dialogue would be mutually beneficial. You might just meet with a group of friends or hold a series of open workshops which any interested citizens could attend.

Finally, the materials provided here will enable a leader to organize and conduct a Disagreement Dialogue workshop with a minimum of preparation. Studying the workshop format, following the guidelines for workshop leaders (found in Part V), and reproducing the instructions and worksheets, are all that should be necessary. I suggest that you begin by reading Parts I and II below, which are the instructions participants read near the very beginning of the workshop.

I. Disagreement Dialogue — General Instructions
Purpose.   The Disagreement Dialogue is designed to help you discuss an important issue with another person who disagrees with you. It is not necessary that either of you change your views in the process, although that might happen. But you can expect to better understand each other and also the sources and complexities of your own views.
Assumptions.   Let's begin with these assumptions. (1) We each

have good reasons for our beliefs; they come from our experiences, and these differ from person to person. (2) A constructive dialogue is necessary if we want to understand each other and/or cooperate with one another. (3) Conflict around ideas and actions is inevitable, but violence is not. Mutually acceptable alternatives to violence can be found if we have the commitment to find them, are patient, and are creative in the search.

Commitments. Three basic commitments should be made and remembered: (1) ''I will try to present my own views in an honest and nonhostile way.'' (2) ''I will assume that my partner is speaking truthfully from his/her experience, and I will make every effort to understand her/his views and the experiences that led to them.'' 3) ''I will continue the dialogue at least until my partner and I have reached a mutually agreed-upon stopping place that represents some progress in our communications.''

Rules. The biggest obstacle to good dialogue is the fact that we seldom really listen to one another; we're usually so busy gathering our arguments and thinking about how to defend them that we only half-listen to what the other person is saying. Rule #1: *Give Your Partner Your Undivided Attention When He/She Is Talking.* Once your partner has finished talking, then decide how you feel about those statements and what you want to say in response; don't try to do it while she/he is talking. But do ask questions if you are unsure about what your partner is trying to say.

Another thing that often happens in arguments about important issues is that we bring so many additional things into the exchange that we soon get ''swamped.'' We overwhelm each other with all sorts of secondary issues, and we get confused, frustrated, or lost. Rule #2: *Take One Issue At A Time And Stay With It.* Other things that you consider important may be brought into the discussion as ''supporting points'' (discussed in Part II) whenever you wish, but try to keep the process as clear as possible.

Most arguments end because one or both persons quit. Quitting may occur for many reasons: getting frustrated or emotional, getting confused about one's own position and not wanting the other person to see that, getting upset and wanting to leave because the other person seems to be winning, or feeling like you are winning and wanting to quit while you're ahead. The Disagreement Dialogue is not a win-lose game, where there must be a winner and a loser. It is intended to be a win-win situation, with both persons gaining something through increased understanding and better mutual cooperation. Rule #3: *Don't Quit!* You may take a time-out any time you wish, and you can stop at a mutually agreeable stopping place whenever you both want to, but don't quit! Let the difficulties be a challenge to your creativity, rather than a threat to your ego.

We often think listeners understand what we are saying when they really don't. Rule #4: *At Any Time, The Speaker May Ask The Listener To Repeat Back What S/He Just Said Until Satisfied That The Listener Does, In Fact, Understand.* This feedback process will help avoid misunderstandings, as well as adding incentive for partners to listen to each other with undivided attention (see Rule #1).

Getting in touch with and sharing inner experiences is a difficult process. One may hesitate, for any number of reasons, to talk about deeper thoughts and feelings with another person, but it is necessary if you really want to grow in understanding. The biggest barriers to sharing are other people's "put downs": statements that belittle, question your intentions or integrity, or in some other way make you want to retreat into your shell rather than be open and trusting. Rule #5: *Assume That Your Partner Is Doing The Best S/He Can At The Moment To Explore And Share His/Her Experiences Honestly; Avoid Putdowns.*

II. Disagreement Dialogue — Procedures

1) After you pair off, take a few minutes to get acquainted. Then decide together on a particular peace issue to discuss. Any issue is acceptable, whether broad or specific, as long as you both consider it important and you clearly disagree in some way about it. (For instance, the issue might be whether the U.S. or U.S.S.R. is more aggressive in its actions, or whether U.S. troops should be used in Central America, or whether a strong military promotes peace.) You should then decide how to phrase your issue so it is in the form of a *belief*, and then write it down at the top of your worksheet (Part IV) in the appropriate place. Using the issues just mentioned, appropriate beliefs might be, "I believe that the Soviet Union is no more aggressive in its actions than is the U.S."; "I believe that the U.S. should regularly keep troops in Central

America''; ''I believe that peace can best be maintained by keeping a strong military defense.'' Make sure that your beliefs are getting to the heart of the issue and that they are clearly in opposition.

2) Now take ten minutes to think through your position, separately, writing down *supporting points* on your worksheet as you go along. Supporting points are any important points you wish to make with reference to your belief. Label each as falling into one of the following categories and then note at the end of the statement which type of supporting point you think it is—use the abbreviations given below:

(a) *Statements of Fact* (SF); for example, ''75% of all − − are − −,'' or ''Research shows that − −.'' (Relating to the issue of Soviet vs. U.S. aggression, a statement of fact might be, ''Over the last 50 years, the Soviet Union has militarily invaded no more countries than has the U.S.'')

(b) *Assumptions About Reality* (AR); for example, ''I think it is human nature to − −,'' or ''I think the world is such that − −.'' (''I don't think the Russians are a trustworthy people.'')

(c) *Thoughts About the Future* (TF); for example, ''If we do − −, then − − is likely to happen,'' or ''If such and such occurs, this is what is likely to follow.'' (''If the U.S. would stop building nuclear weapons, the Soviet Union would do the same.'')

(d) *Moral Convictions* (MC); for example, ''I think it is wrong (or right) to − −.'' (''I don't think it is right to criticize the Soviet Union for dominating Eastern Europe when we do the same in Central America.'')

(e) *Preferences* (P); for example, ''I like this,'' or ''I prefer that.'' (''I like the idea of having U.S. troops in West Germany to help protect it.'')

At times it may be difficult to categorize a particular supporting point, but do the best you can; these categories will help your discussion and understanding. The ten minutes you take to think through your position and write supporting points is not intended to be a complete analysis; it is just an initial clarification of your thoughts to help get the discussion off to a good start. Do not begin your discussion until you have both finished (don't worry that you might leave out some important supporting point; these can be added at any time during the discussion).

3) Begin the dialogue by each of you taking two or three

minutes to explain your belief and the supporting points for it. While your partner is speaking, you should just listen. After each of you has finished, the other can ask questions only to clarify what was said.

4) After your positions have been stated and clarified, open discussion can begin, subject only to the agreed-upon commitments and rules (keep handy the Part III Summary Sheet, which reviews the Commitments, Rules, Procedures, and Supporting Point categories).

5) You may decide at any time to shift the focus of your discussion to another issue, either because some secondary issue seems more important, or a new issue emerges that deserves exploring. If you both agree that you want to move to a new issue, simply take new worksheets, write new statements of belief, and begin a new dialogue. Changing issues is O.K., but don't do it to escape a difficult situation!

6) As your discussion continues, determine whether or not your partner agrees with your supporting points, and make a note to that effect in the right-hand column of your worksheet (Part IV, Supporting Points). You don't have to agree on the categorizing of a supporting point, although a difference of opinion about that might also be worth a little discussion.

7) When you decide to end the discussion, try to come up with a Joint Statement (Part IV) that accurately and fairly represents both of your final positions, and write it down on your worksheets (for example, "We still basically disagree on the issue, but not as strongly as we did in the beginning"; "We agreed on several supporting points, so our positions are not as far apart as we thought"; "We found that we basically agreed on the "statements of fact" and "moral convictions," but disagreed on the other supporting points"; etc.). You should then briefly summarize specific aspects of agreement and disagreement. This summary can serve as a starting point if the dialogue is to be continued later. If it is an important issue, you probably have not exhausted the potential for good discussion in one sitting!

8) Finally, each of you should separately make some *Follow-up Notes* and a *Current Assessment* (Part IV); these are intended only for yourself. Mention your present feelings about the dialogue, avenues you might want to explore in the future, ideas that emerged

during the dialogue that you want to think more about later, and insights that you had during the sessions, whether about yourself, about the interactional process, or whatever. Also note feedback to give to the workshop leader that would help in further development of the workshop.

III. Disagreement Dialogue — Summary Sheet

General Instructions

1) Present your views in as honest and nonhostile a way as you can.

2) Assume that your partner is speaking the truth from her/his experience, and make every effort to understand her/his views and the experiences that led to them.

3) If things get difficult, stick it out at least until you can reach a mutually agreed-upon stopping place that permits some progress.

Rules:

1) Give your partner your undivided attention when he/she is talking.

2) Take one issue at a time and stay with it.

3) Don't quit!

4) At any time the speaker may ask the listener to repeat back what s/he just said until satisfied that the listener does, in fact, understand.

5) Assume that your partner is doing the best he/she can at the moment to explore and share his/her experiences honestly; avoid put-downs.

Procedures:

1) Choose your issue, phrase it as a belief, and write it down on your worksheet.

2) Think through your positions (separately) and write down your supporting points. The categories include the following:

(a) *Statements of Fact* (SF)

(b) *Assumptions About Reality* (AR)

(c) *Thoughts About the Future* (TF)

(d) *Moral Convictions* (MC)

(e) *Preferences* (P)

3) Each present your position, the reasons for it, and answer clarifying questions.

4) Begin the open discussion.

5) Shift the focus to another issue if you wish, starting new worksheets.

6) Note agreement or disagreement on supporting points.

7) When you decide to stop, write down a joint summary statement on your worksheets.

8) Make notes (separately) about present feelings and future possibilities, and feedback that might be helpful to the workshop leader.

IV. Disagreement Dialogue — Sample Worksheets

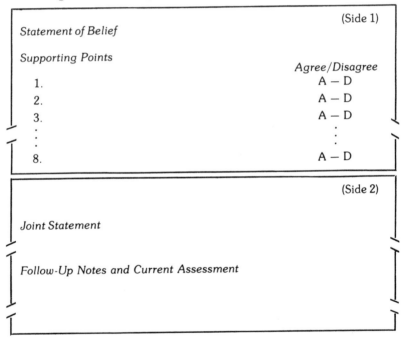

[*When you reproduce your own worksheets, leave room for eight supporting points, perhaps half a page for the joint statement, and maybe two-thirds of a page for the follow-up notes and current assessment.*]

V. For Disagreement Dialogue Workshop Leaders

Here are some suggestions about using the Disagreement Dialogue in a workshop format. The suggestions are minimal, since leading workshops is very much a matter of personal style. Keep in mind that although people meet as a group at the beginning and end of the workshop, the emphasis is on in-depth dialogue between two people.

After some introductory remarks and a get-acquainted process of your own choosing, I suggest that you read to all participants the first two paragraphs of this article. Then hand out Parts I through IV of the workshop and ask participants to read them. Next go over the general instructions briefly to make sure everyone understands them; special attention should be given to the different categories of supporting points. This can be done very effectively by choosing an issue not related to peace and asking the group to give supporting points pro and con, labeling them as they go (a blackboard or writing pad would be helpful).

All of this should take less than an hour, leaving at least another hour for people to divide into pairs and do the dialogue. Encourage the pairs to scatter and find comfortable spots with as much privacy and as little distraction as possible (but not too distant in case some help or clarification is needed). You should let them know 15 minutes before the dialogue time is up so they can complete steps 7 and 8 of the procedures (Part II) before coming back to the larger group.

I would suggest allowing at least 30 minutes (more if possible) for feedback from participants and for group discussion. Group discussion can focus on the issues themselves (further elaboration, etc.), the processes between individuals, feedback to workshop leaders, and where people might go with the issue next (further meetings, etc.). Depending on the group and the degree of trust generated, this can be a very worthwhile activity, but do not pressure anyone to disclose things they might not wish to. A minimum of three hours should be allowed for the workshop. A day would be much better, with breaks for rest and relaxation and additional group interaction.

18

Preparing for Nonviolent Confrontations

George Lakey

The student could scarcely control himself. He was big, bigger than the whites who were taunting him with "Nigger!" and putting mustard in his hair. He dug his fingers into the bottom of the lunch counter stool he was sitting on. Somehow he held on. The next day he came back, determined not to come so close to losing his self-control, wanting to be more composed like his fellow students from the black college on the outskirts of town. The preceding night he'd taken seriously the nonviolence training on campus and even joined in the prayers led by the preacher. He didn't want to fail and hurt the sit-in.

A week later the abuse increased, and a woman was able to push him off his stool. He hit the floor, paused, then slowly got up and, with a noble gesture and a smile, moved a barrier, allowing her to move easily away from the counter. She dissolved into tears and was led from the store by a friend. The young activist experienced in himself a new sense of power. And the woman? A week later she was organizing a women's group in support of the sit-in.

This story, which I learned from the leader of the sit-in, reflects several elements of nonviolent confrontation:

-The goal of the demonstrators, integration as a first step toward racial equality, was difficult to achieve; previous petitions and negotiations had failed, and nonviolent confrontation was required to reach the goal.

-The conflict brought out strong emotions on both sides, as well as the unpredictability that goes with that kind of intensity.

-Deep-seated attitudes are more open to change during crisis; it's as if people, like metal, are more flexible when hot.

-Preparation increased the activists' chances to be creative under stress.

Nonviolent Action: Training and Application

As with any form of protest, nonviolent action requires specific preparation. Training usually involves experiential exercises which enable participants to "feel" their way into the planned action. Some of the tools used in training include role plays, quick-decision exercises, and strategy games. Such preparation helps not only during the confrontation, by building confidence, reducing fear of the unexpected, and learning how to focus on the situation at hand, but also beforehand, by bringing organization and unity to a group as members work together to plan and coordinate an action.

I will not go through the exercises here, as they are covered quite well in several other places: see Martin Jelf's *Manual for Action*, available from International Seminars on Training for Nonviolent Action (P.O. Box 38, South Boston, MA 02127), and *Resource Manual for a Living Revolution* and *War Resisters League Organizer's Manual,* both discussed in Chapter 35. Or locate an experienced trainer by contacting the Movement for a New Society's nonviolent activist network (4722 Baltimore Ave., Philadelphia, PA 19143). The exercises deal principally with how to act toward others to reduce their hostility during confrontations; I want to concentrate instead on how to act toward yourself, what you can do to remain psychologically "balanced" during the chaos and danger of a nonviolent action confrontation.

You should be aware of a number of things as you contemplate and then become involved in nonviolent action. Nonviolent protesters facing life-threatening situations have reported afterward that they felt that even if someone were killed in the confrontation, it would be "somebody else." And like other battlefield combatants, you can expect that you will not freak out if the going gets tough. In fact boredom may be more of a problem than danger, since even the most dramatic confrontation involves a lot of tedium.

The Indian nonviolent leader Mohandas Gandhi suggested that we become fearless; one way to do that is to turn our fear into excitement. Stage performers do this with their jitters on opening night: the adrenalin courses through their veins and adds to the vitality of the performance. Sometimes lovers notice the same on their first sexual encounter with a desired partner; the nervousness adds to the excitement of making love. Gandhi recommended, in fact, that we enter a prison cell with the attitude of a bridegroom entering the chamber of his bride.

If you haven't learned how to shift your fear to excitement and therefore become "fearless," there are a number of ways to at least control it. Share in the group leadership and stay busy attending to the group's needs. This doesn't need formal appointment; just do it! Breathe deeply and remind yourself that love is present. Choose someone who needs support and give it. Relate positively with the police officer or pro-military supporter nearest you. Look at your opponent with as much good will as you can muster. Remember the folks back home who are rooting for you; decide to behave so they will be proud of you. Pray. Visualize Jesus (Moses, Buddha, Confucius, Muhammad,...) holding your hand.

Think how you have controlled your fear in the past and draw inspiration from those times (most of us have survived some scary situations in our lives). Choose the responses to fear that have allowed you to feel in control and do what you needed to at those times.

Adversity, like standing in a freezing rain during a silent vigil, being locked up in jail, being called vicious names, or being shoved during a confrontation, does not have to result in negative feelings. You determine your feelings by how you interpret and think about the hardship (see discussion of the "self-talk monitor" in Chapter 15). You can choose an attitude of self-pity, despair, or worry; you can also choose to see the hardship as a challenge, to you personally and to your cause. You can use the hardship for your own benefit, if you choose. India's first Prime Minister, Jawaharlal Nehru, contended that he was a better leader because of the time he had spent in British jails. A veteran of South Africa's jails told me that when he was being tortured, he found resources within himself he never dreamed he had.

Chaos challenges all of us who like some order in our lives and in our political action. During the Algerian War, French nonviolent activists who opposed French colonialism were frequently attacked by police. They developed a handy rule for themselves: "When in doubt, sit down.'' They found that the level of violence decreased (it's harder for police to keep striking someone who is seated) and they had a better sense of control over the situation — they were more "grounded.'' You might find other ways of attaining psychological order and composure among surrounding chaos, like deep breathing, chanting, holding a rabbit's foot, etc.

The Ups and Downs of Nonviolent Action

Nonviolent confrontation is analogous to white-water rafting; sometimes it can be exciting, and other times it is just plain hard work. You will have a sense that you're not entirely in control, and that there is some danger (although little compared to violent action). As in rafting, you also get a chance to bring 100% of yourself to the moment, to — as they say — "Go for it." This is the personal dimension of nonviolent action. Used correctly, nonviolent confrontation confirms the feminist insight that "the personal is political; the political, personal."

Suggested Readings

Lakey, G. (1985). *Strategy for a living revolution* (2nd ed.). Philadelphia: New Society Publishers. This book presents cases of nonviolent overthrowing of military dictatorships, as well as a framework for how to strategize for nonviolent action.

Pelton, L.H. (1974). *The psychology of nonviolence*. New York: Pergamon. This is a scholarly (but readable and practical) application of psychological theories and research to issues confronted by nonviolent activists. Topics include the nature of social power, the relationship of behavior to attitudes, and the effective use of persuasive communications.

Sharp, Gene (1973). *The politics of nonviolent action* (Vols. 1-3). Boston: Porter Sargent. This extensive study of the nature of nonviolent struggle is in three volumes: *Power and Struggle*, which compares and contrasts the different types of power, *The Methods of Nonviolent Action*, which examines in detail 198 specific methods of nonviolent action, and *The Dynamics of Nonviolent Action*, which investigates exactly how it works against a violent, repressive opponent.

V

PeaceWork:
Getting the Message Out

There are a number of audiences which peaceworkers must reach, and a number of ways of reaching them. Newton presents a comprehensive strategy for reaching target audiences, with a step-by-step program for a campaign for social change, from pre-planning to evaluating effectiveness.

The next paper in the section presents Childers' pointers on writing letters to those connected with or supportive of militarism. Linden Nelson's chapter suggests ways of promoting instruction about nuclear weapons and about war and peace issues in schools, including material relevant to each grade level and how to counter some objections of administrators.

In order to influence government decisions you need to know how governmental policy is set. Williams covers the processes of getting the attention of government officials, influencing government decisions, and following through on how policy is being implemented. He also has a few words on the electoral process.

19

Strategies for Action

James W. Newton

This chapter introduces a cooperative process that your peace group can use to plan, implement, and evaluate activities. This process will be described here within a model called the *Strategy Development Outline*. You can follow this model to construct a campaign that links actions directly to goals which fit the ethical framework of your group. The process supports democratic participation, draws on everyone's knowledge and imagination, encourages solidarity within the group, and allows planning and action to evolve appropriately as you learn from experience.

If those benefits sound like fantasy, let me assure you that this approach isn't based on academic daydreaming. My co-workers and I first developed it while training people in nonviolent action methods during the political struggles of the 1960's. Groups that put it into practice credited it with helping them achieve such diverse goals as closing a Southern California napalm factory, officially banning non-Union farm products from a college campus, and preventing a cut-off of welfare benefits in a major western city. Since then, I've refined it to take advantage of theories and research findings from social psychology.

To show you how it works, I'll first take you step-by-step through a fictional example that introduces both the process and the key factors within it (the key terms are italicized); I'll then review the process and define the terms. A summary of the Strategy Development Outline is included for use as a checklist to guide you through the process of planning your own strategy. It may be helpful as well to refer to the summary as you read through the paper.

THE STRATEGY DEVELOPMENT OUTLINE

I. Set Your Course —

GUIDING STATEMENT:
Express PURPOSES and VALUES
in a few clear sentences

CAMPAIGN GOALS:
State PRIMARY CAMPAIGN GOALS
you intend to achieve directly,
and SECONDARY CAMPAIGN GOALS that
will flow from your campaign's
processes and style.

II. Design Mini-Campaigns —

Identify key *INVOLVED PARTIES*. For each one, form a
TASK FORCE to propose a *MINI-CAMPAIGN* structured
like this:

BACKGROUND INFORMATION   *YOUR GOALS*
(about the involved party)   Decisions
Current Role   Actions
  Goals   (Include a
  Activities   deadline for
  Resources   each decision
Characteristics   *TACTICS*   and action.)
History   Change Tactics
                         Maintenance Tactics
                           For each tactic:
                             Objectives
                             Theory of Influence
                             Evaluation Procedures
                             Ethical Issues
                             Resource Requirements

III. Integrate the Strategy —

An *INTEGRATED CAMPAIGN STRATEGY* consists of MINI-CAMPAIGNS which are linked to be MUTUALLY SUPPORTIVE and PRACTICALLY COMPATIBLE.

Coordinate mini-campaigns, considering:

Anticipated effects of tactics
Timing of need for specific resources
Total resource requirements

Review the entire strategy, with special attention to:

Theories of influence
Evaluation procedures
Ethical issues

IV. Let Strategy Shape Organization —

A *TASK FORCE* implements each *MINI-CAMPAIGN*.

A *COORDINATING COUNCIL* with a representative from each *TASK FORCE* oversees the campaign.

Banning Bombs in Flecha Rota: A Strategy Development Example

Located about 10 miles inland from the San Francisco Bay, the town of Flecha Rota has grown from 20,000 to almost 50,000 people since the Flecha Rota Air Force Base was built in 1966 as a storage and shipping facility for Vietnam war materials. About 5,000 residents are Air Force personnel and their families, while another 10,000 are members of families whose incomes derive from businesses dependent on the Base. The Flecha Rota Municipal Council (FRMC) is, at this writing, composed of two Republicans and three Democrats, including one Democrat who is an environmental activist.

Soon after the Public Broadcasting System aired "Broken Arrow," a documentary on the storage and transportation of nuclear weapons around San Francisco, a group of 10 activists formed Flecha Rota Independent Environmentalists for Nuclear Disarmament and Survival (FRIENDS). With 25 people at their first public meeting, FRIENDS held an initial strategy development session. After the chairperson explained the Strategy Development Outline, *purposes* and *values* were discussed in small groups so that everyone could take an active part. The small group reports revealed a general consensus that led to this *guiding statement*: "The purpose of FRIENDS is to help create a world without war, from which nuclear weapons are completely banned, and in which human beings live cooperatively, in harmony with the earth's natural environment. Membership in FRIENDS means commitment to basic values of equality and democratic decision making, honesty and respect in the way we relate to all people, and principled nonviolence in all actions."

In a ten-minute "brainstorming" session, all were then invited to suggest realistic, achievable campaign goals, expressing each idea in just a few words; no discussion or criticism was to be given at this stage. More than 20 ideas were accumulated in that short time. Small discussion groups were again formed to discuss these. Their reports revealed three ideas that had drawn most attention as *primary campaign goals*, and four that had been most frequently discussed as *secondary campaign goals* — those that could be achieved as by-products of a campaign designed to accomplish the primary goals.

Brainstorming was used to list advantages and disadvantages

of each idea, and two primary campaign goals were chosen: Municipal Council passage of an ordinance prohibiting possession of non-medical radioactive material within the city limits, and voter approval of a resolution calling on the federal government to remove all nuclear weapons from the Flecha Rota Air Force Base. Secondary campaign goals were then easily agreed upon: to raise community awareness of the danger of a nuclear accident in or near Flecha Rota, to promote grassroots democracy by involving more citizens in political action, and to build the foundation for a strong nuclear disarmament movement in Flecha Rota.

Finally, to begin the design of *mini-campaigns*, the group again brainstormed to form a list of *involved parties* — individuals or groups whose decisions and actions could have major effects on the campaign's outcomes. Many came to mind, but only five seemed crucially important: the Municipal Council (FRMC), the Chamber of Commerce (representing the town's businesses), officers of the Air Force Base, the news media, and the general public. Before the meeting ended, a separate *task force* was formed for each involved party to collect *background information* and propose initial *tactics* for a *mini-campaign*.

At the next meeting of FRIENDS, the task forces displayed the findings they collected on large wall charts. Space permits me to summarize only the report of the Municipal Council task force.

The *current role* of the FRMC emphasized support of the Air Force's practice of transporting nuclear weapons through Flecha Rota for storage at the Base; this position furthered FRMC's goal of keeping positive relations between the city and the Air Force in order to obtain jobs for citizens and promote local commerce.

FRMC's *activities* in pursuit of its goal included providing escorts for military vehicles and sponsoring public events (such as school assemblies on military technology) to boost the Air Force's image in the community.

FRMC's *resources* included: control over all city services (such as the police), tax-supported mailings to citizens, ability to arrange public meetings with guaranteed news media coverage, close relations with local political organizations, and financial support from wealthy interests in the community.

Characteristics were listed for each FRMC member — his or her political affiliations, business or professional involvements, membership in religious and social organizations, and value commitments.

The *history* of FRMC's resolutions and official actions with respect to campaign issues was briefly summarized. For example, at one point a parents' group had complained that military vehicles with radiation warning signs routinely passed through a dangerous intersection near the elementary school; in response, FRMC secured a grant to build a by-pass road leading directly to the Base.

The FRMC task force proposed several *decisions* and *actions* the campaign should seek from FRMC. These represented FRIENDS goals for the mini-campaign (referred to as *your goals* in the summary chart), and each had a deadline: (1) Within two months, FRMC should start an investigation of the hazards of transporting and storing nuclear weapons in or near Flecha Rota; (2) Within a year, FRMC should enact an ordinance banning transportation of non-medical radioactive materials in Flecha Rota; and (3) Within a year, FRMC should declare support for a public vote on whether to remove nuclear weapons from the Base.

The FRMC task force proposed a set of initial *change tactics* to influence the FRMC. One change tactic called for well-informed members of FRIENDS to arrange an information meeting with the FRMC. These representatives would give FRMC documentation on the hazards of nuclear weapons transportation and storage in urban areas, relate these materials directly to Flecha Rota, and specify the precise decisions and actions FRIENDS wanted FRMC to take. The *objectives* of this tactic were to educate FRMC members on the issues, to convey FRIENDS' concern for the welfare of the community, to state clearly what FRIENDS wanted from FRMC, to declare the campaign's commitment to nonviolence, and to initiate a relationship of mutual respect between FRIENDS and FRMC.

One *theory of influence* supporting this change tactic is that when a believable source provides well-documented new information that contradicts a person's current beliefs and behavior, the person will experience inner tension ("dissonance") that promotes a change in belief or behavior that matches what the person now knows. [1, pp. 66-72, and pp. 94-100] (Also see Chapters 25 and 26 for more thorough discussion of cognitive dissonance theory). According to a second theory of influence [2], if new information convinces FRMC members that their earlier judgments were poorly informed, the resulting sense of "inadequacy" will result in greater openness to new viewpoints.

An *evaluation procedure* was determined ahead of time, whereby each representative would contact one FRMC member two weeks after the information meeting to inquire about his or her response, and any actions that had resulted. The tactic raised no *ethical issues*, because the actions it called for were consistent with FRIENDS' values. The informed people and documentation needed to fulfill the *resource requirements* of this tactic were already available.

Besides setting change tactics, the FRMC task force suggested a *maintenance tactic* FRIENDS could use to preserve and strengthen present FRMC viewpoints and policies which FRIENDS wished to maintain. This was to be accomplished by FRIENDS supporters who had some positive link to a Council member, such as personal friendship or common membership in a church or social organization. Each FRIENDS supporter was to periodically contact the Council member to express continuing support for the member's position and ask what the member had done recently to promote the cause of FRIENDS. This tactic was intended to help prevent negative changes an FRMC member might otherwise make in response to interest groups opposed to FRIENDS goals. For this maintenance tactic, the task force went through the same considerations it had reviewed for the change tactics: objectives, theory of influence, evaluation procedures, ethical issues, and resource requirements.

The purpose of the second FRIENDS meeting was to approve an *integrated campaign strategy* in which all mini-campaigns would be linked in an efficient, workable manner which all members could understand and really support. One by one, each task force explained its own mini-campaign proposals. Some changes were made after input from other task forces, or when several members found a tactic ethically unacceptable. For example, a proposal to drop leaflets from an airplane was rejected because it would litter city streets. After each mini-campaign proposal was discussed, revised, and approved, small groups formed and met for an hour to discuss whether the different mini-campaigns fit together well into an overall program.

After reconvening, the entire group made a few changes in

strategy. Several tactics were postponed because they involved far more work than members had time for during the upcoming months. Also, a tactic for one of the mini-campaigns was reluctantly cancelled because its expense might exhaust the bank account and thus the resource requirements for other mini-campaigns could not be met. By this point, FRIENDS had its integrated campaign strategy almost finished. Two task forces were asked to carry out their initial tactics, while others gathered additional background information for their own campaigns. The third FRIENDS meeting consisted of hearing reports from all task forces, reviewing the mini-campaigns, and making final campaign decisions.

The Strategy Development Outline

Strategy development begins with a *guiding statement* that expresses the group's *purposes* and *values*; it consists of a few very clear sentences. "Purposes" are grand goals, such as complete nuclear disarmament; "values" are ethical principles to guide action. I recommend arriving at this statement by consensus. Majority rule exercised by voting almost guarantees that people whose serious objections are overruled will form dissident factions and the group will be handicapped by disunity. It may take longer to reach a genuine consensus, but the mutual respect and learning involved will help you remain caring and united.

Next, select *primary campaign goals* — very specific events or policy decision changes that you believe can actually be achieved by your campaign. *Secondary campaign goals* are desirable changes your campaign can bring about as by-products of the primary goals. For example, the FRIENDS primary campaign to stop nuclear weapons shipment and storage in Flecha Rota could also accomplish a secondary goal, such as educating and mobilizing the public for a future campaign on nuclear freeze issues.

Mini-campaigns provide a logical structure for planning and implementing action plans. Each mini-campaign is conducted by one *task force*, and is designed to influence one *involved party*, a person or group whose activities can have major effects on the mini-campaign's outcomes. Please note that I call them "involved parties" rather than "adversaries" or "allies;" these latter terms can color our perceptions and negatively affect our interaction with the group. Accurate *background information* on each involved party will likely require research (discussions with knowledgable people, interviews with involved parties, review of public documents).

The involved party's *current role* in the campaign includes its *goals* relevant to campaign issues, *activities* that promote those goals, and *resources* available to support those activities. Resources aren't limited to money — consider their expertise, access to news media, talents, and links to influential people and groups — anything that may be useful in supporting their goal-oriented activities.

Important *characteristics* of the involved party are such factors as educational level and background, social position, political affiliations, memberships in religious or other groups, personal values, and interests. The involved party's *history* relevant to campaign issues is also crucial; its prior actions may predispose it to work either against you (at least initially) or with you.

With all this background in mind, you should state precise *decisions* and *actions* (representing *your goals*) which you want from the involved party (set *deadlines* for each one). This lets everyone in your group know exactly what you're trying to accomplish; it also makes it easier to assess the appropriateness of the tactics you consider pursuing in each mini-campaign.

Every campaign includes two types of tactics: a series of *change tactics* designed to change an involved party's attitudes or behavior, and a series of *maintenance tactics* designed to maintain desirable attitudes and behavior that might otherwise change so as to hurt the campaign.

Each tactic must have explicit, measurable *objectives*. For instance, appropriate objectives for a march through downtown Flecha Rota were threefold: to notify observers and newspaper readers that FRIENDS existed, to make campaign issues conversation topics in the town, and to demonstrate to FRMC that FRIENDS supporters were willing to stand up for their views in public.

The *theory of influence* (or rationale) for each tactic should be made explicit so that it can be examined critically. Ask yourself such questions as, "How do we expect this action to produce the desired outcomes?" and "What assumptions does this tactic make about how people think, feel, and act, and do we really believe those assumptions are right?"

Evaluation procedures should be determined before you make a
final decision on each tactic. They should be capable of telling you
how well your tactic achieved its objectives, and what sorts of
processes led to that result. They may be as simple as asking
questions over the telephone, or as complicated as conducting a
public opinion poll. Evaluating information about your different
tactics will let you know how the mini-campaign is progressing.

A tactic that seems attractive, workable, and able to be
evaluated, should pass two more tests. First, you should discuss any
ethical issues the tactic raises and discard it if members have
serious worries. An easy way to begin such discussion is to look for
inconsistencies between the tactic and the values in your guiding
statement. Second, be realistic when determining whether the
importance of the objectives to be gained from a given tactic justify
the tactic's *resource requirements* (and decide whether you even
have the resources required). Estimate the money, skills, person
hours, information, special equipment, and other forms of support
needed for successful implementation of the tactic. As you do this,
you may think of less costly variations of the tactic that are
promising enough to substitute.

To stimulate and inform you concerning mini-campaigns and
possible tactics, I suggest that you review thoughtful works on
nonviolent action and social influence. [2,3,4,5,6,7] (Also see
Section VI, which discusses attitude change techniques.)

When all mini-campaigns have been approved in principle
you're ready to link them together to form an *integrated campaign
strategy*. Look at each mini-campaign in relation to the others. Are
they mutually supportive, or is one mini-campaign likely to interfere
with another? This could happen, perhaps, if an involved party is
subjected to so many contacts by your group that it feels harassed
and becomes hostile. Also ask whether the mini-campaigns are
practically compatible, i.e., whether they are coordinated so that
working on two or more at the same time won't overly commit the
group or require the same limited resources. This should also lead
you to consider whether the support you have available matches
your total *resource requirements* for the different mini-campaigns.

Finally, look at your campaigns as a whole and consider three
final issues:
1) *Theories of influence*: What do your mini-campaigns indicate

about your general approach to influencing other people? Is your group oriented toward coercion, persuasion, cooperation, or some other style of action? [8] Does your approach embody your best wisdom about how people act and how they change?

2) *Evaluation procedures*: How will you evaluate progress in the campaign as a whole (just as you would evaluate each tactic)? If you can't judge how well you're doing, you won't know what to do next.

3) *Ethical issues*: Viewed as a whole, does this campaign fully and consistently express the values you've agreed on in your guiding statement?

If you feel uncomfortable with your responses to any of these last three concerns, you will need to reconsider at least parts of your planning.

Conclusion

The Strategy Development Outline is a detailed model of cooperative self-education; it nourishes good working relationships, strong bonds of friendship, and mutual commitment. Naturally, the model can't anticipate every possible occurrence, but it does give you a process to use whenever surprising events or new information signal a need to revise strategy. Notice, too, that the same structure that facilitates planning makes it easy to move directly into action. A task force was set up to conduct each mini-campaign. If you then also form a coordinating council with a representative from each task force, you'll have an organization designed precisely to carry out its key tasks.

References

1. Zimbardo, P.G., Ebbesen, E.B., & Maslach, C. (1977). *Influencing attitudes and changing behavior* (2nd ed.). Reading, MA: Addison-Wesley.

2. Mehrabian, A. (1970). *Tactics of social influence.* Englewood Cliffs, NJ: Prentice-Hall.

3. Abelson, R.P., & Zimbardo, P.G. (1970). *Canvassing for peace: A manual for volunteers.* Ann Arbor, MI: Society for the Psychological Study of Social Issues.

4. Coover, V., Deacon, E., Esser, C., & Moore, C. (1978). *Resource manual for a living revolution.* Philadelphia: New Society Publishers.

5. Lakey, G. (1973). *Strategy for a living revolution.* San Francisco: W.H. Freeman.

6. Pelton, L.H. (1974). *The psychology of nonviolence.* New York: Pergamon.

7. Sharp, G. (1973). *The politics of nonviolent action* (Vols. 1-3). Boston: Porter Sargent.

8. Deutsch, M. (1973). *The resolution of conflict: Constructive and destructive processes.* New Haven, CT: Yale University Press.

20

Correspondents for Peace

Barry Childers

This chapter is released into the public domain, subject only to inclusion of the following statement on each copy reproduced: "Reprinted from Working for Peace, *Neil Wollman, Editor. Impact Publishers, 1985."*

Correspondents for Peace is a network of people who wish to give time to the cause of peace by writing letters. We share the view that non-military means of providing security and resolving international conflicts must be developed. We also think that the responsibility for bringing about the changes necessary for this to happen lies with individual citizens. The most effective way to bring citizens to increased awareness, greater feeling of responsibility, and desire for action is through direct conversation. But often this is not possible, and the only way to reach many people is by mail.

We know that people can be influenced by letters. Amnesty International has been so successful in its letter-writing activities that it received the Nobel Peace Prize in 1977. It has become a commonly accepted practice to "write your Congressperson," and they certainly pay attention when the volume of mail is high. But responsibility for our country's militarism must be shared among many others, including businessmen and their employees in weapon-making firms, scientists and technologists in weapons development, government officials who are linked to the military-industrial complex, academics whose work is military-related, journalists and writers who support current policies, and military leaders. It has not yet become accepted practice to write to such people and hold them accountable. It is time to do so. Given the perceived danger of nuclear war, the conflicts in Central America, and the change in attitude climate generally, these people might be influenced by our personal letters encouraging them to reconsider their positions.

Millions of people all over the world, and from all walks of life, are now speaking out against the increase of nuclear and conventional arms and the failures of governments to seriously pursue nonviolent methods of conflict resolution. Many people in the groups mentioned above (who formerly supported our military policies) are among those speaking out. Correspondents for Peace can contribute to this movement by bringing pressure to bear on all the people who are part of the war system.

Organization and Procedures

People can participate in Correspondents for Peace as individuals or in groups. Groups might be preferable, since mutual support and a sharing of ideas is advantageous. Groups can also divide the work of deciding who to write, obtaining addresses, gathering information about those people, developing ideas for the letters, copying and mailing, etc.

Although it is preferable that letters be individually written, and that they reflect your own personal perceptions and concerns, the following suggestions may be helpful to keep in mind. Whatever your approach, you may want your readers to know some or all of the following:

1. You are writing because you see them as doing or saying things that contribute to militaristic policies, and make war more likely.

2. You see increased military spending as a dangerous thing that no longer provides us with real security, and you believe there are alternatives which are preferable and possible.

3. You do not see them as necessarily being wholeheartedly committed to the military buildup; you are aware that they may be caught up in a process about which they also have questions and doubts.

4. You see them as having the option of changing their position, and the potential to influence policies in their area in a positive direction.

5. You wish to encourage them to explore their options and to consider a different course of action.

In order to try to engage them in dialogue, you may want to do the following:

1. Catch their attention by saying something right away that will make them unlikely to throw your letter away unread; for example, you might begin by asking for a fuller explanation of something they said or did.

2. Present your evaluation of their role in militarism.

3. Present your position.

4. Present your suggestion about what they could do so that they might see it as an attractive, realistic possibility.

5. Leave them with a question that would make it more likely they'll want to answer your letter.

As for general principles, three are sufficient for now:

• Try to plant seeds, or encourage the growth of seeds already planted. Patience and the ability to gain satisfaction from small changes will be helpful in maintaining your interest and commitment over the long haul.

• Different approaches will be effective with different people. You may choose a rational argument, a personal appeal to feelings, a creative stimulation of the imagination, or an eloquent statement of your moral or spiritual convictions. Your choice should be a reflection of your personal style, and the responses of the person to whom you are writing. Other chapters in this book, such as those on attitude change and communication, might be helpful.

• Feedback and discussion of responses should be given a prominent place in your group's activities. You are breaking new ground, and must learn as you go; learn from both your successes and your failures.

You can probably assume that the people to whom you write are very much like you. They want a good life for themselves and their families, they feel insecure in a world that is changing rapidly, and they are looking desperately for ways to understand and control those things that seem most threatening. A major difference may be that they have not had the experiences that would allow them to abandon that basic belief we are all taught, that only through military strength and being more powerful than others can our nation be secure. Another difference may be that they gain money, power, prestige, or something else from their military ties. These things are not easy to give up.

You can also assume that their public positions do not entirely or accurately reflect their personal thoughts about militarism. A person's thoughts and feelings about important matters are far more complicated than surface appearances. One of the main reasons dialogue is so necessary is to explore and share these deeper thoughts and feelings.

All of this suggests that considerable effort should be made to empathize with those to whom you write. Try to "be in the shoes" of the other person; that kind of empathy is crucial to understanding differences and resolving conflicts.

Last, but by no means least, you must assume that other persons (and also you) can change. There is a self-fulfilling prophecy about change: the likelihood of change depends in part on your attitudes and expectations. In much of the current interaction between peace seekers and others there is little real expectation of change, and what often passes for dialogue is more likely to prevent than encourage change.

A Note About Angry Letters

Sometimes there is just no substitute for anger honestly expressed. There is no doubt that there are times when it can have a beneficial effect; however, determining when it can be effective in correspondence is difficult. A flood of angry letters can certainly have an impact on someone, but it may also produce effects that are counter-productive in the long run, like fear and resentment. If you want to engage a person in dialogue, express your anger sparingly and include with it positive statements to help offset the defensiveness and anger it is likely to provoke.

To suggest that letters always be logical and unemotional would be inappropriate. These are issues about which you have strong feelings, and part of the reason for our current dilemma is that there has been too much divorcing of intellect and feeling in responding to peace issues. This is especially true of those who seriously contemplate nuclear war as a military strategy. Encouraging the expression and acceptance of emotion is a worthwhile goal. One of the advantages of a dialogue by correspondence is that it gives the participants time to ponder how they might express themselves more thoughtfully and with more care.

Odds and Ends

How should you start? Sit down and write a letter now! And talk about it with some friends.

Most libraries have standard reference works listing the names and addresses of the persons you will want to write (home addresses are preferable to business addresses). Standard & Poor's *Register of Corporations, Directors and Executives* or Dun & Bradstreet's *Reference Book of Corporate Managements* will do for people in business; *Who's Who in Government, Who's Who in American Politics*, and *The U.S. Government Manual* list government officials. Other useful directories are *American Men & Women of Science, Who's Who in Technology Today, Who's Who in America*, and *Who's Who in the World*. If you can't find the person you want in one of these, try Information Enterprise's *The Directory of Directories*. A list of defense-related companies (and related information) can be obtained from NARMIC, American Friends Service Committee, 1501 Cherry St., Philadelphia, PA 19102.

Correspondence needn't be limited to critical letters; you should occasionally write supportive letters to those opposing military spending. It can be a nice change of pace and will be very much appreciated!

Keeping copies of your correspondence is useful in evaluating and improving your skills and keeping track of your accomplishments. Sharing letters and responses with others in a group can be helpful also.

We must find ways to break down barriers between individuals, in order to end conflicts among people and nations in a peaceful manner. My hope is that Correspondents for Peace program may aid in this. You can help its growth by writing letters and by spreading word of the group. Please copy this article and send it to anyone you think might be interested. Any comments or suggestions to me will be appreciated and responded to (see listing of author addresses).

21

Adding Peace to the Curriculum

Linden Nelson

> *"If we are to have real peace in the world,*
> *and if we are to carry on a real war against war,*
> *we shall have to begin with children."*
> -Mahatma Gandhi

Our children's anxieties about nuclear war and our democracy's requirement of an educated electorate are compelling reasons for teaching in the schools about nuclear war and its prevention. In a recent survey of 900 California adolescents, more than half believed that nuclear war would occur in their lifetimes, and 64% believed that should it occur, they would not survive. [1]

Schools have been reluctant to teach about nuclear war, even though children are concerned about it and citizens need background to intelligently influence national policies. The editors of *Harvard Educational Review* recently noted that U.S. classrooms and textbooks "have been filled with silence" on this issue. [2] A review of 19 current American and world history high school textbooks concluded that "scant attention (was given) to nuclear war and arms limitation." [3] One world history text gave as much space to nuclear war issues as it did to the creation of stained glass windows. A U.S. history text devoted 18 pages to the Revolutionary War and one-half page to all aspects of nuclear war.

While it is disturbing that the educational system has not really taught about the nuclear threat, it is also encouraging to know that you and your co-workers might be the ones who will help introduce peace curricula into the schools. You would have an opportunity to influence children and adolescents who are uninformed on the topic to think intelligently about arms control and disarmament.

Peace Workers' Goals vs. School System Goals

In our desire to have schools teach nuclear issues as we see them, we may forget that many citizens do not share our views about how to further the causes of peace and national security. Many Americans, including school teachers, administrators, and board members, have very strong feelings on this issue. The educational system will resist, and ought to resist, any suggestions that it should develop a political following for arms control and disarmament. The schools should teach about political issues and policy options, but in a way that presents differing perspectives in a fair and respectful way, and that encourages students to form their own opinions.

Your goals overlap with the goals of the educational system, but they are not identical. Knowledge, critical thinking, conflict resolution skills, sensitivity to differing cultures and political views, and citizen involvement in the democratic process are examples of objectives shared by educators and peace workers. Specific policy goals of the peace movement (the freeze, disarmament, defense spending cuts) should not be confused with the goals of educational institutions. You will experience less resistance in your efforts to implement peace education if you openly and conscientiously respect this distinction.

There are some additional constraints in working with educational systems. Superintendents want to know what is happening in their districts; principals are accountable for what happens in their schools. It is wise to inform these people of your plans. Show them your materials, ask for their suggestions, inquire about their rules and procedures, keep them informed, and seek their permission when necessary. While it may be possible to work directly with teachers, doing so without informing their superiors may be harmful in the long run, both to the teachers and to your future work in the district.

Objections and How to Answer Them

Attempts to promote teaching about nuclear weapons issues

are likely to provoke particular objections. Here are some of the objections that parents, teachers, or administrators might raise, and how you might answer them:

- *Children will be emotionally upset by discussing the horrors of nuclear war.*

Answer: Instruction will be age-appropriate. Young children will learn about their counterparts in other cultures and how to peacefully resolve conflicts. Their teachers will learn how to sensitively answer questions about nuclear war, but they will not introduce the topic.

Older children are already worried about nuclear war, and their teachers will encourage them to discuss those concerns. Teachers will also help them understand the likelihood and potential effects of nuclear war, as well as the various efforts of adults to prevent it.

- *Nuclear weapons policy should be left to experts.*

Answer: One reason why experts disagree among themselves is that major policy decisions require value judgments and rely on opinions about human nature. One expert has written, "These are questions in which there is a technical input, but where the fundamental decisions are matters of judgment and common sense. Not only is it possible for an enlightened citizenry to decide matters like this, it is in fact vitally necessary that they do so and that they not leave it to specialized experts." [4]

- *Teaching about nuclear war issues would detract from teaching the basic subjects.*

Answer: Basic skills (like reading, writing, math, and critical thinking) can be practiced using war and peace as subject matter. Furthermore, preparing citizens for self-government should be one of the "basics" for any democratic system.

- *Nuclear war topics cannot be taught in an unbiased way.*

Answer: Teachers can present facts, concepts, and history relevant to nuclear weapons just as impartially as they do other political issues. Teaching materials are available that present information without bias. There are also other resources that discuss various perspectives without making judgments (see the "Resources" section later in this chapter).

When instructors use speakers, readings, and films that take one point of view, they should balance them with other resources representing opposing perspectives. Students should be taught to evaluate evidence, recognize propaganda, think critically, and empathically understand and respect the views of others.

- *Teachers are not trained in the subject matter of nuclear war, nor in the recommended methods for teaching about it.*

Answer: Unfortunately it is true that many teachers are not adequately prepared to teach about the nuclear threat. Teacher training programs in universities are just beginning to acknowledge their responsibilities to educate teachers on this matter. Many teachers, however, have educated themselves. Some of the suggestions offered later in this chapter are directed toward improving teacher training.

What You or Your Group Can Do

- Purchase films, curriculum guides, and other resources for the schools and libraries in your community.

- Sponsor scholarships for teachers to attend relevant classes or training programs. Contact Educators for Social Responsibility to obtain information about Teacher Education Institutes (See "Resources" for their address).

- Organize and distribute to teachers a list of qualified speakers willing to visit classes.

- Compile for teachers a list of resources, such as films, readings, and curriculum guides, that are available in your community. Such resources are likely to be found in your public, school, college, and university libraries. Also check audiovisual services and curriculum laboratories in your schools and universities, and don't forget to check local peace groups for resources they might have or know of in the community.

- Schedule a meeting with a superintendent, principal, or school board member to discuss the possibilities for introducing or improving instruction about nuclear war. (The chapters in this book concerned with communication and attitude change should help in your discussions with these people, or with any others who have a say in determining or influencing peace education policies.)

-Request that your parent/teacher association and school board officially endorse the introduction of curricula and activities for teaching about peace and nuclear weapons issues.

- Contact your representative in the state legislature and request a study about peace education practices within the state.

Join (or form) a local chapter of Educators for Social Responsibility (membership is not restricted to educators).

Ideas for Teaching About War and Peace

As you make contact with teachers, you may want to inform them of some basic things they can try if they want to teach about war and peace. It is possible here to provide only a general outline of the kinds of things they could do in the classroom. See "Resources" below for information about teaching materials that provide detailed suggestions and activities.

In early elementary classes. Plan activities which introduce and illustrate basic notions of cooperation and competition, conflict and conflict resolution, and war and peace. Activities which promote awareness of other cultures are appropriate, as well as exercises which teach empathy and tolerance.

In later elementary through high school classes. Develop age-appropriate lessons or units on nuclear weapons, nuclear war, history of the arms race and arms control, perspectives on deterrence and national security, conflict resolution, Soviet history and culture, current war and peace issues, etc.

In colleges and universities. Prepare lectures to include in existing courses, or consider developing a new course to focus on nuclear and peace issues. In my introductory psychology class, I give one lecture entitled "The Psychology of the Arms Race," and I have taught an entire course with the same title. My research on the effects of these lectures suggests that students become more favorable towards arms control after learning about the probability of nuclear war, the psychology of deterrence, and the influences of competitive thinking and enemy perception as psychological barriers to arms control.

University faculty should also run training sessions for teachers at all levels, and offer relevant extension courses for teachers and other adults in the community; such offerings would provide an essential service to the peace education movement.

In all levels of peace education. (1) Use facts and issues about peace and nuclear war in a variety of contexts within the class; then give assignments that make use of those facts and issues. (2) Demand of authors, publishers, and sales representatives that textbooks acknowledge the importance of nuclear weapons issues. (3) Serve on general education, curriculum, and teacher training committees in order to promote peace education. (4) Sponsor a symposium, film event, peace education week, or other community education project. (5) Ask teachers' organizations and administrators to organize committees and programs on peace education.

Some Encouraging Developments

Educators and the general public are now awakening to the need to prepare children and adults for dealing with the nuclear threat. Consider the following encouraging examples:

- On April 19, 1983, the Milwaukee Board of School Directors approved a resolution that declared it ''appropriate to introduce into the school program, activities and curricula related to peace studies and the dilemma of the nuclear arms race.''

- In Michigan, Governor James J. Blanchard declared May 20-27, 1984, as ''Peace Education Week.''

- The California Legislature passed a law requiring the Department of Education to do a state-wide survey about nuclear age education and to make recommendations for new programs.

- The National Congress of Parent-Teacher Associations passed a resolution in June, 1984, strongly endorsing ''school nuclear education programs'' that might allow students to ''respond to the realities of nuclear developments with accurate information, critical thinking, and full ethical considerations.''

- The National Education Association is organizing ''Peace and International Education'' committees in all 50 states.

- Excellent materials for teaching about nuclear war and its prevention have recently been developed by Educators for Social Responsibility, Ground Zero Resource Center, and other organizations (see ''Resources'' for addresses).

- Major journals for educators have published special issues about nuclear arms education: *Harvard Educational Review* (August, 1984), *Teachers College Record* (Fall, 1982), *Social Education* (November/December, 1983), *Physics Today* (March, 1983), and *Journal of College Science Teaching* (March/April, 1983).

In spite of these encouraging developments, a large majority of students in our schools and universities are not yet being exposed to the educational experiences that could prepare them to think and vote intelligently about nuclear weapons issues. For those of you serious about educating our children to understand and influence the most vital issue of our time, there is much to do in the schools and universities.

Resources
K-12 curricular materials. For curriculum guides, resource lists, role playing games, audiovisuals, etc., contact: Educators for Social Responsibility, 23 Garden St., Cambridge, MA 02138, and Ground Zero Resource Center, P.O. Box 19329, Portland, OR 97219.
University curricular materials. For suggestions on developing lectures and courses in a variety of disciplines, see "Nuclear War: A Teaching Guide," edited by Dick Ringler, in *Bulletin of the Atomic Scientists*, Vol. 40 (December, 1984), a 32-page supplement. This issue includes an excellent resource guide and information about obtaining copies of sample course syllabi. Also see the manual, *Organizing the Campuses to Prevent Nuclear War*, published in 1985 by United Campuses to Prevent Nuclear War (UCAM), 1346 Connecticut Ave., NW, Suite 706, Washington, DC 20036.
Readings for high school-university. The following are examples of publications that make serious efforts to be unbiased or balanced. They are listed in order of increasing sophistication:
Public Agenda Foundation (1983). *Nuclear arms and national security.* Dayton, OH: Domestic Policy Association. (5335 Far Hills Ave., Dayton, OH)
Mayers, T. (1984). *Understanding nuclear weapons and arms control.* Arlington, VA: Education in World Issues. (Box 1355, Arlington, VA 22210)
Bender, D.L. (1982). *The arms race: Opposing viewpoints.* St. Paul, MN: Greenhaven Press.
Sedacca, S. (1984). *Up in arms: A Common Cause guide to understanding nuclear arms policy.* Washington, DC: Common Cause. (2030 M Street, N.W., Washington, DC)
Harvard Nuclear Study Group (1983). *Living with nuclear weapons.* New York: Bantam Books.

References
1. Doctor, R.M. cf. D.K. Miller (1984). *Psychologists for Social Responsibility Newsletter*, 3 (1), 1-2.

2. The Editors (1984). Preface to a special issue: Education and the threat of nuclear war. *Harvard Educational Review*, 54 (3), v.

3. Fleming, D.B. (1983). Nuclear war: What do high school history textbooks tell us? *Social Education*, 47 (7), 480-484.

4. Shulman, M. (1982). The process of governmental policy-making in this area. In H. Dunathon (Ed.), *The role of the academy in addressing the issues of nuclear war*. Geneva, NY: Hobart and William Smith Colleges.

22

Influencing Government Policy

Leonard Williams

Why should you bother to learn the basics about government policy-making? Quite simply, because your ultimate goal is to influence what governments do about problems of conflict and war. Knowing how policies are made will help you influence government decisions. In what follows, I will briefly discuss the process and stages of political decision-making and their relevance for peace workers trying to influence governments. [1] [2]

Getting Attention

Public policies (what the government says and does about our problems) are the result of a fairly complex process. The first stage involves getting the attention of the public at large and of people in government. These often go hand in hand, since getting the attention of government officials often means arousing enough citizens or a significant interest group (the American Medical Association nationally, for example, or a Chamber of Commerce locally) to demand governmental action.

Getting officials to respond usually requires persuading the public that a problem exists, that the government can and should act upon it, that there is a particular kind of solution to the problem, and that they need to make their feelings known to officials. Perhaps the most influential way to do this is to make skillful use of the media. Individuals generally have less impact on media coverage than groups, since groups are more likely to do something that is newsworthy. No single strategy will work in all cases, but in general, your group should try to use the media to (a) arouse public interest in an issue, (b) demonstrate the group's unity and commitment, and (c) provoke public or governmental response to your concerns. [3]

Effectively using the media means recognizing that their coverage is often limited to comments and events that contain drama or controversy, that bring conflicts between villains and heroes into focus. [4] Thus, statements by local clergy about the moral issues of working in defense plants may be enough to get media attention and focus public debate. The drama or controversy need not be explosive, however. All that may be needed to attract media attention is to invite a government official to a town meeting on peace issues, to hold such a meeting (open to the media and filled with "photo opportunities"), and to report on the official's participation.

Effective use of the media also means recognizing the importance of symbols. For example, to counteract the Pentagon's use of terms such as "credible nuclear deterrent" or the "Communist threat," which are in essence symbols, your group might stress the need to "save the children" from nuclear war or "love thy neighbor." Both symbols and slogans (such as the popular ones "No Nukes" or "Give Peace a Chance") are valuable aids in presenting a simple and direct message to people through the media. Part of Ronald Reagan's political success has been attributed to his staff's ability to offer a single, direct (and occasionally dramatic) message to the public. Such a strategy can help peace workers, too.

Nevertheless, even given these general guidelines, it is difficult to make blanket statements about what particular events the media will cover. Demonstrations, guerrilla theater presentations, and conferences, for instance, have all attracted attention at some times and been soundly ignored at others. Many factors will determine whether a particular event will be covered; your best bet is to look at the kind of events your local media usually cover, and make plans around that. For instance, do they concentrate more on events that are unusual or fairly routine, peaceful or violent, serious or "happy news" oriented, more local or national in scope? The timing of an event is important as well. For example, does it tie into the current interests of the media, does it in some way fit with the nature of the day or season (tax day, Christmas, Veterans Day, etc.), does it occur on an otherwise busy or a slow news day? Though you often cannot plan on having a slow news day, you can do other things in planning and timing your events to improve the chances the media will cover you.

There are a variety of books and pamphlets that can help you put the above guidelines into practice. They offer specific suggestions on getting media attention and on translating public awareness into political influence. I would recommend, first, the Friends Committee on National Legislation's (FCNL) "How-To Series" of pamphlets. Also valuable is the section on media and advertising in *How to Win an Election.* [5] Both sources offer important hints on preparing press releases, writing letters to newspaper editors and legislators, and "packaging" both candidates and issues. You may also wish to consult the Public Media Center (see "Organizations" at the end of this chapter) or the book *We Interrupt this Program... A Citizen's Guide to Using the Media for Social Change* (cited in Chapter 35).

Approaching Government Officials

The next stage in policy-making involves making direct appeals to government officials. This requires presenting information and policy recommendations about specific problems. When you talk to government officials, you need to give details about the policy you suggest. For instance, don't just say that we need to have a nuclear freeze; talk about matters like constitutional authority (which level of government has the power to act on an issue), the verification of arms control treaties, the maintenance of a strong defense, and the pros and cons of differently worded freeze resolutions. Translate general concerns for peace into specific proposals and reasons for government action. Support your arguments with well-researched information.

You should also be prepared to make your case repeatedly. A good policy idea usually needs a long period of discussion, bargaining, and compromise before people in government even consider making a final decision on it. Be ready to face the same issues and arguments time and time again, and use as many forums as possible: public hearings held by government bodies, face-to-face meetings with officials and their aides, media interviews or articles, letters, phone calls, telegrams.

It is important to take your proposals to the right people, and at the right time. It does little good, for example, to share your new approach to US-Soviet relations with a city council member (though the Council member is appropriate for a local "nuclear-free zone" resolution). Instead, seek out officials who debate and heavily influence foreign policy, such as a member of the Senate Foreign Relations Committee. Remember, however, that your own Representative or Senator, regardless of the issue, should be your first target. One thing you might do is to send copies of your correspondence with your own representatives to the chairs of the relevant congressional committees.

Most policy decisions are made by small groups of people who are considered experts on an issue, and who have some stake in the final decision. This is especially true at the national level. For instance, important policy decisions about defense are often made by congressional committees after hearing the views of Defense Department officials and leaders of interest groups (such as the conservative American Security Council, and the liberal Friends Committee on National Legislation). Your best chance at influencing this process lies in making regular contact with your representatives and working with interest groups who will give their views on debated legislation.

Even if you can influence policy debates, the checks and balances of American democracy usually do not permit swift and major policy changes. If this is true, how can you persuade people in government to enact peace-oriented reforms? There is, of course, no magic answer. Yet there are several keys to influence. First, get a sense of what motivates government officials. Officials are people, too. They are moved by their concerns as individuals, as people in a given job, as members of groups, and as people concerned with what is good for society. Get to know your officials and appeal to the concerns that motivate them. The best course is probably to develop a long-term relationship with them by writing letters, and by meeting face-to-face when possible.

Second, be aware of the groups in your community which influence your elected officials. Decision-makers respond to different circles of people at different times and on different issues. Try to find an influential group that you can work with to influence the official. For instance, if the representative has a health science or medical background, you might do well to get involved with the American Medical Association or Physicians for Social Responsibility.

Third, remember that accurate information is important in politics. Dedication to peace is helpful, but it does not get you very far unless it is informed. Your credibility is hard to establish but is easy to lose, and once lost, it is gone forever. Fourth, when you lobby people in government, be brief, direct, well-organized, and focus on one issue at a time. (See the FCNL's pamphlet, "How to Visit Your Congressman," for concrete suggestions and advice.) Follow other suggestions given in this book for developing good communication and changing opinions. Fifth, encourage the official to take some specific concrete action. This allows you to discuss the merits of the action, rather than having an official agree with your general principles without having any intention of taking the action you would like. Finally, when people in government do something right, let them know. This will make personal access to government that much easier the next time you have something to say.

Following Through

The final stage of policy-making occurs when the policy is put into effect and its costs and benefits are measured. Frequently, activists work hard to get policy reforms made and then quit, thinking the game is over. It's not. A policy is not self-executing; decisions still need to be made about money, staffing, and other matters that often mean the difference between good policy and bad. Policies may be undermined by the officials whose duty it is to put them into effect. Thus, you need to carefully watch the actions of government on those policies you helped influence.

On a national level, publications like the *National Journal*, *Congressional Quarterly Weekly Report*, the *Washington Post*, and the *New York Times* can help you monitor government activities. Your local library probably subscribes to these periodicals.

Three groups who can help you on legislative peace concerns are: The State Legislators Network on Arms Control and Foreign Policy, the Peace Network of State Legislators, and the National Caucus of Peace Legislators (contact the Conference on Alternative State and Local Policies for more information on these groups — see "Organizations" at the end of this chapter).

You could also consult publications by the General Accounting Office for evaluation of specific government programs (see "Organizations" section). The point is that your efforts should not stop with getting a new policy; make sure that the policy was implemented as intended, and that it is working effectively.

Elections

This chapter has thus far offered some general guidelines on influencing government policy. These suggestions all relate to working with existing policy-makers, with current government officials. Research suggests, however, that fundamental policy change most often occurs through the *replacement* of government officials. This was true of the election of young Democrats in the "Watergate election" of 1974, and of the election of Ronald Reagan in 1980. So get involved in the electoral process.

First and foremost, of course, vote according to your convictions and encourage others to do the same. Elections can be won by getting enough "my-vote-won't-make-a-difference" folks to the polls. And sometimes a few votes do make a difference, as seen in the 1984 four-vote re-election margin of Indiana U.S. Congressman Francis McCloskey.

Second, support your candidate through financial contributions and volunteer labor (telephoning, door-to-door canvassing, distributing literature). While your goal is to help a peace candidate win, working for a candidate also helps you bring issues to public attention and develop skills for your own peace work.

Finally, work through one of the two major political parties. This means contributing money, attending party rallies and meetings, seeking party office or a seat at a party convention, and encouraging people (even yourself) to run for office. Opportunities for participation are great (especially at the local level), and you should take advantage of them. Concrete suggestions for participation can be found in *How to Win an Election* [5] and in the FCNL's pamphlet "How to Work for the Congressional Candidate of Your Choice." And, of course, many of the other chapters in this book contain ideas which are applicable to campaigning.

Conclusion

Peace workers trying to influence government need to be aware of the many features of the policy-making process. It is a complex and lengthy process, and obviously cannot be covered in detail in a short paper. Nevertheless, knowing the basics, as described here, should help in your attempts to influence government policy.

References
1. Dubnick, M., & Bardes, B. (1983). *Thinking about public policy*. New York: John Wiley.
2. Anderson, J. (1984). *Public policy-making* (3rd ed.). New York: Holt, Rinehart and Winston.
3. Cobb, R. & Elder, C. (1983). *Participation in American politics* (2nd ed.). Baltimore: Johns Hopkins University.
4. Henry, W. (1981). *News as entertainment.* In E. Abel (Ed.), *What's news* (pp. 239-252). San Francisco: Institute for Contemporary Studies.
5. Huseby, S. (1983). *How to win an election: A complete guide to running a successful campaign.* New York: St. Martin's Press.

Organizations
Conference on Alternative State and Local Policies (2000 Florida Ave., NW, Washington, DC 20009). The CASLP publishes a regular newsletter on progressive state and local policy-making (*Ways and Means*) as well as other materials on specific issues and recommendations for action.

Friends Committee on National Legislation (245 2nd St., NE, Washington, DC 20002). FCNL publishes a monthly *Washington Newsletter* which contains information on major peace issues and legislation before Congress. The group also provides important research and testimony on these issues. Additionally, FCNL has an excellent "How To" series of pamphlets on lobbying, letter-writing, and other means of political influence.

General Accounting Office (U.S. GAO, Document Handling and Information Services Facility, P.O. Box 6015, Gaithersburg, MD 20877). The GAO publishes a *Monthly List of GAO Reports*, a catalogue of reports on the implementation of important national policies. Selected reports deal with national defense and international affairs. Single copies of the reports are available free.

Public Media Center (25 Scotland St., San Francisco, CA 94133). The Center provides information on using the media for social change. In some cases it can assist in organizing a media campaign.

Suggested Readings

Ginosar, M. (1982). *How to influence Congress to reverse the nuclear arms race.* (See description in Chapter 35.)

Norwick, K.P. (1982). *Lobbying for freedom in the 1980's: A grassroots guide to protecting your rights.* New York: Perigee (Putnam Publishing Group). Though not relating specifically to peace, this valuable book discusses the operations of state legislatures, as well as how lobbying groups can influence legislators' votes.

Simpson, D. (1974). *Winning elections: A handbook in participatory politics.* (See description in Chapter 35.)

Walzer, M. (1971). *Political action: A practical guide to movement politics.* Chicago: Quadrangle Books. Walzer provides many useful hints on topics ranging from using the media to working in coalitions.

VI

Peaceful Persuasion: Changing Attitudes

Whether you label the techniques here *education* or *persuasion*, you can use them to lead your listeners to political opinions more supportive of the peace movement. To be persuasive, you may first need to reduce the hostility some citizens feel toward peace activists. The "image" chapters, made up of papers by Melburg & Tedeschi and Tinker & Eckhardt, cover that assignment, and also give other hints on how you can present a positive image.

The second Tinker and Eckhardt piece, on attitude change, and the chapter by Wollman and Keating, present a number of principles of attitude change and apply them to peace issues. Tinker and Eckhardt deal first with reaching people and then with ways to change their minds by creating doubts, repeating ideas, and supporting small shifts in attitudes. Wollman and Keating cover a number of other important principles of opinion change and how they can be applied in your work, including ideas for tailoring your arguments to your listeners, making your arguments persuasive, and creating moods and associations which will enhance the impact of your message.

The next paper, by Linden Nelson, Wollman, and Hunn, is concerned specifically with changing attitudes on nuclear weapons issues. Many suggestions are given on how to develop relevant arguments, point out faulty assumptions in current nuclear policies, reframe issues in a way favorable to your cause, and formulate appealing arms control proposals. You'll likely find some suggestions relevant to non-nuclear concerns as well. The Manhattan Project paper, prepared by Wendy Mogey, concludes this section with twelve guidelines for changing attitudes which she discovered in her own work for peace.

23

Enhancing the Image and Credibility
of Peaceworkers I

Valerie Melburg and James Tedeschi

The only knowledge most people have of peace workers is through the mass media, and such coverage usually focuses on the dramatic actions peace workers sometimes take to bring public attention to an important issue. Yet those actions may sometimes be considered so radical by the public as to nullify their effectiveness. This chapter will examine the negative impressions that may be planted in the minds of audiences, how they affect the processes of persuasion and influence, and what you can do to retain a positive image while taking actions to promote world peace.

Actions and Negative Impressions
    The formation of impressions, while complicated, essentially involves two processes: (a) the observer examines the *effects* of a behavior to evaluate whether the behavior and the person are to be considered "good" or "bad," and (b) the observer infers the *intentions* of the person. The public may see the effects of a behavior differently than does the person involved.
    You may view your dramatic action (eg. hanging a banner on a public building) as an important public statement, bringing attention to your cause. You hope others will wonder why you would risk imprisonment, and will realize it is because the issue is very important to you. You probably believe your action will cause others to think about the issue and join your movement.
    For most Americans, a behavior is "bad" if it violates the law. Peace activists shown on television being carried to a police van or

chained to a fence at a military base will very likely be viewed by others as "deviants," perhaps as "wild-eyed radicals." The mass media may focus attention on the most unkempt and unruly members of your demonstration, and hence reinforce that impression. This occurred during the large protests staged against the American military presence in Vietnam. Large groups of well-dressed, middle-class people who participated were not shown on television. Instead, young people with long hair, beards, t-shirts, jeans, and marijuana caught the camera's not-so-allseeing eye.

In addition to labeling your *actions* as "good" or "bad," the public attempts to determine your *intentions*. This process of judgement goes on within the particular social context and belief system of the observer. Americans in the 1980s have been bombarded with anti-Soviet messages, supported by a massive build-up of U.S. military forces that might be called the "propaganda of the deed." (That is, the belief that the Soviet Union *must* be a real danger to us is backed up by the expenditure of enormous sums of money to "protect" ourselves.) The Russians have also been portrayed as two-faced: while they are trying to gain military advantage over us, they engage in propaganda for peace. Their stated concern about peace is said to be insincere.

In the context of those beliefs, there are two likely ways in which your dramatic action for peace might be viewed. The more favorable image is of a person who has good intentions but who has been taken in by Russian propaganda or perhaps is just plain foolish. Even if they recognize your good intentions to end conflicts around the world or prevent nuclear war, observers are likely to believe that if they support the cause of peace activists, the opposite will happen. Trusting the Russians to keep treaties, or failing to "protect our interests" around the world or to build an adequate nuclear defense are considered dangerous policies.

Some observers, of course, will see your civil disobedience as "communistic" or anti-American. Instead of "well-intentioned but foolish," peace activists are seen as attempting to undermine the strength of America and to promote the cause of communism. This perception is reinforced because many left-wing individuals are a part of the peace movement. As a result, you may be considered a traitor who is cooperating with the enemy.

Either of these two images of peace workers can make your

audience unreceptive to persuasive communications. Obviously, if you want to do more than experience the emotional release of making a personal statement, you will need to consider ways of countering or avoiding such negative images.

Promoting a Positive Image

There are a number of actions which will project a more positive image to audiences. *Establishing credentials* can be an important step. ''Concerned Physicians'' or ''Federation of Scientists'' (or, nationally, ''Physicians for Social Responsibility'' and ''The Union of Concerned Scientists'') are names which suggest groups that contribute to education about the consequences of nuclear war in a way that does not alienate the audience. The status associated with physicians and scientists, and the fact that well known individuals may endorse the groups establishes their credentials as patriotic and informed citizens.

Make an effort to *direct your criticism toward both sides.* In discussing peace issues, avoid appearing to support the Soviet Union's policies. Criticism of the arms race or of military intervention in the Third World should be directed at both the U.S. and the U.S.S.R. Keep a balance between criticism of the Soviet Union for its aggressive actions and calling for a need to work with the Soviets in order to have peace in the world. Complement this by subtly or openly expressing your patriotism, as well as emphasizing the patriotic values which your position embodies — justice, seeking to live in peace, freedom of expression.

Others are likely to view you more positively and to be more persuaded by your positions if they see you as *similar to them in attitudes and values.* Focus on such similarities as dress, manner, and communication style. Politicians have learned to wear war bonnets on Indian reservations, cowboy hats in Texas, and tuxedos at parties in the Nation's capitol. Peace activists can similarly benefit from ''blending'' with their audiences and appearing less different or deviant. It may be necessary to choose between being ''yourself'' and being effective.

Finally, *clear and uncomplicated arguments* should be given to support the policies advocated. Mass movements are seldom based on complex arguments such as those given in books and classroom lectures. Instead, the most effective arguments may be those that can be stated in simple slogans and bumper stickers. Since social issues have become popular as TV movies and other media activities, dramatic ways of presenting peace issues through the mass media can be effective in gaining audience attention. The ABC television movie, "The Day After" was effective in stating the *problem;* now there is a need to dramatically present some *solutions.*

Your image is an integral part of your message.

Suggested Reading

White, R.K. (1976). *Nobody wanted war.* Garden City, NY: Doubleday Anchor. White presents an analysis of the role of misperceptions in the Vietnam and other wars.

24

Enhancing the Image and Credibility
of Peaceworkers II

Lorena Jeanne Tinker and William Eckhardt

In order to reach the minds of listeners in the first place, peace workers must reduce the distance between themselves and their audiences. Bridging that gap can be accomplished through a number of active steps by the peace activist or sponsoring group:

Stress Similar Characteristics and Values.
There is a great deal of research evidence which indicates that a speaker's similarity to the audience promotes acceptance of a persuasive message. This principle should be applied to messages about peace and arms control. Profession, status, politics, place of residence, age, interests, memberships, hobbies, religion, ethnicity,... All such characteristics offer areas of possible "common ground" which can help to establish rapport.

Create a good impression.
Peace activists will often be in contact with total strangers in public places. There is a desire to attract attention to peace issues and perhaps to persuade the strangers to support or oppose various policies or actions. The impression strangers form of the peace activist is critical for determining their reactions.
First impressions often affect the entire course of a relationship. [1] A "warm" individual will be viewed very differently from a "cold" person, even though they say exactly the same words. The activist can convey a "warm" impression by smiling, maintaining eye contact, and offering a handshake after a verbal greeting.

We pretend that "appearances are deceiving" and that "one cannot judge a book by its cover," but packaging is just as important for people, especially those who seek to influence others, as it is for consumer products. The proverbial "little old lady in tennis shoes" may not be taken seriously when she talks about significant political issues. (See Chapter 5 for more suggestions about improving your personal appeal.)

Be seen as possessing high credibility and other persuasive personal traits.

Your ability to change attitudes is greatly affected by the credibility you have with your listeners. If you appear credible your listeners will be more likely to accept what you say.

Your chances of establishing or maintaining credibility are best if you do a number of things: present accurate, dependable information which can be documented; be a reliable and trustworthy person whose information cannot easily be discounted; be well-prepared with specific facts and figures.

One excellent way to establish your credibility as a speaker is to *bring along witnesses* — individuals who can testify to and give evidence for the argument you are trying to make. In 1984, for instance, children from around the world who had been tortured traveled across the United States, speaking under the auspices of various peace groups. Presentations are more convincing when made more concrete through use of pictures, films, slides, recordings, demonstrations, or exercises.

Association is another key principle from social psychology which has application here. Peace activists can gain respect by association with high-prestige individuals and groups, and dissociation from disliked or hated persons or groups. This is not to argue against involvement with unpopular individuals or causes, but it should be recognized that your effectiveness *may* be diluted by doing such association. Integrity is always of top priority, of course.

Stress similar traits and concerns.

Whenever possible, use speakers who are similar to your audience and will thus be seen as "one of them." For example, if a local labor union asks for a speaker on the effects of military spending on local jobs, send a well-prepared blue-collar peace worker, rather than a university professor (who may be an expert on the subject but has no personal background in unions). The union leader's message will be better accepted. Similarly, community leaders you are trying to influence may relate best to peace workers who are similar regarding professional and status level. For such an audience, in order to be considered "one of them," you need to have sufficient standing in a given field to merit credibility.

You can reduce the barriers between peace workers and audiences by using speakers who *specifically discuss concerns or values which match those of the audience*. For instance, Kathy and Jim McGinnis have found their "Parenting for Peace" presentations well received when they address groups concerned with proper child-rearing. In this situation, both the presenters and the audience share a common concern regarding the effects of war and violence on children; this concern increases the likelihood that the McGinnis' message about peaceful ways of parenting will be accepted. Regardless of your particular audience, you will likely be viewed more favorably if you emphasize those values of the peace movement which the general public typically endorses, like dignity of life and abhorrence of violence.

For audiences concerned with authority, being similar and having the same concerns may not be the key factors in making your listeners identify with you. What may be most important is that they see your speaker as an *authority figure*. By associating with an authority figure, they can experience feelings of power and security. This effect may explain why certain parishioners accept the peace message of priests and nuns who have drawn from the bishops' pastoral letter on war and peace (*The Challenge of Peace*). The "similarity" factor should not be forgotten, however; "authority figure" speakers will be best accepted when they also emphasize similarities with their listeners. For instance, one Catholic bishop told a military-related group how his experience as a World War II pilot led him to his peace commitment.

It is not necessary to compromise your beliefs or principles in order to appear credible and attractive to others, but it is vital to *be* both credible and attractive if you are to win others to the movement for peace.

Reference
1. Berscheid, E., & Walster, E.H. (1978). *Interpersonal attraction* (2nd ed.). Reading, MA: Addison-Wesley.

Suggested Readings
Tinker, L. and Eckhardt, W. (1983). *Attitude change and peace action.* St. Louis, MO: Peace Research Laboratory (1115 Magnet, St. Louis, MO 63132). This is a more comprehensive presentation of the information in this section of *Working for Peace,* based on a review of attitude research in psychology.

Mitchell, G. (Ed.) (1982-85). *Nuclear Times,* Vol. 1-4. New York: Nuclear Times, Inc. (Room 512, 298 5th Ave., N.Y., NY 10001). This is a contemporary magazine which monthly is filled with practical ideas for peace makers who want to reach people with their peace messages.

Keyes, K. (1982). *The hundredth monkey.* Coos Bay, OR: Vision Books. Ken Keyes, in this delightful, very important (although also a fun) book to read, says: "There is no need to feel helpless or get paralyzed by hopelessness. We know we have the power to make changes if we can join together and raise our voices in unison."

Zimbardo, P.G., Ebbeson, E.B., & Maslach, C. (1977). Influencing attitudes and changing behavior (2nd ed.). Reading, MA: Addison-Wesley. This readable introductory attitude text presents the major theories and research, along with practical application. In particular, see the section near the end of the book called "postscript on becoming a social change agent" for some very valuable hints.

25

Attitude Change and Peace Action

Lorena Jeanne Tinker and William Eckhardt

This chapter presents two basic steps necessary for doing successful peace work. First, we as peace workers have to reach people. Too often, we talk only to each other. We prepare programs that are of interest only to "insiders." We write articles in newsletters and magazines that interest only those already committed to peace. Second, we must change the attitudes of the people we do reach. Without such change on a large scale, ours will remain a militaristic society.

Reaching People's Minds

There are four important questions to ask as you set the stage for attitude change. First, is your information relevant and important to those you are trying to reach? Second, is the information readily available to your listeners? Third, have you contacted leaders among the population group you are trying to reach? Fourth, are you using language your listeners can understand and with which they can identify?

Is your information relevant and important to those you are trying to reach? [1] Your information, whether presented in casual conversations or formal programs, must be relevant to your listeners. If you will be doing a formal program, give the sponsoring group an opportunity to choose a topic they want to hear about.

The Corpus Christi Ground Zero group, for instance, prepared a list of topics its members could speak on and presented it to various organizations. Two Rotary clubs responded, one choosing the topic "Accidental Nuclear War," while the other selected "Nuclear Weapons and the Just War Theory." Both talks received excellent responses, at least partly because they were relevant to listeners' interests. If at all possible give your audience a choice; don't assume that because two groups seem similar they will have the same particular interests.

Betty Bumpers, wife of the U.S. Senator from Arkansas, talks to women about the safety of their children. She is quite effective as she presents the very real possibility of nuclear war, and the need for mothers to work to prevent it. Her information is relevant to her audience.

Is your information readily available to your listeners? Peace messages and publicity about events should be widely circulated in the community and the local media. Prepare press releases and public service radio announcements, hold press conferences (with written hand-outs available), present programs on cable TV public access channels (stations must provide instruction in the use of video equipment), publicize that you have speakers available (for conferences, TV and radio interviews, organizational events, classroom talks, etc.), serve as a resource for community and church groups who are studying war and peace issues, print reader-relevant announcements in newsletters and bulletins of various groups (churches, labor unions, women's clubs, business groups, service clubs, parent-teacher groups), run ads in "trading post" type magazines, write letters to the editor, display information on large rented billboards, leave newsletters, magazines, and other materials where they will be read (libraries, laundromats, subways, buses), list events in community calendars or other information services, and place flyers or peace-oriented stickers at different locations (cars, your home mailbox, envelopes). Be creative; you will surely think of additional ways to keep people informed (also see Chapter 4 for more ideas on getting out the peace message).

Have you contacted leaders among the population group you want to reach? Focus some of your attitude change attempts on leaders of groups you want to influence (service clubs, unions, parent-teacher groups, business associations, local governments, athletic clubs, civic associations, professional organizations, etc.). If you can reach people like these, they may influence not only members of their group, but also other influential community leaders with whom you might never have direct contact.

Are you closing the distance between you and your listeners by using language that your audience can understand and with which they can identify? It is important that you present messages framed in a language that your listeners regularly use and understand. Be aware, for example, that "average citizens" might not understand the terms "non-intervention," "zero-sum situation," or "economic conversion." However, most people would understand "agreeing not to invade another country," or "in some situations only one side can be a winner," and they would probably be interested if you talked about "adding new jobs that don't make weapons." If you address special interest groups (religious, athletic, political, ...), use terminology and concepts with which they are familiar and can identify.

Sometimes the idea of using the right language must be taken literally: How many peace workers try to reach Hispanic Americans, whose primary language continues to be Spanish? There are some encouraging beginnings: both the American Friends Service Committee and the Earlham College Peace and Global Studies Program have produced some peace materials in Spanish. But this is only one step; you must not only hold programs using the language of your audience; you must hold the programs in their neighborhoods. Is it any wonder that the peace movement is confined principally to middle and upper-middle class white Anglo Americans?

Changing the Minds You Reach
The balance of this chapter is devoted to a discussion of three methods which we consider among the most effective in helping people change their attitudes from nationalistic and militaristic to compassionate and peace-oriented: (1) *stimulate imbalance and doubt in listeners;* (2) *repeat ideas, both within a message and over time;* (3) *support those whose attitudes are changing.*

Stimulate Imbalance and Doubt in Listeners
People continually try to keep consistency among their values, behaviors, and beliefs. [2] Attempting to maintain beliefs or take actions which are inconsistent with each other causes uncomfortable feelings; psychologists have labeled these feelings "cognitive dissonance." [3] The more important a topic is to a person the greater the uncomfortable feelings will be.

For example, someone who smokes three packs of cigarettes a day and believes that smoking causes cancer will likely experience cognitive dissonance. She will wish to alleviate those feelings and can do so by changing her beliefs or actions so they are consistent. She has a number of options: "kicking the habit," repressing the fact that smoking causes cancer, disbelieving (or distorting) the evidence linking smoking with cancer.

If you present new information (a peace message) which your listener accepts as true but which is inconsistent with the listener's political beliefs, the imbalance can cause anxiety and raise questions in the listener's mind about the validity of his present attitude. If the imbalance and anxiety are felt strongly, the discomfort can lead to a change in attitude. [4]

In her speeches, Dr. Helen Caldicott (formerly active with Physicians for Social Responsibility and now with Women's Action for Nuclear Disarmament) has stimulated dissonance, anxiety, and questions about nuclear weapons policies. She does this by making vivid the fact that nuclear war can indeed occur, and that stockpiling nuclear weapons will lead almost inevitably to nuclear holocaust.

"Walking in another person's shoes" may create such an imbalance in a person's attitudes. Role playing has been used effectively to simulate such experiences. [5] All kinds of art — drawings and paintings, films, songs, poetry, drama, mime, literature, clowning — can help stimulate empathy for another's point of view. If the new perspectives differ from their own, audiences may question their present attitudes and perhaps begin to change them.

You can create dissonance in others in another direct way: Acknowledge that you know your listeners are interested in peace, and that *they* are concerned individuals. Then note that if *they* do not raise their voices or take appropriate action we will never have peace in the world or avert nuclear war. Point out possible inconsistencies in their politically-related behaviors or attitudes. If you can, tell them about specific actions/inactions of theirs that are hurting the cause of peace (especially those they can freely change).

Of course, when people question their own attitudes, the resulting imbalance can be very uncomfortable, even painful. Such conflict may lead the person to defend the previous attitude. People with jobs in nuclear weaponry or other military industries have vested interests which are in conflict with peace messages. Those who are convinced by political leaders (such as Ronald Reagan) that stockpiling nukes keeps the peace will be defensive in response to messages of peace workers.

When peace makers succeed in stimulating listeners to question militaristic attitudes, opportunities should be available to deal with these questions. Discussion periods, preferably with people in small groups, are helpful. Relevant literature also is very useful, and can extend the impact of your peace message.

We as peace makers are responsible, when our messages arouse anxiety, to help our listeners deal with it constructively. Otherwise original attitudes may be clutched and defended, with the peace message minimized, ignored, or attacked — sometimes along with the peace worker!

Repeat Ideas — Within a Message and Over Time

When you give a speech, separate it clearly and distinctly into parts, and give brief summations after each part. Making the same point two or three times is good, but don't repeat identical information or it will lead to boredom and hinder attitude change.

Make the same point using different terminology, examples, or presentation style (for instance, sometimes use rhetorical questions: "And why was it wrong to invade Grenada?" They are effective when used with strong arguments [6]). Similarly, conferences consisting of speeches and workshops which don't repeat information but give different aspects of a topic can also change opinions.

Don't expect listeners to become committed to peace after hearing an argument for peace just one time. However, if someone is exposed to a consistent message over time, with new information and arguments included at each presentation, attitude change could very well result. [7]

Repetition can be offered in various formats: conversations with friends and other individuals, speeches and programs which get media coverage, press releases, newspaper ads, bumper stickers, letters to the editor and to legislators, and literature distributed to the public or within newsletters and brochures of churches and service clubs. It is also effective to have different communicators presenting the same basic arguments.

Support Those Whose Attitudes Are Changing
A shift in attitude from a militaristic to a peaceful orientation may be temporary and subject to reversal. There are certain things you can do to make it more likely that changes in attitudes will endure.

Many of those who attend meetings and begin to change their attitudes will become lost in the crowd unless you take certain steps. Invite them to future meetings and activities, and stress the importance of their participation. Ask them to begin taking some small actions to promote peace, such as writing letters to elected officials (see Chapter 10 on getting new people to work for peace). Have them take literature, talk to others, express their new feelings and fill out information cards about themselves. Request their permission for a group member to contact them individually in a more informal setting.

New attitudes are more likely to become firmly entrenched if a person formally joins a peace group and becomes integrated into its structures. This means assuming responsibilities within the group, developing relationships with group members (have old members initiate contacts with new members), and receiving extra support from group members if he still has ties to others who influence his attitudes toward militarism. (For instance, a churchgoer who has joined your group but whose church and congregation are pro-military will need as much support as your members can give). Getting individuals to join the group is important because of the influence groups can have over individuals. For example, members tend to conform to the attitudes of a group and to use the group as a standard to evaluate the correctness of their behavior.

One psychologist has recommended doing several things to stabilize attitude change. (8) Discuss the newly-formed views with the person, and stress why such views are good. Also, "inoculate" the individual against reverting to her old attitude by presenting criticisms against the new attitude, but then giving reasons why the criticisms are not valid. Additionally, in whatever way seems appropriate, subtly let the person know that she voluntarily came to this new position.

Provide appropriate rewards (encouragement, congratulatory notes, political support, etc.) to individuals or groups who begin going public in their support of peace (making public statements, passing resolutions, talking to friends about peace, engaging in demonstrations). Such rewards will help those who have changed their attitudes to become social change agents themselves.

Conclusion

To change militaristic attitudes to those of compassion and peace with justice, peace workers can make use of knowledge developed by social scientists.

It is obvious that we must first *reach* the minds of our listeners; then our arguments must be presented such that they will *change* the minds we reach. The three major approaches described in this chapter — raising doubts in the minds of your listeners, repeating your message often, and providing support to those whose attitudes are beginning to change — have solid research evidence to support their effectiveness.

Changing and helping maintain new attitudes is not an easy process. It takes care and nurturing, but it can be encouraged by the practical application of the proven techniques of attitude change discussed here.

References

1. Katz, D. (1963). The functional approach to the study of attitudes. In E. Hollander, & R. Hunt (Eds.), *Current perspectives in social psychology* (pp. 340-351). New York: Oxford Press.
2. Heider, F. (1958). *The psychology of interpersonal relations*. New York: Wiley.
3. Festinger, L. (1957). *A theory of cognitive dissonance*. New York: Row, Peterson.
4. Cooper, J., Zanna, M.P., & Taves, P.A. (1978). Arousal as a necessary condition for attitude change following induced compliance. *Journal of Personality and Social Psychology*, 36, 1101-1106.
5. Elms, A., & Janis, I. (1965). Counter-norm attitudes induced by consonant versus dissonant conditions of role playing. *Journal of Experimental Research in Personality*, 1, 50-60.
6. Burnkrant, P.E., & Howard, D.J. (1984). Effects of the use of introductory rhetorical questions versus statements on information

processing. *Journal of Personality and Social Psychology*, 47, 1218-1230.
7. Tinker, L. (1985). *Peace-minded south Texans: Selected in-depth interviews*. St. Louis, MO: Peace Research Laboratory. (1115 Magnet, St. Louis, MO 63132)
8. Johnson, D. (1960). Attitude modification methods. In F.H. Kanfer, & A.P. Goldstein (Eds.), *Helping people change: A textbook of methods*. New York: Pergamon Press.

Suggested Readings

Eckhardt, W. (1972). *Compassion: Toward a science of value.* Huntsville, Ontario: CPRI Press. (Huntsville, Ontario L9H 4E5, Canada). Background book for peacemakers who want to learn about philosophy and values of peacemaking with compassion as the norm.

Eckhardt, W. (1980). *A manual on the development of the concept of compassion and its measurement, 1962-1978.* St. Louis: Peace Research Laboratory (1115 Magnet, St. Louis, MO 63132). A very helpful manual for those who want to develop ways to measure attitudes in the populations with which they work. Useful validated scales are included.

Mitchell, G. (ed.) (1982-1985). *Nuclear Times*, vols. 1-4. New York: Nuclear Times, Inc. (Room 512, 298 Fifth Avenue, 10001). Excellent contemporary magazine with many good ideas for peacemakers — according to actual feedback from those in the field.

Tinker, L. (1982). Attitude formation and attitude change: A review of literature relevant to peace (mimeo). St. Louis, MO: Peace Research Laboratory (see address above). Two-page paper listing many ideas for changing American attitudes toward peace. Based on extensive review of the psychological literature on attitude formation and change.

26

Principles of Opinion Change

Neil Wollman and John Keating

This chapter presents a number of principles of attitude/opinion change which are applied to peace concerns. The suggestions here, along with those in the other chapters in this section, can help you become an effective social change agent.

Get At the Reasons for Your Listeners' Beliefs

People hold beliefs for particular reasons, and you will need to take this into account when you try to change those beliefs. [1] Here is a detailed example of how this principle can be applied. Let's say you are talking to someone who feels that the United States must be very aggressive in its dealings with the Soviet Union. She might not state this directly, but it would emerge in her arguments concerning policies the U.S. should pursue, weapons it should produce, or tactics it should take in disarmament talks. In a case like this, rather than initially discussing specifics of foreign policy, it would be better first to explore the underlying reason for those specific beliefs. Ask *why* the U.S. must be aggressive with the Soviets; after she gives her response, ask "why?" again. Gently probe deeper into the person's attitude structure. She will be more open to talking about such matters if at the same time you reveal the underlying reasons for your own beliefs.

Assuming the circumstances allow you to probe your listener, determine the apparent reason for her aggressive beliefs. Is it a desire to appear "strong?" Is it a (superficially) well-reasoned view of the global situation? Is it a need to maintain a "good guy vs. bad guy" view of the world? If it is the latter, for example, make an appeal which takes this reason into account. Show similarities between U.S. and U.S.S.R. global policies. Try to satisfy a "good guy vs. bad guy" view by shifting it to another perspective — for example, that the good guys are those working hard for peace and the bad guys are those pushing for more armaments.

Admittedly, it is not always practical or possible to first explore underlying reasons for beliefs and then plan an appropriate and successful argument. However, if you have the time, energy, and desire, doing so could make a difference — especially if you will be talking to someone over a long period of time. (The *War Resisters League Organizer's Manual* — see description in Chapter 35 — gives hints on appealing to various constituencies, such as religious groups and labor.)

Don't Use Arguments Too Extreme for Your Audience

People judge new information and appeals in terms of how they already feel about a topic. Any argument that differs too much from their current beliefs on a topic will be rejected. [2] Thus, for example, if you know that your listener believes that every weapons system on the drawing board should be produced, don't push for a bilateral nuclear weapons freeze; he will probably reject your proposal outright (and be even more rigid in his beliefs). Instead, a more moderate appeal, perhaps suggesting that the U.S. not build a *particular* weapon, might be more effective. When dealing with staunch anti-Communists, rather than advocating a total non-involvement policy in Central America, suggest a more limited involvement. It all depends on where your listeners are on the topic to begin with. Remember two things: don't decide on the arguments to use before you find out the person's attitude, and don't expect a major change from that attitude unless you plan on working to change that attitude gradually, over time.

Develop Persuasive Arguments

Compare benefits of your policies with alternatives. Let your listeners know what they and our country will gain by adopting your policies rather than the alternatives. For instance, you might note that we already have far more than enough nuclear weapons to deter the Soviets from attacking us. Building more would produce few, if any, additional benefits. If we stopped building more weapons, each citizen would have more money, more could be spent on health care and other benefits, and we would be looked upon favorably by the world for our peacemaking efforts. (Chapter 27 discusses advantages of arms control proposals over current military ones.)

Arouse Fear Under Certain Conditions. Arousing fear in an audience — perhaps regarding the nuclear threat or the possibility of a military draft — can be a very effective means of changing an attitude. [3] Researchers have noted, however, that the danger must seem real, and that an audience — even when fearful — will not adopt the proposed new attitude or behavior unless they feel that doing so will counteract the feared outcome (nuclear war, the draft). Thus, if you use scare tactics, be sure also to present specific concrete actions your audience can do to help prevent the feared outcome. Presenting your audience with a list of peace activities they could engage in (see Chapter 4), and discussing past successes of the peace movement, can help people feel they can do things to work for peace. Without such options, your audience will remain threatened and will likely discount your message.

Use New Arguments. Good arguments which the audience has not heard are tremendous catalysts for persuasion. [3] It is important, then, to remain up-to-date on peace issues and to introduce new information and arguments (or twists on arguments) within your same basic theme. This is especially true of the nuclear debate. In our society, debates about the deployment and use of nuclear weapons have permeated even the most isolated communities. When surveyed, people have expressed impatience over hearing what they consider to be repetitious arguments on both sides of the subject. Consequently, you should use novel approaches in presenting material and introduce recent findings. For instance, you might compare the destructive capacity of a single missile of today with the total power of the A-bomb used on Hiroshima; this is an approach to the issue your audience may not have considered. Or, for example, point out recent findings about the effects of nuclear war. At the time this chapter was being written, the phenomenon of a "nuclear winter" was emerging as a likely consequence of nuclear war. New arguments contain the potential for effectively reaching people who previously had been bored by the repetition of the nuclear debate.

Make Your Conclusions Obvious. Don't just present the facts, but also clearly draw the conclusions to your argument. [3] All too often speakers believe that if they clearly state the facts, the audience will be capable of drawing the desired conclusions and deciding on the appropriate actions to take. Research shows that this is the case only when your audience is highly intelligent and the conclusion is *exceedingly* obvious.

Know Whether Peace Issues Are Important to Your Listeners

There is evidence that the more important an issue is to someone, the more she will be affected by the quality of the arguments (if understood) than by ''secondary'' factors — those not related to the argument itself, but to aspects of the speaker, the listener, or the situation (e.g., the similarity of the speaker, or whether the discussion occurs in a pleasant setting). [4] Secondary factors become more influential when the issue is less important to a listener. Also, as you might expect, a change of attitude brought on by arguments (rather than secondary factors) will last longer and influence behavior more. These findings point out the value of knowing how important a topic is to your listeners before speaking to them. When you address a politically sophisticated audience, be aware that secondary factors like flashy language, good jokes, and neat appearance won't be particularly effective unless your political arguments are sound, and that weak arguments can really damage your case. On the other hand, when you address people who are not highly motivated politically (a majority of our citizens), concern yourself more with those secondary factors. Research has even shown that for those who have little concern about a topic, the number of arguments presented may affect persuasion more than the strength of the arguments. [4]

Create Good Moods, Bad Moods, and Word Associations

Research has shown that a person who happens to be in a good mood while listening to an argument will be more receptive to the message. [5] You might employ this principle, for example, by serving food at some peace-oriented activity, or by presenting peace literature at a county fair booth.

You can also apply this principle by linking your position or argument together with political or other ideas which listeners would likely feel good about. For example, associate your suggested policies with a popular past president ("The policy is in the tradition of John Kennedy."), or say that your position is "patriotic" or "morally right." Or you might do as one peace worker did and use a political bumper sticker ("Nuclear Freeze") along with a heart-warming, non-political one ("Hugs are better than drugs").

Likewise, use ideas which associate bad feelings with a position you oppose: link U.S. Central American policies with those leading to the Vietnam War. Or refer to a government as a "bandit," when it "steals" money that could go to help needy people, using it to make more weapons.

Similarly, use terms together regularly in various communications so that listeners will begin to think of one word when they hear the other. For instance, you may wish to add the term "terrorist," when referring to the Nicaraguan Contras (i.e. "Contra terrorist"). You might counter images presented by the media by using a term such as "Democratic Sandinistas." Words help shape the way we see the world and form opinions. Use them to your advantage.

Make Your Listeners Uncomfortable

You can create "cognitive dissonance" — a feeling of psychological discomfort which occurs when one holds incompatible beliefs — by pointing out inconsistent government policies (relevant to your conversation) which your pro-military listener(s) may very well support. This will result in dissonance because the listener is made aware that he is holding beliefs (concerning government policies) which are not consistent with each other. The more inconsistencies you can point out, the greater the dissonance. [6] (See also Chapter 25.)

Here is a wide-ranging list of inconsistent U.S. policies which you can use in your arguments: supporting rebels in some countries (Nicaragua) and denouncing them in others (El Salvador); building more sophisticated nuclear weapons that frighten the Soviets and are more prone to accident, thus actually making us less secure; supplying weapons to both sides of military conflicts (such as the Middle East); condemning human rights violations in Communist nations but excusing them in our allies (such as South Africa); condemning a relatively few welfare cheaters while allowing weapons manufacturers to make millions in cost overruns;

supplying aid and weapons to the ''Contras'' trying to overthrow the Nicaraguan government while criticizing that government for seeking weapons to defend itself; not allowing citizens to withhold that portion of their taxes going for military purposes while allowing many large profit-making companies to legally pay little or no tax at all. The inconsistencies go on and on; it's not hard to make a collection of them — they emerge with surprising regularity in our government's policies.

You can also help your listeners to be more active on their own in recognizing government policy inconsistencies. For instance, ask whether it is right for a strong military power to invade a weaker one for the security of the weaker country. Note that the U.S.S.R. took this position after its invasion of Afghanistan. If the listener says no, then bring up the U.S. invasion of Grenada. Or ask whether it is right for a country to supply arms to rebels who are trying to overthrow a government — as our government claims the U.S.S.R. has done in certain Central American countries. When the listener says it is not, raise the issue of U.S. support of rebels in Nicaragua.

You can set up similar questions from the list of inconsistent policies mentioned earlier; also check the November, 1984 issue of *Psychology Today* magazine, p. 48, for other items which reflect U.S.-U.S.S.R. similarities. [7] Take care in using this approach because it has the potential of making listeners feel stupid. Be gentle and make your statements in a way that your listeners know you are trying to inform them rather than show them up.

Once dissonance is created, you should present specific new beliefs (about government policy) that your listener could adopt so that he no longer supports and believes in inconsistent policies. Accepting these new beliefs about appropriate government policies would remove the dissonance. Thus you might point out how the U.S. and U.S.S.R. are similar in many ways in foreign policy and could decide to cooperate and become peaceful, or that all countries are sovereign and no major power has a right to intervene in local disputes, or that if we already have sophisticated enough nuclear weapons for deterrence, we should instead use our money to handle our many domestic needs.

It is important to present specific and sensible alternative beliefs (about policies), because otherwise your listeners may reduce their dissonance by rejecting or distorting the new information you have presented them. They may do this anyway to maintain their basic attitude structure. The more deeply ingrained the structure, the less likely they will accept new information and make an attitude change.

If your listeners are to make a basic attitude change, they will need to feel psychologically secure with the new beliefs you propose; this is true whether the change is caused by cognitive dissonance or some other factor. Thus, for example, if you suggest that the U.S. reduce its conventional or nuclear forces, be sure to present an alternative policy with which your listeners can feel safe (you might need to explore this during the course of the conversation). People will feel more secure if they do not see their attitude (or behavior) change as an abandoning of relatives and friends who share their political outlook. Try to convince your listeners that their relatives and friends, who are similarly concerned about world tensions, would likely find your arguments sensible as well. [8]

Get Your Listeners to Do Something Small for Peace

Sometimes individuals do not form their opinions until they become fully aware of their own behavior. [9] For example, someone may realize she is in love with another person only after becoming aware that she always gets excited around that person, spends a lot of time around the other, and often gets presents for the person. But why do we form opinions this way? Because we need to explain our behavior to ourselves. If we start taking certain actions, we feel it tells us something about what kind of person we are or what we believe in.

You can apply this principle by getting people to voluntarily make any statements or take any actions that are favorable to your cause. After they do so and then become aware of their small support for peace, they will begin to feel more favorable to the cause.

Urge Small Statements and Behaviors Supportive of Peace. Try (in a noncoercive way) to get others involved in small activities favorable to peace: signing a petition, giving a small donation, reciting back to you some of your arguments, becoming involved in any activities at a peace group meeting, or publicly making or endorsing any statements favorable to promoting peace.

For example, at a presentation you might ask for a show of hands from people who believe that "peace is the first order of business for all countries." Or during a presentation to a pro-military audience, lead listeners through an exercise in which they imagine and describe the steps needed to peacefully resolve or lessen a particular world conflict (the arms race, a war in Central America or the Middle East): Ask members of the audience to consider on their own what specific actions are required to peacefully resolve or lessen the conflict. Then break the audience into small groups (or pairs if small groups are not feasible) to share their ideas.

Note that the above exercise can cause attitude change in two ways: it induces individuals to make statements favorable to peace, and it has those individuals thinking about peaceful solutions. The more a person thinks over an argument without criticizing it in his mind, the more favorable he will become toward it. [4] Thus you might ask listeners to think over your argument on their way home that day. They'll be more likely to do so if you tell them that you will do the same if they have ideas they wish to share.

Balance Your Presentations. If your arguments are so one-sided that you seem to misunderstand the complexity of an issue or to miscomprehend the other side's arguments, your audience will see you as unknowledgeable. Consequently, you will be more persuasive if you present both sides of an issue, showing that you understand those points an adversary might make against your proposal for peace. [3] After you present both sides, then offer clear rebuttals to the main thrusts of opposing arguments. (The exception to this rule is that you should not present both sides if you are absolutely sure your audience is familiar with only your position or is already completely in agreement with it — don't put opposing ideas in their heads.)

Make Peace Work Enjoyable

Reward Appropriate Statements. Another way to get a listener to start talking more favorably about peace is to reward her whenever she makes *any* statement which supports the cause of peace. Rewards come in many varieties: nodding your head, giving particularly good eye contact, giving (legitimate) compliments, promising (and then doing) a favor, etc. [3] Remember to give rewards only when listeners agree with your statements or make statements favorable to peace interests; don't give them on a continuous basis. As long as your listeners don't feel they were forced into behaving or saying what they did, or that they did so only to get a reward, they probably will see their actions as representing some part of who they are or what they believe in. This should lead to attitude change.

Conclusion

A number of basic principles for changing attitudes have been presented. Each has something a little different to offer on the subject, and they are better seen as complementary approaches than as opposing ones. Explore how you can use them together in your work. For instance, give a presentation which uses new arguments and doesn't deviate too far from the listener's original attitude. If you are creative in using and combining the attitude change approaches presented here (and elsewhere in this section of the book), you'll give yourself the best chance of changing people's opinions on peace issues.

References
1. Katz, D. (1960). The functional approach to the study of attitudes. *Public Opinion Quarterly*, 24, 163-204.
2. Sherif, C.W., Sherif, M., & Nebergall, R.E. (1965). *Attitude and attitude change: The social judgment approach.* Philadelphia: Saunders.
3. Middlebrook, P. (1980). *Social psychology and modern life* (2nd ed.). New York: Alfred Knopf.
4. Petty, R.E., & Cacioppo, J.T. (1984). The effects of involvement on responses to argument quantity and quality: Central and peripheral routes to persuasion. *Journal of Personality and Social Psychology*, 46, 69-81.
5. Staats, A.W., & Staats, C.K. (1958). Attitudes established by classical conditioning. *Journal of Abnormal and Social Psychology*, 57, 37-40.
6. Festinger, L. (1957). *A theory of cognitive dissonance*. New York: Row, Peterson.
7. Plous, S., & Zimbardo, P. (1984, November). The looking glass war. *Psychology Today*, pp. 48-59.

8. Rosenberg, M., Verba, S., & Converse, P.E. (1970). *Vietnam and the silent majority*. New York: Harper & Row.
9. Elms, A., & Janis, I. (1965). Counter-norm attitudes induced by consonant versus dissonant conditions of role playing. *Journal of Experimental Research in Personality*, 1, 50-60.

Suggested Readings
Deaux, K., & Wrightsman, L. (1984). *Social psychology in the 80's* (4th ed.). Monterey, CA: Brooks/Cole.   This is a good social psychology text which nicely summarizes attitude change research and theory.

Cialdini, R.B. (1984). *Influence: How and why people agree to do things*. New York: William Morrow. Using everyday language and examples, Cialdini creatively examines a number of factors which influence citizens and consumers..

Mehrabian, A. (1970). *Tactics of social influence*. Englewood Cliffs, NJ: Prentice-Hall. This small book distills key psychological ideas and principles so that anyone can use them to promote personal change or influence other people toward change. Includes clear, everyday examples.

Zimbardo, P. (1972). The tactics and ethics of persuasion. In B.T. King, & E. McGinnies (Eds.), *Attitudes, conflict, and social change* (pp. 84-99). New York: Academic Press. This is a small chapter in an older, but still relevant book. It focuses on useable peace-oriented suggestions rather than on a presentation of attitude change research.

27

Disarming Support for Nuclear Weapons

Linden Nelson, Neil Wollman, and Jeff Hunn

Public opinion surveys show that about eighty percent of U.S. citizens favor a mutual and verifiable nuclear freeze. [1] Yet there are other indications that public support for arms control is weak.

In one study, 80 percent supported a freeze, until the question specified that a freeze at present levels would give the Soviets superiority in land-based long-range missiles; then the support dropped to 40 percent. [2] It is obvious that public demand for arms control in the U.S. has been too weak to lead citizens to widespread social action or to elect a president who will negotiate seriously for an end to the arms race.

What can be done to change this picture?

The previous chapters in this section offer general principles for effective persuasion; they are applicable to nuclear weapons policies or other peace issues. This chapter describes three general approaches to changing opinions about nuclear weapons policies. The first discussion presents suggestions for *developing relevant anti-nuclear arguments*. Next we describe effective methods for *challenging pro-nuclear policy assumptions* and *reframing the nuclear debate* in a way that is favorable to our cause. The third part of the chapter gives ideas on *presenting arms control proposals* so they will appeal to your audience of citizens or policy makers.

Developing Relevant Arguments

Recent studies of public attitudes toward arms control have important implications for peace workers. Several themes turn out to be particularly relevant, and should be emphasized in the arguments you present: (1) the Soviets don't want nuclear war, nor a costly arms race, and they have in the past complied well with verifiable agreements; (2) arms control would improve U.S. security and Soviet security; (3) acquiring more nuclear weapons or achieving "nuclear superiority" will not improve deterrence; (4) attempting to gain superiority prolongs the arms race; (5) nuclear war is probable if the arms race continues — it is the arms race that is the major threat to our national security; (6) nuclear war would be catastrophic, especially given that the resulting "nuclear winter" could end all life on the planet.

What's so important about these themes? Research shows that people who favor arms control (compared to people who are unfavorable or uncertain) tend to believe (1) that the Soviets desire, and will comply with, arms control agreements, (2) that nuclear superiority is not required to restrain Soviet aggression, (3) that nuclear war is probable if the arms race continues, and (4) that nuclear war would be an extreme catastrophe. [2,3]

Support for arms control is directly related to *how many* of these four beliefs an individual holds; the percent of people favorable to arms control increased from 17% to 94% as the number of these beliefs they held increased from none to four. (2) This implies that you should address as many of these issues as you can in your attitude change attempts.

Widespread public education needs to be done in several of these areas. A 1984 survey found that 39% of adult Americans believed that "the U.S. should always have more nuclear weapons than the Soviets," 61% believed that "the Soviets have cheated on just about every treaty," and 58% believed that nuclear war is unlikely in the next ten years. [4]

Research on the effects of the ABC television movie "The Day After" has illustrated the limitations of an appeal based on just one issue, in this case, the catastrophic consequences of nuclear war. The movie persuaded many viewers that the consequences of nuclear war were more horrible than previously believed, and it made viewers more anxious about the possibility of nuclear war. (2) The movie did not, however, address the other issues, nor did it offer any arms control solutions. While "The Day After" did not change viewers' opinions about arms control, it did appear to motivate political activity in viewers already favorable to the cause. [2]

In contrast, university students became more favorable toward arms control after hearing *lectures* covering four key issues: Soviet treaty compliance; deterrence and nuclear weapon superiority; the probability of nuclear war; and the consequences of nuclear war. [3,5] Students whose beliefs changed on two or more of the issues became more favorable toward arms control than students whose beliefs changed on only one or none of the issues. [3]

Other chapters of this section offer many suggestions for presenting these arguments in persuasive ways. The last part of this chapter discusses ways to accompany those arguments with specific and attractive proposals for arms control. First, however, we'll look at ways to confront the arguments supporting current nuclear policies.

Challenging assumptions and reframing issues

[Many of the suggestions in the remainder of this chapter have been adapted, with permission of Dr. Baruch Fischhoff, from the article, "Social science and the politics of the arms race" by Baruch Fischhoff, Nick Pidgeon, and Susan T. Fiske. The article appeared in the Journal of Social Issues, *1983, Vol. 39, pp. 161-180. References for supporting research may be found there.]*

Want to increase your chances of persuading your listeners? Frame discussions of the arms race differently, by shifting the focus to more human and personal dimensions, such as human suffering, the unhealthy psychological effects of the arms race, and the destruction of civilization.

Because they created the arms race, those favoring military solutions have attempted to maintain their favorable position by shaping *how the public looks at the issues*. Debates about nuclear war usually focus on causes and effects that are readily quantifiable, like megatonnage of weapons, numbers of warheads, expected body counts, and economic costs. There is room to argue on some of those specifics, but if debate centers just around numbers and counts, listeners can remain detached and analytical about the arms race; if they do not experience fears and emotions about the nuclear threat, they will not be stirred to oppose it.

Personalize statistics so that people can relate to them. Rather than simply stating how many people will be killed in a nuclear blast, compare that number with your town's population. Or talk about the likely effects a nuclear war would have on individuals. Mention some of the direct blast effects, and also include some effects that people may not immediately think about, such as the inavailability of food, water, and medical attention, or the loss of loved ones and property (don't be too gory in your descriptions, however, or your listeners may just tune you out).

Encourage your listeners to consider the *long-term* impact of building and maintaining weapons. The costs of weapons and the risk of war over a lifetime are much greater than those that exist in any moment, day, or even year. Effects are also cumulative; point out how the benefits from gradually reducing weapons become greater over an extended period of time. Mention how much money goes to the military over a 10-year period and thus how much is lost to schools, health care, consumer products. Point out that even if the chance for nuclear war were, say, only one in a hundred for any one year, that over 100 years the chances for having a war at some point would be nearly two out of three.

Instead of the usual focus on military proposals, shift the debate to concrete non-nuclear (or non-military) options for maintaining national security, such as more serious negotiations between nations. Or tell your listeners about *nonviolent* means of national defense (such as the program of civilian-based defense researched and advocated by Gene Sharp, director of the Program on Nonviolent Sanctions in Conflict and Defense at Harvard University's Center for International Affairs, 1737 Cambridge St., Cambridge, MA 02138, 617-495-5580).

Military strategies are often based on faulty (or at least questionable) assumptions about human nature and abilities; point out these assumptions in your talks and debates. Some strategies assume, for example, that human operators will act calmly and make decisions rationally during the stressful times preceding a possible nuclear war. Similarly, civil defense planning assumes that citizens will remain relaxed and trusting during times of nuclear emergencies. (There are numerous other faulty assumptions made by policy makers and citizens concerning nuclear policies and national security. [6(Chapter 2), 7])

Many assumptions actually valid for conventional warfare are false when applied to nuclear warfare. [8,9] Examples include the following: superiority improves deterrence; war can be won; war can be controlled and limited to combat zones; there is a defense for every offense; a country needn't cooperate at all with an adversary to provide for its own security.

Remind audiences of Albert Einstein's famous words, "The unleashed power of the atom has changed everything save our modes of thinking, and thus we drift toward unparalleled catastrophe." [7]

The public generally assumes that military planners and leaders are experts who know proper military strategies and policies because of their training and their access to particular classified information. You can erode the credibility of such "experts" by pointing out mistakes of the military (and government) in weapons design and construction, weapons purchases, and weapons negotiations (which have only led to more weapons on both sides). Just by showing that there is an alternative analysis of the weapons situation you have undercut the experts' credibility. The public can see that other sources of research and information exist, and that national security issues can perhaps be perceived in new ways.

Sometimes the most important message you can present is that there is enormous uncertainty about nuclear issues. For instance, no one *knows* whether our weapons will deter the Soviets, *exactly* where our (or their) missiles will land, whether our (and/or their) complex computer systems will *work*, how great the damage will be, or whether a "nuclear winter" will end life on our planet. You can help cast doubt on military proposals by conducting (and publicizing) your own analyses of these questions that draw different conclusions from those of the military.

This approach is particularly applicable, for example, in debating the merits of the Strategic Defense Initiative (the "Star Wars" proposal). Constructing a defense against ballistic missiles would initiate an expanded arms race involving defensive weapons, countermeasures to defenses, and new offensive weapons. [10] The resulting complexity in the balance of U.S. and Soviet forces would raise uncertainties about each nation's ability to retaliate to a nuclear attack, and might therefore allow an aggressive leader to believe that nuclear war was winable. The possibilities for war by miscalculation, accident, or aggressive strategy would multiply. [11] Proposals for arms control have more appeal when current and planned nuclear war policies are shown to be more uncertain and more dangerous.

Presenting Attractive Proposals

To successfully argue for an end to the arms race, for disarmament, or for any other peaceful strategy, you'll need to offer specific and understandable alternative proposals. Try to select proposals that promise tangible, attainable, and verifiable results.

Formulate peace proposals that are at least as satisfying to your listeners as the military alternatives. Typical "peace" or disarmament proposals require people to give up something concrete (arms, territory) in return for something intangible (reduced probability of war). Since intangibles are not always valued highly, your proposals for military conversion will be more attractive if they offer tangible returns.

Here are a number of potential economic returns that would be attractive to many people: increased trade, greater productivity, conversion of weapons research to consumer product research, and reduced defense spending (which could lead to a "balanced budget," lower taxes and/or more money for community needs and social services). Of course, you will also need to gather relevant facts and figures to back up such proposals.

By their very nature, many military proposals give their supporters the opportunity for a small victory each time a new weapons system is adopted or expanded. Disarmament proposals need to offer their supporters similar small psychological boosts. The vague hope that sometime in the future all weapons will be abandoned is not enough; such a victory will be a long way in the future, and people will tire of focusing on it if they don't see progress along the way. Focusing attention on intermediate steps, such as nuclear freeze resolutions, would be one way of setting up goals that are more achievable in the near future.

Show your listeners that small steps of progress have already been made, and that such progress is due to the work of peace activists and the support of the public. Point out the postponement or cancellation of specific weapons systems, the continuing pace of arms reduction talks, and the increasing public sentiment against nuclear weapons (polls show support for a nuclear freeze, and many town councils have passed resolutions supporting anti-nuclear policies, nuclear free zones, and "Jobs with Peace" initiatives).

Military proposals will seem less satisfying if you can show how little opportunity there is to verify their validity. For example, the public must take it on faith both that new arms systems will deter the Soviets from military attack, and that the weapons will work as designed if they ever have to be used under real conditions. Avoid public uncertainty about your own proposals by including verification measures within them. For instance, give specific plans for how the U.S. and Soviets can have mutually verifiable weapons reductions, how conventional forces can be built up to replace nuclear ones, or how countries can live together more peacefully through various cultural, economic, and educational exchanges.

The proposed Comprehensive Test Ban Treaty is a good example that fulfills all of our criteria for an attractive peace proposal. It is specific and understandable — all underground explosions of military significance (over one kiloton, for example) would be prohibited, thereby severely hindering the development of new nuclear bombs. The result would be tangible — the testing of nuclear bombs would cease. The goal is attainable — there are no technological obstacles and there is considerable support for the proposal in the U.S. Congress, the Soviet Union, and other nations. Finally, the results would be verifiable — "there appears to be no technical obstacle to monitoring with great confidence underground nuclear tests releasing as little as one kiloton or less of energy" (p. 44). [12]

Conclusion

Your anti-nuclear activity will be most effective if you take these steps: *persuasively address the issues* discussed near the beginning of this chapter, such as Soviet trustworthiness in regard to arms control; *reframe questions addressed*, and *point out faulty or uncertain assumptions* about current policies; *present anti-nuclear proposals that have public appeal*, and which, if adopted, would make significant steps toward ending the arms race and achieving nuclear disarmament.

References
1. Milburn, M., Watanabe, P., & Kramer, B. (1984, August). The nature of attitudes toward a nuclear freeze. Paper presented at the

meeting of the American Psychological Association, Toronto, Canada.

2. Nelson, L., & Slem, C. (1985). Attitudes about nuclear arms control and effects of "The Day After." Manuscript submitted for publication.

3. Nelson, L., & Perner, L. (1985). Opinions about nuclear arms control and effects of classroom instruction. Manuscript submitted for publication.

4. Doble, J., & Kingston, R. (1984). Public attitudes: Conflict. In D. Yankelovich, R. Kingston, & G. Garvey (Eds.), *Voter options on nuclear arms policy* (pp. 26-37). New York: Public Agenda Foundation.

5. Slem, C., & Nelson, L. (1985, April). Enhancing the effects of "The Day After" with an educational intervention. Paper presented at the meeting of the Western Psychological Association, San Jose, CA.

6. Lifton, R., & Falk, R. (1982). *Indefensible weapons: The political and psychological case against nuclearism.* New York: Basic Books.

7. Holt, R. (1984). Can psychology meet Einstein's challenge? *Political Psychology,* 5, 199-225.

8. Frank, J. (1983). Nuclear arms and prenuclear leaders: Sociopsychological aspects of the nuclear arms race. *Political Psychology,* 4, 393-408.

9. Nelson, L., & Beardsley, G. (1985). Toward an interdisciplinary model of barriers to nuclear arms control. Manuscript submitted for publication.

10. Bundy, M., Kennan, G., McNamara, R., & Smith, G. (1984/1985). The President's choice: Star wars or arms control. *Foreign Affairs,* 63, 264-278.

11. Glaser, C. (1985). Star wars bad even if it works. *Bulletin of the Atomic Scientists,* 41, 13-16.

12. Hafemeister, D., Romm, J., & Tsipis, K. (1985). The verification of compliance with arms-control agreements. *Scientific American,* 252, 39-45.

28

Depolarizing Discussion:
Guidelines for Peaceworkers

The New Manhattan Project,
American Friends Service Committee

(This article is slightly modified from "Depolarizing disarmament: Twelve guidelines to help us reach new people" prepared by Wendy Mogey for the New Manhattan Project. New York: American Friends Service Committee, 1979. Permission to reprint has been granted by the New Manhattan Project of the American Friends Service Committee, New York Metropolitan Region.)

From my experience in peace work, I have discovered twelve guidelines which may help you in your attempts to reach new people.

1) Don't ever assume that your audience (whether one person or a crowd of a thousand) is either totally with you or totally against you.

2) Beware of labeling new people — "right wing/left wing," "conservative/liberal," etc. — as you talk with them. Once someone feels that his/her alternatives are either remaining a "conservative" or turning into a "liberal," s/he may decide that it is safer to stay where s/he is.

3) Be sensitive to the presence of hidden agendas in dialogues about militarism. Listeners may have underlying psychological reasons (vulnerabilities) for supporting a strong military. Don't deal only with rational arguments; also listen to the emerging feelings of your listeners.

4) Make sure other people understand what you are saying. Explain ideas and terms well and ask for audience feedback regarding what they are hearing.

5) Make sure you understand what people are saying; ask for clarification if necessary.

6) Don't push people into a corner so that the only way they can change their attitude is to admit vocally they were wrong; give people a less threatening or embarrassing way to adopt a new attitude.

7) Don't limit yourself by your own arguments or responses. If you are arguing that a specific military policy or weapons system is counterproductive, listeners might falsely assume that you do approve of other policies or weapons systems. Be sure also to argue that our military policies and weapons systems in general are counterproductive and will make us less secure.

8) Let your audience know if you don't know something; you are showing them that a person doesn't have to know every fact on a topic to know that certain actions, like building more nuclear bombs, are morally wrong. Also, giving information that is false might hurt your credibility.

9) Help people see the consequences of their beliefs, even though they remain closed to alternative ideas.

10) Keep the discussion on the right questions. Don't get bogged down on specifics like exactly how much nuclear megatonnage we and the Soviets have, or how to calculate the amount of military aid needed to counteract Soviet influence in Central America; raise the deeper question of the morality of nuclear weapons and of U.S. intervention.

11) Don't be afraid to present your underlying values, assumptions, experiences, doubts, fears, and personal commitments. At some point in a discussion it's better to reveal such things than to give just more facts.

12) Be willing to "let go" of a discussion at the right time. Don't try to "convert" a person on the spot; your responsibility is to say the truth as you know it and then to "disengage" to allow a change process to develop.

VII

Pieces:
Other Tools for Peace Work

Psychologists are not the only ones with valuable suggestions for peace workers. The first four chapters in this section apply the arts to peace work. Most of the material is geared toward reaching the public, but some is relevant to keeping spirit and creativity within your own group.

Rogers opens the section with practical, hands-on suggestions for the various art forms (music, drama, visual arts). Philbin concentrates on music, dealing with application of the talents of trained musicians. Friesen focuses on drama and summarizes different dramatic formats, such as guerilla theatre, tableaux, and church plays. In her second paper, Philbin briefly discusses creative arts projects from around the U.S. (e.g., billboards for peace, exhibitions, peace quilts, and radio programs). She also lists numerous arts organizations working for peace.

The paper by Zimmerman is more than comic relief on the serious subject of peace. He offers concrete suggestions for using humor in various ways: attitude change, relieving tension, keeping up spirits at group meetings. Humor is a valuable tool; here's how to use it.

Ganong and James discuss a topic only now coming into its own, heretofore receiving little formal attention in peace literature: the use of computers. The authors outline how to set up operations and how to apply computers in your peace work (word processing, mailing and membership lists, computer communication, graphics, and spreadsheets). The final piece by Ed Nelson suggests a number of books (and pamphlets) which take other approaches (most are non-psychological) to peace or political work. Some selections are described, others merely listed. Nelson's sampling ranges from ''nuts and bolts'' handbooks to philosophically oriented works; all are useful for peace workers.

29

The Arts in Peacemaking

Ingrid Rogers

Many of the experiences that are most meaningful to us are difficult to express in words. And so we turn to something else to capture the essence of those experiences. If we can't say it, we sing it, dance it, mime it, play it, paint it, shape it — recreate it in some way that will tell others what we feel. Thus we communicate (and educate) not only with words, but with our whole beings.

Why Use Art?

Using art in peace education has many advantages. It appeals to young and old, it stimulates curiosity, and it involves people intellectually and emotionally. Speakers on peace issues often get pulled into debates and arguments, which may become hostile interchanges. In contrast, art works at breaking down barriers. It is at times as provocative as the most radical speech, but it is distant enough from reality (a mirror, as Shakespeare put it, but not reality itself) that we venture to take a look. Humor makes the confrontation even easier. Think of the truth people allow a clown to present, or the subtle satire of a cartoon. People laugh and are ready to think about a message they would otherwise reject.

Another advantage of art is that it can be used together with other strategies for changing views and feelings about peace. Sometimes the sole focus of a peace gathering might be an artistic event such as an exhibit, an evening of songs, or a dramatic performance. Other times certain art forms may be integrated into a "regular" program to attract people and to enliven the event. A creative drawing or graphic, for instance, may attract people's attention to a flyer advertising a peace gathering. Likewise, banners can have an important function at a demonstration, signalling either aggressiveness or a longing for peaceful cooperation; they can profoundly influence the general population's reaction to the event.

Music also can be an enriching addition to an event; it can be used both in public events and also for gatherings involving only peace group members. A song at the beginning of a public or private meeting relaxes people and draws the group together. During longer sessions, singing gives a change of pace and raises the mood of participants. A song expressing hope and togetherness is a good way to end an event; it tends to energize people at the closing.

Getting Peace Workers Involved in Art

The simpler the art, the better the chance that peace workers will get involved in the project. Take a skit about the arms race, for example: few volunteers have the time and energy to memorize lines and attend dozens of rehearsals for a sophisticated two-hour production, but a five- to ten-minute skit which requires fewer than a half-dozen players and only a few simple props is easy to stage and can be an effective consciousness-raising tool.

Or to popularize visual arts, how about having each group member add a little something to a peace picture, or draw a symbol of peace on a poster or banner? We need to teach peace at the grassroots level, getting as many people involved as possible; the artistic approach allows this to happen.

Following are suggestions on how you can work for peace through art. Even if you are not artistically inclined yourself, you will find many of the suggestions useful. Perhaps "creativity" is a better word for what we want to appeal to; everyone has it — it waits to be awakened.

Music

There are many advantages to making music a part of a peace event. Only one leader is necessary, and no preparation by the group is required. Plenty of songbooks, records, and cassettes are available as resources. Music allows spontaneous group participation, and singing is good for building unity and group spirit. Here are some suggestions:

1. Invite your group to an event where a musician presents his or her songs about peace. Set up a resource table with cassettes and records of peace songs. Publicize the event in the local media. Sponsoring such an event is an excellent way to support a singer/songwriter who works for peace; it can also be a good fund-raiser for peace groups.

2. Share a record or cassette of peace songs; give one as a gift to a friend. For a resource list contact the New Song Library, P.O. Box 295, Northhampton, MA 01061.

3. Use peace songs to educate children. The "heroes" they see on TV are fighters who combat evil with violence. As peacemakers you can tell alternative stories of people who used their courage constructively and who valued human life. Some of these stories have been set to music. Children remember what they sing better than what they are told. Play songs for the children, discuss them, and sing along. Good collections are *I Can Make Peace*, distributed by Herald Press, Scottdale, PA 15683, $8; and *Peace Be Unto You*, by I. Rogers, 707 N. Sycamore St., N. Manchester, IN 46962, $5.

4. Teach peace songs. If there are several stanzas, project the words on a screen with an overhead projector, particularly for a large gathering. Shorter songs can be written on posterboard. Ditto or photocopy the songs and let people share the songsheets to promote unity. Use some of the standards that people are likely to know already, like "Last Night I Had the Strangest Dream," "We Shall Overcome," and "If I Had a Hammer." Or have a singer/guitarist lead sing-along *Peace Gathering Songs* available from the New Song Library (see above). These songs have easy refrains, basic guitar chords, simple words, and catchy tunes. How about a peace "sing-a-thon" for a fundraiser?

Drama

Drama is an extremely effective way to present the peace message, because the audience gets involved in a life-like situation and identifies with the characters. Drama also tends to be the most entertaining of the art forms. Here are suggestions on using drama without getting bogged down in months of practice:

1. With a group of friends, read some of the peace plays from *Swords Into Plowshares*. This collection of short plays is available from Brethren Press; call toll-free 1-800-323-8039. When you feel you are ready, give a public reading, or try performing one of the skits at church services or in street theater.

2. Tape a discussion concerning a peace issue, then turn it into a short play.

3. Show the videotaped play "Changing the Silence" (available from STOP, Box 232, Northfield, MA 01360). It presents a group of

high school students expressing their anger, grief, and pain about living under the nuclear shadow. Encourage viewers to verbalize their own feelings as if they were one of the players.

4. Conduct a workshop or presentation in which participants role-play a conflict situation and then brainstorm to find a peaceful solution.

5. Set to mime peace songs; for instance, from *Peace Be Unto You* (see "Music" above), try "The Wall," "The Weight of a Snowflake," and "Telemach."

6. Use simulation games relating to peace to effectively teach junior high and high school students. For instance, the game "BAFA BAFA" teaches the frustrations, joys, and insights that come from interacting with a foreign culture (available from Simile II, 218 Twelfth St., P.O. Box 910-A B, Del Mar, CA 92014). The game "Star Power" helps promote empathy for the powerless in society (available from Western Behavioral Science Institute, 1150 Silverado, La Jolla, CA 92037). For younger children, try puppetry to play out a conflict and its resolution.

Visual Arts/Crafts

One advantage of this medium is its continuing availability once it is created. Posters and pictures can be reused and offer a steady visual background during a peace event. Here are some suggestions:

1. Advertise a peace event by enlarging your favorite logo or symbol for a poster or newspaper ad. Your local quick-print store should be able to help you with this suggestion, and also the next one.

2. Insert cartoons or peace symbols into newsletter mailings and private correspondence. One year I put a flower at the bottom of our Christmas letter with the words, "War is not healthy for children and other living things," and a picture of a dove emerging from a broken bomb.

3. Plan a peace exposition. Invite friends for an evening of poster-making or banner-making, and then display the creations for the larger community. Offer your best work to churches or community rooms for permanent display. Display peace posters or banners on the walls during public meetings. Share children's peace pictures in the community, or even at regional or national conferences.

4. As parents and educators, encourage children to paint peace pictures. Children can express their feelings through art before they can put them into words. Drawing and painting allow them to get in touch with their fears and their hopes. Seeing their dreams for a peaceful world helps us as adults to recall our responsibility for their safe future. Parents: consider sending the finished pictures, with a letter, to your Congressional representatives.

5. Organize a peace-crafts event: participants bring their own creations and materials, and teach others how to make them.

6. Cut out logos and cartoons from peace publications and assemble them on posterboard for display, or use them to make a letterhead on your stationery. You could also paste these on the backs of letters, as you would a sticker.

7. Send short messages on peace postcards. Very good sets with peace messages are available from the Fellowship of Reconciliation, Box 271, Nyack, NY 10960; Communicators for Nuclear Disarmament, P.O. Box 1283, Cambridge, MA 02218; and Kimo Press, P.O. Box 1361, Falls Church, VA 22041. Kimo Press also has eye-catching bumperstickers, buttons, magnets, and embroidered peace patches.

8. Give a presentation at your church describing various peace symbols which have a religious origin (swords into plowshares, rainbow, world unity symbols, linking hands, etc.). Perhaps a group of people will be inspired to make a peace-quilt or banner using these symbols.

9. Crafts are an excellent way to help children develop peace awareness in school, Sunday School, or at home. Use the traditional peace symbols (paper crane, dove, rainbow, lion and lamb, butterfly, outstretched hands, etc.) for peace mobiles, glass painting, simple banners, needlepoint, wood working, or printmaking (ask or read about these simple techniques if you are unfamiliar with them). Talk with children about the symbols and issues as you work. Most importantly, listen to children as they express their feelings. If appropriate, completed art work can be exhibited temporarily at a local event or at a more permanent location.

Art can not only help you educate others for peace; it can also inspire your own peace-making. Let the creativity within you work for peace.

30

Music as an Instrument of Peace

Marianne Philbin

Music is a very powerful form of expression and communication. Whatever kind of peace event you may be organizing, you can include music to increase its effectiveness.

Music as an Organizing Tool

Music can be a political and spiritual call to action, a means to help rally diverse groups to a common cause. Use music as the focus of an event, as a component, or just as a background to help motivate people and bring them together into a more cohesive group.

Use a song to open or close an event, to arouse a speaker's audience, to set the mood for a march, or to begin educating others on an issue. An anthem or "theme song" can bring a movement together, becoming identified with a particular campaign the way "We Shall Overcome," for example, became identified with the civil rights movement. For any kind of ongoing campaign, select or write a theme song to help focus attention on the campaign and unify the program.

Whether you stage a one-time event or a long-term campaign, consider ways in which music might be incorporated. And if you can include old songs along with the new, the music helps create a sense that working for peace is an integral part of our heritage, a goal pursued by thousands of people over generations and generations.

Consider creating a soundtrack to accompany whatever event or project your peace organization is sponsoring. Even if you're simply setting up a booth or literature table at a local community festival, include music to draw supporters to your area, and select songs to communicate the goals and interests of your organization. If no other sound system is available, play a tape of selected peace songs on a portable cassette player or "boom box." To select songs, consult the listing in the back of the book *Give Peace a Chance*; it lists nearly 2,000 songs on peace and related topics (available from The Peace Museum, 430 W. Erie St., Chicago, IL 60610, $8.95).

The Appeal of Popular Musicians

The desire for peace has been a traditional theme for decades in American popular music. It is reflected in songs ranging from "I Didn't Raise My Boy to Be a Soldier" (1912) to Pete Seeger's "Where Have All the Flowers Gone?" (1961) to James Taylor and John Hall's "Children's Cry" (1982) to Steve Van Zandt's "Los Desaparecidos" (1984) about Central America. Work with local musicians to present a festival in celebration of music for peace, or work with the history and music departments of an area university or college to present a workshop or conference on the role music has played in peace efforts. Such events could include films, videos, lectures, and naturally, concerts.

Build a program around the music or work of a particular musician. Some folk and rock musicians who have written peace songs or been involved in peace efforts include Joan Baez, Africa Bambaata, Jackson Browne, Harry Chapin, Bruce Cockburn, Crosby Stills Nash & Young, The Clash, John Denver, Bob Dylan, Arlo Guthrie, John Hall, George Harrison, John Lennon, Yoko Ono, Holly Near, Randy Newman, Bob Marley, Rita Marley, Country Joe McDonald, Laura Nyro, Peter, Paul, & Mary, Tom Paxton, Malvina Reynolds, Paul Robeson, Gil Scott-Heron, Pete Seeger, U2, and Stevie Wonder. The program could be designed to focus attention on a particular issue, or to motivate people generally toward peace. If you are doing the former and can pick someone who is interested in or identified with the issue you are working on, so much the better. For instance, Country Joe McDonald has worked extensively with veterans organizations, while Holly Near has been outspoken on a number of issues, including intervention in Central America.

Invite the musician for a personal appearance, but if that is not possible, seek the musician's cooperation in other ways; an endorsement, a telegram which can be read at the event, a videotaped message, etc. Additionally, local musicians could perform a revue of the musician's best-known songs, and music writers and critics, historians, fans, and family members of the musician could give lectures.

Sometimes a musician who is sympathetic to an organization's work but who is unable to perform a special concert will agree instead to help in other ways — making an appearance, for example, as a special guest at a reception, or agreeing to shake a few hands or sign a few albums in order to help out an organization.

Another possibility is for an organization or institution to award a musician (or a representative) in recognition of his or her work for peace. The Southern California Alliance for Survival, for example, presented Graham Nash with "The First Annual Woody Guthrie Humanitarian Award" for "Outstanding Contributions Toward Peace and a Nuclear-Free Future." The award was given in part for Nash's work in organizing the massive Peace Sunday concert in 1982. Presentations of such awards can help generate publicity, encourage the involvement of others, and focus attention on the issue being highlighted.

Concerts or other events featuring popular musicians can draw new people to the organization or the movement, since individuals having little familiarity with peace issues or a particular peace group will come because they are fans of the musician. And in the course of the concert, workshop, reception, or other event, members of the the audience naturally learn more about working for peace and perhaps are inspired to follow the musician's example, seeking ways to work for peace that best suit their own particular interests and talents. For many people, musicians are heroines and heroes, role models who set examples, and they can be a powerful force for promoting peace.

Other Ways to Work With Music or Musicians

Sponsor a peace musical with help from your community theater group or university drama department. Consider *Peace Child*, *Alice in Blunderland*, and *Lubov Means Love*, for example. Information on these plays is available from The Peace Child Foundation, Box 33168, Washington, DC 20033, (202) 628-6262.

Introduce peace themes into traditional seasonal activities such as caroling during the Christmas holidays. Rather than just singing standard Christmas carols, organize a group of "carolers for peace" to sing popular peace songs while they collect donations for local peace groups.

Collaboration between local musicians and peace organizations can also produce a wide variety of exciting projects. Present concerts (built around a peace theme) which showcase the talents of local musicians. Sponsor competitions inviting local songwriters to compose a song for peace; the winning composition can be performed at a special event or aired on local radio. Encourage musicians to create programs on music and peace and perform them in schools.

Radio As a Way to Educate

Work with your local radio station, or with an individual disc jockey who is particularly interested in peace issues. Propose that the station schedule a program or set aside a special day featuring music on war and peace. A day featuring peace music can be tied to a holiday such as Veterans Day or Memorial Day, or to the anniversary of an event such as Woodstock, or to the birthday of a musician such as John Lennon. Keep in mind that a station geared toward popular music and concerned about ratings will be more likely to schedule such a program if it's tied to something positive or upbeat, as opposed to something like Hiroshima Day, which station managers might fear would turn off listeners.

Encourage a local radio station to co-sponsor a music-related peace event, such as a concert, dance, or festival. In Chicago, for example, a local radio station has regularly helped present "Give Peace a Dance" at a popular night club to benefit a peace organization. The station's most popular disc jockey hosts the dance, spinning records from Motown to modern with a healthy sprinkling of danceable peace tunes like the Talking Heads' "Life During Wartime," or U2's "New Year's Day," Elvis Costello's "Goon Squad," Edwin Starr's "War," and XTC's "Generals and Majors."

Music is a powerful means of affecting and motivating people — both you as a peace worker and those you are trying to reach. Learn to use it where you can and your work will become more effective.

31

Teaching Peace Through Drama

Lauren Friesen

While drama is an art form and is often judged on its artistic merits, it can also be useful as a means to educate about peace. There are many types of drama which can help you communicate your peace concerns. This paper will review them and suggest certain scripts you might consider performing.

Before doing this, however, it is important to ask why one would choose drama to educate about peace; there are certainly other methods. The answer may lie in the power of drama's effects. As performers create a play before an audience, the play, the performers, and the audience change. As the plot unfolds, the audience responds with understanding or confusion. As the characters develop before their eyes, viewers begin to recognize themselves, their families, neighbors, or forgotten friends. In the scenery, the spectators see their own houses, apartments, villages, or cities. The line which separates the stage from the audience becomes thin and nearly invisible as the plot unfolds and the audience responds with laughter, tears, or awed silence.

The difficulties of characters and the changes in plot bring out many emotions, attitudes, and personal struggles within the audience. Any sensitive viewer must consider the complexity of human relationships, the value of human dignity, and the peaceful or violent consequences of human actions. The story on stage does not present an escape from reality, but rather an unfolding of events which are common and true to humanity. No wonder drama is such a powerful means to educate, about peace or any other concern.

Types of Drama

Professional theatre. After such a lofty introduction it is time to turn to practicalities. An obvious first step would be to convince a professional theatre company to produce a peace-oriented play. A professional company with an established reputation would attract an interested audience and make a considerable contribution to peace awareness. Many examples from theatre history support the claim that plays, on the professional stage, can have a considerable influence upon the public. Plays such as Bertolt Brecht's *Mother Courage*, Bernard Shaw's *Arms and the Man*, and Megan Terry's *VietRock*, have all influenced public opinion on peace issues.

The strength of professional theatre performance resides in its potential to affect a large audience. Many people see plays in the professional theatre and are influenced by them. The play receives publicity and critical response.

The weakness of professional theatre is just that: It is professional. Normally, only persons with considerable talent become directly involved. Also, because of the subject matter of a peace play, potential investors may not come up with the money to finance the play if they do not agree with the message or expect the play to make a profit.

Nevertheless, when a peace play is produced professionally, it can be a great opportunity for peace workers. The Church Council of Greater Seattle organized groups to attend plays and then meet for discussion and action. If a peace play is produced in your city, don't ignore it, support it.

Church drama. This consists of church-sponsored plays, with cast and crews from within the church. During World War II Howard Thurman had the Fellowship Church in San Francisco produce Sophocles' ethical play, *Antigone*. If nuclear war is a concern of your church, the short play *The Last Word*, by James Broughton, would be a good choice.

A play could be produced for an evening or Sunday afternoon performance, or as part of a worship service. Careful work with appropriate church boards and pastors might result in sizeable church and community response.

An important factor and strength of the church play is that all interested persons, young or old, can have an opportunity to participate. The play achieves goals beyond the production itself, such as community outreach or peace education within the congregation. An additional strength is that the group process in a dramatic production contributes to the church's community of faith; this evolves as people share responsibilities, challenge each other's discoveries, and learn from the peace-oriented content of these plays. The collection of peace plays by Ingrid Rogers, *Swords Into Plowshares*, is a valuable resource.

An obvious weakness of church drama is that it may be difficult to find persons who will make the time commitment necessary for a quality production (a poor production of a play may be a counterproductive witness for peace). It is a general rule that for each page of script, a cast should schedule one hour of rehearsal. Plays often have scripts that run over seventy pages, which would necessitate considerable rehearsal time! A church doesn't necessarily have to stage a major play, however; one-acts, scenes from longer plays, or short skits on peace themes can also be used effectively. These shorter works can be performed during worship, evening programs, at camps, or in nonchurch settings like fairs, peace demonstrations, or other community activities.

Tableaux. If you have not been invited by a church or other organization to help produce a play, or if your group does not have the resources to do so, there are alternatives. You could create the dramatic "tableau," or representational scene. If your concern is the brutality of violence and torture, for example, have three or four persons dress in appropriate costumes and perform a scene at the entrance of a convention hall or on a street corner. Enact a thirty-second torture scene in which two "soldiers" beat a "victim" with rifle butts until the victim falls. Eventually allow the victim to rise, and begin the action from the start. While these actions occur, a fourth person could be reading the names of those who have been tortured by governments around the world, or who have suffered other forms of violence. Other brief scenes and readings of names could celebrate global peace workers who have been harassed, misunderstood, or forgotten. The repetition of the scene gives a sense of the repeated nature of these unjust acts.

The strength of a tableau is that in a very short time, relatively inexperienced actors can select and develop a powerful scene. The weakness stems from the nature of the activity; once people have seen it, they will want to move on. There is no plot or character development to sustain the interest in the audience. But a tableau provides a chance, however short, to affect the consciousness of the audience.

Guerrilla Theatre. This form of theatre normally takes place inside a church or convention hall, during a traditional meeting of a committee, worship service, corporate meeting, city hearing, political rally, or lecture. Members of the theatre group walk into the meeting or auditorium carrying banners or signs to draw attention to their cause. They may engage the speaker or presiding officer in dialogue, or just stand in a highly visible location.

The strength of this format is that concerned persons who feel ignored by political or other power structures can draw attention to their concerns. It takes little training or experience to do this, and it can focus the attention of the audience on the issue of interest.

A disadvantage of guerrilla theater involves the public's general discomfort with socially disruptive tactics; even those who may sympathize with the group's cause may feel uncomfortable with a staged confrontive method of expressing that concern. Be aware that guerrilla theatre methods may alienate an audience, obstruct cooperative work among peace groups, and inhibit collaboration with community organizations.

Street Theatre. This is a short theatre piece performed in the street (or sidewalk) for all who pass by. Short comic or serious routines relating to peace can be developed. Actors normally dress in costumes authentic for the situation portrayed, and street theater can be particularly effective with clowns, large puppets, mime artists, or music. Smaller local parades (and some major ones) accept entries from community-sponsored groups; this can provide your peace group with the opportunity to build a float, large puppets, etc., allowing many people in an area to become familiar with your work and cause. Bread and Puppet Theatre of Vermont has gained international attention from their street theatre work focusing on peace and environmental themes.

Some strengths of street theatre are that it is short and it enables the audience to respond and possibly enter into dialogue with the cast. One weakness is that with a short script, the impact on the audience may be rather superficial; however, this is better than no impact at all. Another problem is finding the next stage when the parade is over; otherwise large investments in costumes, puppets, and time may all focus on one short production.

The amount of preparation time for street theatre is more than for guerrilla theater or a tableau. Plots will need more attention, costumes will need to be appropriate and attractive, and puppets (if employed) will require considerable craftsmanship.

There are many ways to educate others about peace. One very powerful way is through the use of drama, which affects people's emotions as well as their thoughts. Perhaps this is what it will take for the world to turn from war.

Catalogs of Plays
Baker's Plays, 100 Chauncy St., Boston, MA 02111
Dramatic Publishing Co., 4150 N. Milwaukee, Chicago, IL 60641
Dramatist Play Service (DPS), 440 Park Ave., New York, NY 10016
Samuel French (SF), 45 W. 25th St., New York, NY 10010

Suggested Plays
Anderson, Maxwell. *Winterset.* (SF)
Arden, John. *Sergeant Musgraves' Dance.* (SF)
Berrigan, Daniel. *Trial of the Catonsville Nine.* (SF)
Brecht, Bertolt. *Mother Courage.* (SF)
Brook, Peter. *Conference of the Birds.* (Dramatic Pub.)
Broughton, James. *The Last Word.* (SF)
Euripides. *Trojan Women.* (SF)
Fry, Christopher. *A Sleep of Prisoners.* (SF)
Fuller, Charles. *A Soldier's Play.* (DPS)
Fugard, Athol. *Master Harold and the Boys.* (DPS)
Giraudoux, Jean. *Tiger at the Gates.* (SF)
Goldemberg, Rose Leiman. *Marching as to War.* (DPS)
Goodrich and Hackett. *The Diary of Ann Frank.* (SF)
Hellman, Lillian. *Watch on the Rhine.* (SF)
Miller, Arthur. *Incident at Vichey.* (DPS)
Rabe, David. *The Basic Training of Pavlo Hummel.* (DPS)
Rogers, Ingrid (1982). *Swords into Plowshares.* (Elgin,
    IL: Brethren Press, 1-800-323-8039).   Collection of one-act
    peace plays.
Shaw, George Bernard. *Arms and the Man.* (SF)
Shaw, Irvin. *Bury the Dead.* (SF)
Taylor, C.P. *Good.* (DPS)
Terry, Megan. *VietRock.* (SF)
Ustinov, Peter. *The Unknown Soldier and His Wife.* (SF)
Weiss, Peter. *The Investigation.* (DPS)
Wibberly, Leonard. *The Mouse that Roared.* (SF)

32

Creative Arts Projects and Organizations

Marianne Philbin

There are many ways in which the arts can be used to help motivate and involve people in working for peace. This chapter is a sampling of the wide variety of creative projects which have been undertaken.

Exhibitions. Numerous exhibitions on peace themes have been presented by organizations around the country. Some of these groups make exhibits available for travel to other cities. Amnesty International, for example, frequently has exhibits available for loan, as does The Peace Museum in Chicago.

Exhibitions available through The Peace Museum include "The Unforgettable Fire," drawings by Hiroshima and Nagasaki survivors; "Dr. Martin Luther King, Jr.," on King's work for civil rights and peace; and "Give Peace a Chance," on music and the struggle for peace (contact The Peace Museum, 430 W. Erie, Chicago, IL 60610).

Amnesty International has exhibits on Cambodia, political prisoners, and other topics (contact Amnesty International, 304 W. 58th Street, New York, NY 10019).

Many organizations have sponsored peace exhibitions of work by local artists: "What Artists Have to Say About Nuclear War" (May-June 1983), Nexus Gallery, 360 Fortune Street, Atlanta, GA 30312; "Target L.A.," a series of anti-nuclear events and exhibitions sponsored by L.A. Artists for Survival, Southern California Alliance for Survival, 1503 N. Hobart, Los Angeles, CA 90027; "ArtPeace" (August 1983), an exhibition on the theme of a nuclear-free planet, sponsored by the Popular Arts Workshop, P.O. Box 15052, Lansing, MI 48901.

Similar exhibitions have been presented in other cities on a variety of peace-related topics. On the national level, recent exhibitions include "Disarming Images: Art for Nuclear Disarmament" (1984-85), featuring work by artists such as Ed Paschke, Claes Oldenburg, Robert Rauschenberg, and others. A 70-page exhibition catalogue is available from The Art Museum Association of America, 270 Sutter Street, San Francisco, CA 94108.

Billboards. Artists in the Berkeley area rented 12 x 25 ft. commercial billboards and hundreds of poster displays in buses and rapid transit cars. The billboard campaign focused on the insanity of the arms race and nuclear stockpiling. In Los Angeles, a chapter of Women Strike for Peace sponsored billboards which asked the public "What Do You Do in Case of Nuclear War? Kiss the Children Goodbye..." In Michigan, a woman rented a billboard and put up a peace message as a Christmas gift for her daughters. For information on billboard campaigns, contact the Berkeley Billboard Project, Bay Area Artists for Nuclear Sanity, 981 Creston Road, Berkeley, CA 94708.

Quilting Projects. Taking the traditional "friendship quilt" a step further, women in Boise, Idaho, began their first peace quilt project in 1982, and by 1984 had created more than eight quilts on a variety of themes. When completed, each of the Boise Peace Quilts is awarded to an outstanding peacemaker. Recipients of the quilts have included singer-songwriter Pete Seeger, Physicians for Social Responsibility leader Dr. Helen Caldicott, the late Sen. Frank Church, Norman Cousins, and the women of the Greenham Common Peace Camp in England.

Hundreds of individuals have participated in the making of the Boise Peace Quilts, each of which is unified by a different theme: wildflowers common to the U.S. and the U.S.S.R., popular peace songs, children's drawings on peace, a celebration of individual peacemakers, etc.

"The patchwork quilt is really a symbol of the world which must come," Pete Seeger has said. "One new design made out of many old designs. We will stitch this world together yet."

For information on how to organize a peace quilt project, contact: Heidi Read, Boise Peace Quilt Project, 1820 N. 7th Street, Boise, ID 83702; Connecticut Peace Quilt, Piece for Peace Productions, Box 202, RFD 2, Carter Road, Pomfret Center, CT 06259; San Francisco Peace Quilt Project, c/o Saybrook Institute, Dept. V, 1772 Vallejo Street, San Francisco, CA 94123.

The Ribbon. A nationwide project involving thousands of people, The Ribbon consists of 2' x 3' fabric panels, embroidered, appliqued, painted, or decorated in other ways with illustrations expressing the hopes and fears of people living in a nuclear age. Contributors were asked to create panels focusing on what they cherish most and what they cannot bear to think of as lost in a nuclear war. Some sewed in snapshots of their families, while others created images of their homes, their favorite artists or musicians, friends, animals, etc.

The panels were joined together to create a ribbon fifteen miles long. On Hiroshima Day, 1985, the fortieth anniversary of the bombing, the Ribbon was assembled in Washington, DC, where it was "tied" around the Pentagon, the Capitol, and the Mall near the White House and Lincoln Memorial. Thousands of volunteers formed a human chain to hold the Ribbon, encircling a symbol of war with this very unique symbol of peace.

The Ribbon Project was originated by Justine Merritt, a mother of five and grandmother of six. State coordinators worked for over two years in many states, coordinating contributions. For information contact Justine Merritt, The Ribbon Project, P.O. Box 2206, Denver, CO 80201.

Radio Programs. Peace-oriented shows can be prepared in conjunction with local radio stations, the broadcast department of a local university, or with freelancers familiar with radio production. In Seattle, for example, a program on the history of U.S. peace movements before Vietnam was produced and aired over a local NPR (National Public Radio) affiliate, with a panel discussion and listener call-in following each of the four shows in the series. For information on the radio project, contact Doug Honig, Project Director, "Quest for Peace," 831 N.E. 57th Street, Seattle, WA 98105. For several years the North Manchester, Indiana, chapter of the Fellowship of Reconciliation produced a weekly half-hour program for the Manchester College radio station. Both local and visiting peace makers were interviewed about their peace activities and concerns.

Poster and Essay Contests. A 10-page handbook on "How to Organize a Peace Essay Contest in Your Community" is available from Sandra Fluck, Lancaster County Friends Meeting, 110 Tulane Terrace, Lancaster, PA 17603. Information on running a poster contest can be obtained from the Union of Concerned Scientists (UCS), 1384 Massachusetts Avenue, Cambridge, MA 02238. The UCS has run contests on topics such as motivating individuals to action and the threat of nuclear war.

US-USSR Reconciliation Projects. The Fellowship of Reconciliation has established a number of art-related projects which attempt to further communication between United States and Soviet citizens. Projects include the sending or exchanging of photographs, flower seeds, paintings, and letters/poems. Perhaps you can get individuals or groups in your area to become involved in these programs; they help break down barriers to peace by "humanizing" the supposed enemy. For information contact the US-USSR Reconciliation Program, Fellowship of Reconciliation, Box 271, Nyack, NY 10960, (914) 358-4601.

Other Projects. Numerous additional ventures, such as dances, art auctions, peace fairs, poetry readings, film nights, theatrical presentations, and festivals, are possible. An imaginative guide to organizing a variety of art-oriented projects is *Our Own Show: Organizing Cultural Programs for Working People,* available for $2.95 from District 1199 Bread and Roses Project, 310 W. 43rd Street, New York, NY 10036, 212-582-1890.

Some of the organizations involved in promoting peace through the arts are listed below:

Artists Against Nuclear Arms, P.O. Box 431, Canal Street Station, New York, NY 10013.

Artists Against Nuclear War/Reactors/Waste, 537 Jones Street #9970, San Francisco, CA 94102.

Artists for Disarmament, 65 Inman Street, Cambridge, MA 02139.

Artists for Nuclear Disarmament, 7 E. 15th St., Suite 407, New York, NY 10003.

Artists for Social Responsibility, 520 E. 12th Street, New York, NY 10009.

Artists for Survival, Artists West, 144 Moody St., Waltham, MA 02154.

Artists Speak for Peace, P.O. Box 931, Miami, FL 33133.

District 1199 Cultural Center, 310 W. 43rd St., New York, NY 10036.

Foundation for the Arts of Peace, 1615 Broadway #670, Oakland, CA 94612.

Gallery 345, 345 Lafayette, New York, NY 10012.

L.A. Artists for Survival, 1727 N. Spring Street, Los Angeles, CA 90012.

Musicians Against Nuclear Arms, 2161 Massachusetts Ave., Cambridge, MA 02140.

The Peace Museum, 430 W. Erie St., Chicago, IL 60610.

Performers and Artists for Nuclear Disarmament, 225 Lafayette St. #207, New York, NY 10012.

Performing Artists for Nuclear Disarmament Action, P.O. Box 740, Cambridge, MA 02139.

Poets for Nuclear Disarmament, 66 Grove Hill, Newton, MA 02160.

33

Humor for Peace

Gary A. Zimmerman

You can't say civilization don't advance. In every war
they kill you in a new way. - Will Rogers

A government that robs Peter to pay Paul can always
depend upon the support of Paul. - George Bernard Shaw

Military intelligence is a contradiction in terms.
                                        - Groucho Marx

ICBM, SLBM, ABM — every time you turn around lately
there's another BM. Seems like there are stockpiles
everywhere you look. Proliferation of BMs and their
payloads is a sticky problem. How to get rid of them?
There's no easy answer. It should be a simple matter of
elimination, yet it has become a stooltifying situation.
Do you know your BM? Can you keep pace with all the
different types? Before you get wiped out, get to know
what's up in your arsenal. [1] (p. 62).

The benefits of humor
    The benefits of humor and laughter have been widely
acclaimed:
1. Laughter is healing [2,3], is socially contagious [4], improves
learning [5,6], and reduces tension [7,8,9,10].
2. Laughter liberates us from fear, sorrow, and inhibition [11].
3. Laughter releases embarrassment and low levels of fear and

anger, making it possible to think more clearly [12,13].

4. Laughter helps calm us during uncomfortable, awkward, or terrifying situations [11].

5. Laughter can create a mood in which other positive and beneficial emotions, such as zestfulness and hopefulness, can emerge [2].

6. Laughter enables group members to release anxiety, stress, and conflict, and brightens members' outlooks and spirits [15].

7. Political or educational messages can be presented effectively through the use of humor [14].

8. Finding humor in a troublesome situation allows us to see the problem in a different perspective [14].

The benefits of humor for peace work

Humor (and its accompanying laughter) can be important in a wide variety of ways in the peace movement, whether the sayings or jokes you use are related specifically to peace or not. For example, humor can be used:

- To reduce tensions during conflict, such as in a demonstration, a mediation session, or a discussion with others about peace.

- To help people's minds better absorb the information and message you are sharing in a speech or in a letter to the editor.

- To set a positive tone at the beginning of a group meeting.

- To help put you and the other person at ease when you canvass door-to-door.

- To help alleviate burnout that you or co-workers are beginning to experience.

- To make peace work more fun.

These are but a few examples of how humor can help in particular situations that arise in peace work. Look over the group of benefits listed earlier; stay attuned to situations in your work in which such effects would be helpful, and use humor when it seems appropriate to the situation.

Some Hints On Improving Your Use of Humor

> *Some bright boy over at NBC once told me there were only thirty-two basic jokes. Another bright boy reduced it to eleven. Somebody else has it down to two —*
> *comparison and exaggeration.* - Fred Allen

Using comparisons or exaggeration are two ways to create humor and make people laugh. Comparisons are made automatically by the mind. If you present an idea which is out of context, unexpected, illogical, unreasonable, exaggerated, or inappropriate, the incongruity between the new idea and a related one already in the listener's mind creates laughter and a release of tension. For example, you can put two sayings together in a new way: "The meek shall inherit the earth — but not the oil rights." [14] Or you can change a word in a popular phrase or saying: "The CIA and the KGB are equal opportunity destroyers"; or "Some songs are anti-folk songs."

Exaggeration can also elicit laughter, again because of the incongruity involved. For example: Did you hear the new "hits" on the "Nuke Top 40" list? "There'll Never Be Another You," "Blowin' in the Wind," "Hit Me with Your Best Shot," "Oh, Say, Can You See," "Thanks for the Memories," "All of Me" [1] (p. 52).

One of my colleagues sometimes utilizes exaggeration in letters to the editor. Here's an example: [16]

Dear Editor:

I am irritated by all the long-faced pessimists who are bad-mouthing our defenses because of "nuclear winter." Since the prestigious National Academy of Sciences reported in December that even half the world's arsenal would blacken the sky for, perhaps, 4 or 5 months, certain sadsacks have been whining away about the bad climatic effects of nuclear war.

Why can't these doomsday nuts ever see the silver lining in the nuclear cloud? Why can't they see that advantages can balance out disadvantages in a temperature drop of 18-55 degrees? Think of the business for ski resorts, and during summer vacation! Think of the increase in tourism for Florida and the Sun Belt, all summer long, when rates are cheap and facilities uncrowded. Think of the economic boom for the clothing industry, snow shovels, heating oil, and cough syrup. I don't suppose these wet blankets have thought that cloud cover might save Africa from further drought and starvation, or that farm surpluses in the U.S. could be eliminated, saving hard-earned taxpayers' money. Or that deer hunting could last longer.

Why do some people always look at the bad side of everything? It's time we started accentuating the positive to make this country great again. God's miracle of a snowflake should be appreciated all year long. That's easier to do if we can have them around to see, even in July.

Yours truly,
Ken Brown

What can you do to improve your ability to make people laugh? Work at developing your own humor [11,17]; read more about how humor works [17,18,19]; read humorous peace sources. [1, 20, 21, 22, 23] Cut out relevant comic strips or editorial cartoons; start a file of them, and use them on your peace group's bulletin board, your refrigerator door, or your office door. Jot down good jokes that you hear, and also the humorous sayings that appear on bumper stickers, buttons, or T-shirts: "One Nuclear Bomb Can Ruin Your Whole Day;" "The Pentagon: Bombs Я Us." [14]

Some of you may not have laughed yet while reading this chapter. Is that because I'm saving the best jokes for the end, or for my own book? No. Your mind and its characteristics are different from mine. I may not have used the best exaggerations, incongruities, or comparisons for you personally. But more importantly, you are probably reading this to yourself, and we tend not to laugh when we are alone. [4,14] Try some of the humor in this chapter on a group of people. Have fun laughing with co-workers, the people you canvass, your Representative, or your neighbor who supports the military. They will be more relaxed if you do, and will be more likely to let some of your ideas into their heads.

References

1. Langer, V., Thomas, W., & Richardon, B. (1982). *The nuclear war fun book*. New York: Holt, Rinehart, and Winston.
2. Cousins, N. (1979). *Anatomy of an illness, as perceived by the patient: Reflections on healing and regeneration*. New York: W.W. Norton.

3. Moody, R.A. (1978). *Laugh after laugh: The healing power of humor.* Staunton, VA: Headwaters.
4. Chapman, A.J., & Foot, H.C. (1976). *Humor and laughter.* London: Wiley.
5. Kaplan, R.M., & Pascoe, G.C. (1977). Humorous lectures and humorous examples: Some effects upon comprehension and retention. *Journal of Educational Psychology,* 69, 61-65.
6. Zillman, D., Williams, B.R., Bryant, J., Boynton, K.R., & Wolf, M.A. (1980). Acquisition of information from educational television programs as a function of differently paced humorous inserts. *Journal of Educational Psychology,* 72, 170-180.
7. Freud, S. (1905). *Jokes and their relationship to the unconscious.* New York: Norton (1960).
8. Berlyne, D.E. (1971). *Aesthetics and psychology.* New York: Appleton-Century-Crofts.
9. Mendel, W. (1970). *A celebration of laughter.* Los Angeles: Mara.
10. Nichols, M.P., & Zax, M. (1977). *Catharsis in psychotherapy.* New York: Gardiner.
11. Mindess, H. (1971). *Laughter and liberation: Developing your sense of humor, the psychology of laughter.* Los Angeles: Nash.
12. Jackins, H. (1973). *The human situation.* Seattle: Rational Island.
13. Scheff, T.J. (1979). *Catharsis in healing, ritual, and drama.* Berkeley: University of California.
14. Peter, L.J., & Dana, B. (1982). *The laughter prescription.* New York: Ballantine.
15. Chapman, A.J. (1977). *It's a funny thing, humor.* New York: Pergamon.
16. Brown, K. (1985, March). Winter winners (Letter to the editor). *Foretell,* p. 2. N. Manchester, IN: Fellowship of Reconciliation.
17. Bailey, J. (1976). *Intent on laughter.* New York: Quadrangle/Times.
18. Eastman, M. (1938). *The enjoyment of laughter.* New York: Simon & Schuster.
19. Gruner, C.R. (1979). *Understanding laughter: The workings of wit and humor.* Chicago: Nelson-Hall.
20. Munnik, L. (1983). *Nothing to laugh about.* New York: The Pilgrim Press.

21. Staff. (1982, Fall). Nuclear arms and terrific legs. *Harvard Lampoon Parody of Newsweek*, pp. 20-22.
22. Staff. (1982, Fall). Military shoots its wad. *Harvard Lampoon Parody of Newsweek*, pp. 26-28.
23. Lippman, D. *George Schrub speaks: Declassified documents from the Committee to Intervene Anywhere*. San Francisco: Author. (Several songbooks and cassettes of activist humor available from Dave Lippman, P.O. Box 40800, San Francisco, CA 94140.)

34

Computers in Peace Work

James Ganong and John S. James

Notice: This chapter is released into the public domain without restriction. If you republish this chapter, we would appreciate receiving a copy. Please send it to Computer Professionals for Social Responsibility, Santa Cruz Chapter, P.O. Box 7708, Santa Cruz, CA 95061. Please include the above address in your publication, and also indicate that the original article appeared in Working for Peace, *edited by Neil Wollman, Impact Publishers, 1985.*

Computers have entered practically all aspects of our lives. They are tools that can be used for either good or bad, and we feel it is time they were used more fully for the good of promoting world peace. In a short chapter, we cannot include the details of computer operation; however we can help you begin to put a computer to practical use. We'll do this by giving some basic suggestions on obtaining, running, and using a computer in your work for peace. Some good sources for additional information will also be suggested.

Getting a Computer
One option for obtaining a computer is to buy a new one; prices have been dropping steadily in recent years. Perhaps your group can split the cost with one or more individuals who will also make personal use of the equipment. Before shopping for a computer, check with other organizations or individuals and see how theirs

have worked for them. Don't worry about buying the latest, fastest, and most powerful machine; if a less-advanced computer serves your purposes, it can keep on doing so for years (even if your office gets a new computer for other tasks). You could buy a used computer, but avoid taking in computer junk (obsolete or other equipment that doesn't quite work and no one quite knows how to fix). Usually it's more trouble than it's worth.

There are alternatives to buying a computer. Many home computers now gather dust in closets or attics; find someone who could donate, share, or lend their unused (or underused) machine. Additionally, sometimes people who buy computers don't have any particular use for them except to learn computer operation and programming; they and your group could both benefit if they could be persuaded to make their computer available to your peace group.

One final note. At this writing, Apple Computer Company is granting computers to non-profit groups who can propose creative ways to employ them for particular uses, including citizen action. Each grant is to a network of 3-5 non-profit organizations who want to share information. Contact Community Affairs Grant Program, Apple Computer, 20525 Mariani Ave., M/S 23L, Cupertino, CA 95014. You might also ask them about ways others have reported using the computer; some of those ways might help you in your own peace efforts.

Who Runs the Computer?

For a group to use computers, at least one person must take the time to learn about them, get the equipment set up, keep it running smoothly, and show others how to use it. This coordinator doesn't need computer experience to start, though it would be helpful to find someone who wants to learn about computers anyway, so that the time required to do the job will not be a sacrifice. It is also important to have a source of good advice, such as an experienced computer user who can volunteer a little time to answer questions, or people you meet in a local computer club or "user's group."

While the coordinator and advisor(s) may be recruited from outside the main core of the organization, there should be one core member (a paid staffer, a director, or another key member of the group) who has overall responsibility for managing the computer project. Too often equipment gets into offices and then sits idle for lack of real interest by the leadership. The manager must make sure the group sees a real use for the computer equipment in the first place, and then must maintain good communication on computer projects with group members.

Uses for Computers

How can computers help your organization? Here are the principal uses and benefits we have seen:

Word Processing. In word processing, the computer replaces the typewriter for preparing documents of all sorts: articles, proposals, letters, budgets, etc. Productivity improvements can be dramatic; businesses often find a three-to-one increase over doing the same work by typewriter.

Word processing lets you make corrections quickly on the screen, and easily re-arrange your rough draft by moving words, sentences, or paragraphs from one part to another. You don't need to retype successive drafts of the same document; instead you can print a fresh one at any time from the computer's memory. This allows you to carry a manuscript with you without worrying about losing the only copy, and without worrying about marking changes on the only original. When the document is ready:

- You can check its final appearance, and perhaps change its layout on the page to make it more attractive. This procedure, called "formatting," can be done quickly and easily, and thus allows volunteers to produce a professional-looking document.

- You can print any number of copies, each different if desired, quickly and easily.

- You can send the document by telephone to colleagues in different cities if both you and the receiving party have "modems" to use with your computers. The receiving party can then print copies immediately, add his/her own changes before printing, or transmit the paper somewhere else.

- You can send your work to "computer bulletin boards" (see Computer Communication below), where it can be read by thousands of people.

- You can send your text to a typesetter to be published. Typesetters are beginning to accept word-processor text, either by telephone or by computer disks carried into their shop; this avoids the expense and errors of re-typing material.

- You can use word processing to work on statements which must be reached by consensus. Changes can easily be tried out without retyping, and fresh working drafts can be distributed to group members at any time.

Mailing Lists and Memberships. Computerized mailing list and membership information can improve the quality of a group's communication with the world.

- Zip-sorted bulk mailings become much easier; the computer can arrange and print labels for letters or newsletters in zip code, alphabetical, or any other order you desire, saving much sorting time later.

- With a mailing list management program, the computer can personally address a duplicate letter for each group member.

- Selective mailings to only one subgroup of members, such as those having particular zip code numbers, can be easily done by a computer with the proper filing program.

- Organizing your mailing list can improve office procedures. Member names are no longer in separate folders or on scraps of paper, and full or selective list copies can be printed without fear of losing or misplacing the information.

- Incidentally, we should mention that commercial mailing-list services can provide selected mailing lists (for example, all churches in your state). You can buy a set of labels to use for only one mailing, or you can sometimes purchase use of the list for a longer period.

Computer Communication. This very important area, just coming into widespread use, will open the doors to whole new kinds of organization.

You can use your computer for "electronic mail," a sending of messages through the telephone system to avoid postal delays. Across oceans and international borders, electronic mail may be the only feasible way to maintain close working relationships. The peace group SANE (711 "G" Street SE, Washington, DC 20003) uses computers in its network of 50,000 political activists who can be reached for "action alerts;" contact them for more information.

"Computer conferencing" is a kind of electronic mail useful for groups of people to discuss issues as a community, where they can develop consensus and plans together. There are three different types of computer conferencing. One, sometimes called a "chat mode" or "CB simulator," works like a citizens-band radio, but for written messages; a channel is selected, and all messages sent go to everyone on that channel at that time. The participants, who can be anywhere around the world, decide on certain times and channels for holding the "electronic meeting."

A second kind of computer conferencing, which we have found even more useful, lets you leave written messages where they will be available to the rest of your group or to the public. You also, then, can read the messages and replies of others. The big advantage here is that everyone can use the system at their convenience. National organizations can "meet" continuously, not only at annual conventions. And at such computer "meetings," you needn't hurry to speak, nor be pushy to get your message across.

There is a third type of conferencing called "voice mail." It's new — as of this writing we don't know of any use in peace work — but it will be important. Acting as a complex answering machine, it allows one person to leave a message for many people in a telephone network without the individual receivers having a computer or answering machine of their own.

By "computer conferencing" you can get your message out to thousands of people, and find others who share your interests, whether you are located in a big city or a small town. Those interested can reply immediately, and others attracted by the messages can join in the conversation, and perhaps join your cause. Computer conferencing thus allows for widespread discussion and information-spreading about peace concerns.

Conferencing includes "computer bulletin boards" and "information utilities." Bulletin boards are telephone-accessible systems run by individuals or small organizations and are usually available free to anyone who wants to use them; information utilities are large commercial networks with thousands of subscribers. Some information utilities let individuals and organizations earn money by setting up special-interest computer conferences; they then receive royalties based on use by other subscribers. This can be an easy entry into "electronic publishing" for those who have an interest.

These computer bulletin boards are under political attack because a few have been used to organize illegal entry into computer, telephone, and credit-card systems. Nevertheless, it is important to understand the importance of maintaining this medium as a *two-way* form of mass communication. Citizens can be actively involved in spreading ideas to the community or the country, rather than just passively receiving messages via television or other media.

You can also use computers to connect with research "data bases" to get immediate, valuable information on almost any question involving public issues. For example, one law data base indexes everything that appears in over 600 law journals around the world; you can immediately search for any subject or combination of subjects you want, find relevant sources and related topics, and then refine your search and try again. Hundreds of similar data bases cover subjects in government, business, technology, medicine, academic research, associations, foundation grants, etc. If anything has been published on a given subject, you can probably find out about it in a few minutes from your office or home. Often article summaries are given in English even when the original work is in another language. You can also locate specific people and organizations to contact on particular questions and concerns. Often such experts welcome the chance to talk with someone interested in their own special area.

We cannot recommend specific databases necessarily useful for peace workers, since most are designed primarily for corporate business. Your selections will depend very much on your particular focus of interest. The *Omni Online Database Directory* (by Mike Edelhard and Owen Daves, Collier Books, New York, NY) shows the great variety of databases available. Or check with university librarians, who often use these systems.

With other services you can get the AP and UPI news-wire reports from your office or home, and select stories on subjects you request. Sometimes these stories include in-depth information which never appears in print. Also, your organization could review the news-wire for a breaking story involving itself, in order to quickly prepare informed statements for reporters who might call.

There are drawbacks to computer communication, however. Many systems were poorly designed and are hard to learn or awkward to use, although they are likely to improve in the future. Some services cost too much for most people (for example, fifty dollars an hour or more at this writing), but some cost about eight dollars an hour during nights and weekends, and many others are free (contact Information USA, Inc., 4701 Willard Ave., Suite 1707,

Chevy Chase, MD 20815, 301-657-1200, for a free sample copy of their monthly newsletter, "Data Base Informer," which gives information on many low-cost or free data bases).

If you're just getting started in computer communication, you should know that it's usually easiest to use your computer and "modem" (telephone connection) as a "dumb terminal," meaning that you can type information to a distant computer and see the results it sends back. The alternative, a "smart" terminal, is usually a software program which runs on your computer. These programs offer valuable capabilities, but many of them are difficult to learn how to use. Find someone with experience to show you how to begin using one or two communication or research services.

Graphics. Some computers can help you prepare posters, charts and graphs, logos, slides, pictures, and images of all sorts. Even non-artists can design presentable newsletter and poster graphics in a few minutes, without the specialized tools of a graphic artist. You will have the advantage of being able to create complete posters and flyers without the delay and expense of typesetting. With the right software, you can even create your own automated "computer slide shows" to use at meetings, fair booths, and other occasions.

Spreadsheets. Spreadsheets are calculation programs used for financial planning. For example, tentative budgets can be prepared which project specific amounts for income and expenses; you can then insert a new hypothetical amount for a specific expense, and the program will recalculate new amounts for sources of income so that the budget remains balanced. Such calculations can help a group do better financial planning.

A Word to the Wise

One practical point relevant to word processing, mailing lists, graphics, spreadsheets, and nearly all other uses of computers: machines do break down, or get reserved for somebody else's work, sometimes just before important deadlines. Organize projects to avoid complete dependence on your computer. For example, when we wrote this chapter:

- We composed it with pen and paper, often in coffeehouses or libraries with no computer nearby, then later re-read the draft and marked revisions by hand.

- A short session with the word processor transformed the marked-up handwritten copy into a freshly-printed draft, with no erasures, etc. This new draft could then be revised by hand, anywhere, and the corrections could be typed into the computer at any convenient time.

- We periodically (every page or two) ''saved'' our revised work onto the computer disk. This minimized the amount of retyping we would have had to do if the power had gone off while we were working. (Revisions that you make on the screen exist only in the computer's electronic memory until you ''save'' them onto a disk.)

- We systematically made ''backup'' copies of our work, stored on several computer disks, in case of damage to one of the ''original'' disks.

- We minimized the time needed with the computer in order to keep a low-budget operation. This chapter required only a few hours of actual computer use, and those few hours could have fit into whatever time was available without significantly holding up the project. This allows many different people and projects to share the same equipment, greatly reducing the cost.

These things helped us avoid complete dependence on the computer. Even if the equipment became unavailable, the project could have been continued manually (on a typewriter) without a hitch. One major strategy to reduce dependence on your particular computer is to select a machine which is compatible with those of your friends and colleagues; that way you can share equipment when necessary.

For More Information

The best way to find out about computers is from other people. Find the computer clubs in your area. Many of these are users' groups, which specialize in particular kinds of computers or other special interest areas. Other computer club members can be very helpful to you as you get started.

Also read some computer books and magazines; select those that are clear and understandable to you. Many are not as informative as they could be because of their bias to cover the latest products, rather than those most practical for their readers. But few are technically incorrect (except those which are out of date), so if a book or magazine speaks to you, it's probably a good choice.

Suggested Readings
Brand, S. (Ed.), (1984). *Whole earth software catalog.* New York: Quantum Press/Doubleday (available in bookstores, $17.50). This book is filled with good and thorough evaluations of computers and software programs.

Rotenberg, M. (1984). *Nonprofits enter the computer age.* Washington, DC: Community Careers Resource Center (1520 16th St. NW, Washington, DC 20036, 35 pages, $6.95). This excellent overview was prepared by the founder of the Public Interest Computer Association in Washington, DC. It includes discussion on needs assessment and planning, information about purchasing hardware and software, a large bibliography, and a list of groups which can provide computer assistance.

35

A Bibliography of Nuts and Bolts and Other Tools

Compiled and annotated by Ed Nelson

Alinsky, S. (1972). *Rules for radicals.* New York: Vintage Books (196 pages, $3.95). Like Alinsky's earlier *Reveille for Radicals*, this is a classic among guides to movement activism, organizing, and trouble making. The blunt-spoken Alinsky gives little attention to such specifics as poster design or the fine points of handbilling; his goal is to help you increase your influence with "the masses." There are chapters entitled "Tactics," "A Word About Words," and "Of Means and Ends." Alinsky's approach is: Make the right enemies — loudly. He insists that a group should seek power before deciding on policy ("No one can negotiate without the power to compel negotiation." p. 119).

Saul Alinsky was an inspired trouble maker and polarizer. Whether or not you agree with his overall philosophy, you can likely find something of value in his methods. If you pick this book as your guide, you'll find it outspoken, provocative, and rich with anecdotal illustration.

Coover, V., Deagan, E., Esser, S., & Moore, C. (1985). *Resource manual for a living revolution.* Philadelphia: New Society Publishers (4722 Baltimore Avenue, Philadelphia, PA 19143, 330 pages, $9.95). The "tools" offered here aren't the "nuts and bolts" of organizing you might be accustomed to; they are procedural devices — group exercises, roleplaying, brainstorming, simulation games, and the like. There are sections on a wide variety of topics, such as consciousness raising, community building, taking action, working in schools, fundraising, and cooking for large groups. Many case histories and examples clarify proposed procedures and processes. Your group will profit from familiarity with these techniques.

Desai, M. (1982). *Handbook for satyagrahis.* New Delhi, India: Gandhi Peace Foundation, & Philadelphia: New Society Publishers (4722 Baltimore Ave., Philadelphia, PA 19143, 57 pages, $3.95). This brief handbook outlines basic principles of nonviolence and offers suggestions which you can practice in your own life and in your interactions with others. For local peace groups in the U.S., the book may appear handicapped by its roots in a very different culture, but this very weakness can sometimes be a strength. If you have an open mind, you can find specific suggestions for new types of attention-getting devices. For instance, Desai mentions both fireworks and kites as possible tools; the two-stick kite of your childhood may not be adequate, but bigger kites might lift your banner high above a rally or demonstration. There are also basic hints on developing good interaction among peace group members and with the general public.

Although this product of an Indian publisher and printer requires a little extra understanding from U.S. readers, it is a useful handbook.

Ginosar, M. (1984). *How to influence Congress to reverse the nuclear arms race.* Sacramento, CA: Author (2645 La Mesa Way, Sacramento, CA 95825, 16 pages, $1.00). The wordy title may be more appropriate to a scholarly paper, but Ginosar's casually printed pamphlet presents a carefully thought out, detailed program for choosing and influencing swing members of Congress — by mail. A minor activity for a peace group? No, not when you recall the critical votes that have been decided by a single member.

Besides, you're likely to have some committed supporters who can't or won't get involved in public picketing or demonstrating; they could become a superb letter-writing task force. Letter-writing shouldn't be just "busy work" to occupy shy colleagues; it is an important task. (See Chapter 20).

Hedemann, E. (Ed.), (1981). *War Resisters League organizers manual*. New York: War Resisters League (339 Lafayette St., New York, NY 10022, $8). This is as fine a piece of work in the field as you're likely to find, and should be a basic in your peace worker library. It's unusually broad, yet packed with detail. Hedemann contributed ten of the forty-four short chapters, concentrating on basic organizing techniques, literature production, and "action." His product is very readable; the abundant, clear illustrations are used to advance your understanding. Every peace group should have a copy.

League of Women Voters of the United States (1979). *Simplified parliamentary procedure*. Washington, DC: Author (1730 M Street NW, Washington, DC 20036, 9 pages, 75 cents). You think I'm joking, that this can't be a serious citation? Wrong. Your success requires that your group members get along well in making decisions.

"We'll just reach our conclusions informally," you say? "We don't want to get all tangled up in points of order"? That's just the reason for a pamphlet such as this. Even with as few as a dozen people at your meetings, you'll need some rules in order to discuss issues, plan strategy, and make decisions efficiently. The total text runs only to 40-odd brief, clear paragraphs, making no effort to cover everything in the 300-plus pages of *Robert's Rules of Order Newly Revised*; it aims simply to set out the system for fair and orderly decisions.

Other League publications are also valuable. Check the "Media Kit," a collection of five short LWVUS pamphlets, all of which you can apply to your group's campaign. Included are *Breaking into Broadcasting*, *Reaching the Public*, *Getting into Print*, *Projecting your Image: How to Produce a Slide Show*, and *Speaking Out: How to Set Up a Speakers Bureau*; send $2 to receive all five. And when you write to the League, get a copy of its publications catalog.

Simpson, D. (1974). *Winning elections: A handbook in participatory politics*. Chicago: Swallow Press (order from Harper & Row, New York, $9.95). Simpson, a successful academic-humanist-politician-clergyman, led the brief 1969 Eugene McCarthy for President compaign in the Chicago area, created the Independent

Precinct Organization (IPC) to battle the famous Daley mayoral machine in Chicago, and later was the IPC aldermanic candidate in his home ward, becoming Chicago's lone independent alderman; *Winning Elections* tells how.

Wilson, A. (1983). *The disarmer's handbook of military technology and organization.* New York: Penguin Books (40 West 23rd St., New York, NY, 318 pages, $4.95). If you're looking for a pocket-size reference book on peace and war topics, this is the one to get. Though relatively small in page length, it is diverse in coverage. Wilson's aim was "to give everyone engaged in fighting the arms race (or following moves to reverse it) a compendium of facts with which to be as expertly informed as any professional who opposes them, whether on technology, military organization, or the 'logic' of nuclear deterrence..." (p. 9). The book's topics range from the psychology, theory, economics, history, and ethics of war, to specifics on biological warfare and nuclear missiles. This is an excellent reference book.

Here is a list of some other books or pamphlets that focus on specific topic areas:

Anti-Nuclear Legal Project (1980). *The national no nukes trial handbook.* Boston: Author. (People's Energy Project Clearinghouse, c/o Massachusetts Lawyers Guild, 120 Boylston St., Room 1011, Boston, MA 02116, 50 pages.)

Berson, G. *Making a show of it — A guide to concert production.* Oakland, CA: Redwood Records. (Redwood Records, 476 MacArthur Blvd., Oakland, CA 94609, 101 pages.)

Brigham, N. (1976). *How to do leaflets, newsletters, and newspapers.* Boston: The Boston Community School, republished in 1982 by PEP Publishers (distributed by Hastings House Publishers, 10 E. 40th St., New York, NY 10016).

Flanagan, J. (1977). *Grassroots fundraising book.* Washington, DC: Youth Project. (1000 Wisconsin Avenue, NW, Washington, DC 20007.)

Gordon, R. (1978). *We interrupt this program . . . A citizen's guide to using the media for social change.* Amherst, MA: Citizens Involvement Training Program. (225 Furrolo Hall, University of Massachusetts, Amherst, MA 01003.)

Oppenheimer, M., & Lakey, G. (1965). *A manual for direct action*. Chicago: Quadrangle Books. (Out of print but available at many libraries.)

San Francisco Study Group for Peace and Disarmament. *Thinkpeace* (a bi-monthly newsletter containing creative ideas for promoting world peace. 2735 Franklin St., San Francisco, CA 94123, (415) 673-7422).

Union of Concerned Scientists. *Organizing manual: A guide for planning educational activities on nuclear war and arms control*. Cambridge, MA: Author. (26 Church St., Cambridge, MA 02238.)

Index

DO YOU KNOW SOMEONE WHO
WOULD LIKE TO KNOW ABOUT THIS BOOK?

We welcome your comments on *Working for Peace*, and invite your recommendations of other peace activists or groups who might be interested in the book...

- for personal use
  - to aid the effectiveness of an organization
    - as a course text or supplemental reading
      - as a discussion guide for a church or social action group
        - or...?

To have announcement information sent to your friends and colleagues, please give us the name of the person or organization, and full address, including zipcode.
Please send your comments and recommendations to: *Working for Peace*, Impact Publishers, P.O. Box 1094, San Luis Obispo, CA 93406.

Many thanks for your cooperation.